Well-Being

Well-Being

Happiness in a Worthwhile Life

NEERA K. BADHWAR

OXFORD
UNIVERSITY PRESS

Oxford University Press is a department of the University of Oxford.
It furthers the University's objective of excellence in research, scholarship,
and education by publishing worldwide.

Oxford   New York
Auckland   Cape Town   Dar es Salaam   Hong Kong   Karachi
Kuala Lumpur   Madrid   Melbourne   Mexico City   Nairobi
New Delhi   Shanghai   Taipei   Toronto

With offices in
Argentina   Austria   Brazil   Chile   Czech Republic   France   Greece
Guatemala   Hungary   Italy   Japan   Poland   Portugal   Singapore
South Korea   Switzerland   Thailand   Turkey   Ukraine   Vietnam

Oxford is a registered trademark of Oxford University Press
in the UK and certain other countries.

Published in the United States of America by
Oxford University Press
198 Madison Avenue, New York, NY 10016

© Oxford University Press 2014

First issued as an Oxford University Press paperback, 2017

Library of Congress Cataloging-in-Publication Data
Badhwar, Neera K
Well-being: happiness in a worthwhile life / Neera K. Badhwar.
pages cm
Includes bibliographical references and index.
ISBN 978-0-19-532327-6 (hardcover : alk. paper); 978-0-19-068207-1 (paperback : alk. paper)
1. Conduct of life.   2. Virtue.   3. Happiness.   4. Well-being.   I. Title.
BJ1595.B235 2014
171'.3—dc23
2013045705

For Annika and Aidan
Wishing you much Happiness in a Worthwhile Life

CONTENTS

ACKNOWLEDGMENTS

I've thought about the main idea of this book since I started thinking about "life," but the seed of the book was probably sown when I read and wrote a response to Wayne Sumner's book, *Welfare, Happiness, and Ethics*, for the Fellows' Seminar at the University Center for Human Values at Princeton in 1996–1997. Many thanks to the faculty and the Fellows for making my year there an intellectual feast, and to the University of Oklahoma and Ray Elugardo, then chair of the philosophy department, for supporting my leave in 1996–1997. It was many more years, however, before I decided to use the response as a springboard for this book. A sabbatical at the Social Philosophy and Policy Center in Spring 2008, and an Earhart Foundation grant in 2010–2011, enabled me to make headway on the project. I thank the SPPC and the Earhart Foundation for their support, as well as the University of Oklahoma and Hugh Benson, then chair of the philosophy department, for supporting my leave in 2008.

Many people have helped me whip this book into shape by commenting on one or more chapters. Andrew I. Cohen organized a workshop on the manuscript at Georgia State University in August 2011, and he, Andrew Altman, Andrew J. Cohen, Marilyn Friedman, Christopher Freiman, Eddy Nahmias, Richard Parry, George Rainbolt, and Hal Thorsrud participated in the workshop. Lawrence Becker was unable to attend, but sent me copious comments. I am immensely grateful to Andrew I. Cohen and the Philosophy Department at Georgia State for the workshop, and to all the commentators for taking several days out of their busy schedule to read, comment on, and discuss the manuscript.

In September 2011, William Glod organized a workshop at the Institute for Humane Studies and commented on several chapters. I am very grateful to him and to all those who took the time to give me comments and participate in the discussion: Ben Chambers, Alexander McCobin, Gordon Shannon, David Schmidtz, and Jason Walker.

I also received invaluable comments on one or more chapters from Erik Angner, Heather Battaly, Sarah Buss, Gary Chartier, John Christman, Amihud Gilead, Daniel Haybron, Brad Hooker, Julia Driver, Michael Lacewing, Duane Lewis, Mark Sagoff, Christine Swanton, Denise Vigani, Sam Wren-Lewis, Linda Zagzebski, and anonymous referees of OUP. Julia Annas, Pete Boettke, Fred Miller, David Schmidtz, and Wayne Sumner supported my project in various ways. My heartfelt thanks to all of them.

I also thank my students in my Graduate seminars on Virtue Ethics (1997), Ethical Naturalism (2005), Immorality (2006), and Happiness (2008) at the University of Oklahoma. I learned a great deal from their comments and questions. For the intellectual curiosity and excitement he brought to the classroom, I give special thanks to Shyam Patwardhan.

Earlier versions of most of the chapters of my book were presented, with great profit, at University of North Carolina at Chapel Hill, Duke University, University of Texas at Austin, University of Colorado at Boulder, University of Denver, Washington University, St. Louis University, University of Virginia, College of William and Mary, Bowling Green State University, University of Missouri, Ryerson University, York University, George Mason University, Universidad Torcuato Di Tella School of Law, Haifa University, Potsdam College, and at the following conferences: Moral Judgment (University of Arizona); Emotions (Arizona State University); Royal Ethics Conference (University of Texas at Austin); Rocky Mountain Ethics Conference (Boulder, Colorado); Happiness: East and West (University of Hong Kong); Ethical and Social Scientific Perspectives on Well-Being (California State University Long Beach); Virtue Ethics and Moral Psychology, Carl M. Williams Institute of Ethics and Values (University of Denver); Happiness (Santa Barbara Community College); and Joint Session of the Mind Association and the Aristotelian Society (Kent University).

An earlier version of chapter 5 was published as "Is Realism Really Bad for You? A Realistic Response" in the *Journal of Philosophy*, February 2008, and chapter 6 contains some material from "The Limited Unity of Virtue," *Nous*, September 1996, and from "The Milgram Experiments, Learned Helplessness, and Character Traits." *Journal of Ethics*, September 2009. Thanks to all three journals for permission to use these articles for my book. Many thanks also to my editor, Peter Ohlin, for encouraging me to write this book(and believing that I would finish it).

My husband, Larry White, has supported me in more ways than one over the years. I thank him for his love and support. I dedicate this book, with love, to our grandchildren, Aidan and Annika, and thank their parents, Pranav and Ellen, for bringing them into the world and helping shape them into the lovable individuals they are.

PART ONE | Well-Being

CHAPTER 1 | Introduction

"You're not happy unless you think you're happy."

—GRETCHEN RUBIN

"What a wonderful life I've had! I only wish I'd realized it sooner."

—COLETTE

1.1 Varieties of Well-being/Happiness

They both have a point: a life of happiness or well-being must be wonderful and also seen by the person whose life it is to be wonderful. But wonderful how? Colette probably means, blessed by good fortune. But many people would say that a wonderful life must also be objectively worthwhile and psychologically fulfilling, and psychologically fulfilling largely (but not wholly) by being objectively worthwhile. Of course, everyone does not share this view. According to some—maybe many—people, all you need for well-being is psychological fulfillment, or that plus success in meeting your own standards. There are no objective standards of well-being, so the objective worth of your life is irrelevant to your well-being.

Let us dub the proponents of the first view objectivists, and the proponents of the second view subjectivists. Subjectivists make a sharp distinction between a life's *prudential value* on the one hand, and its *moral value* on the other, between the idea of *the highest prudential good for an individual* and the idea of *her objective goodness as a person*. Objectivists, by contrast, hold that the moral or perfectionist value of a life is partly constitutive of a life's prudential value, and that the idea of *the highest prudential good for an individual* entails the idea of *her objective goodness as a person*. In recent years, subjectivism about the prudential good has been on the ascendancy, gaining strength and respectability from its alliance with empirical studies of subjective well-being, while objectivism has been on the retreat. I hope to show that objectivism need not and should not leave the field to subjectivism. My main aim in this book is to vindicate the idea that when well-being is understood as the individual's highest prudential good (HPG), it entails not only a sense of fulfillment but also objective worth, and that objective worth entails, at its best, a life of the central moral virtues, such as justice, integrity, kindness, and the practical wisdom implicit in these. Thus virtue and virtuous actions are partly constitutive of well-being. Less controversially, they are also a means to well-being. Aspiring to and achieving well-being is, therefore, not only desirable, but also admirable, and aspiring to and achieving virtue is not only admirable, but also desirable.[1] Clearly, however, the claim that well-being requires a virtuous life is true only on a certain conception of well-being and a certain conception of virtue. One of my substantive tasks, then, is to vindicate these conceptions of well-being and of virtue as plausible in their own right.

My thesis is neo-Aristotelian insofar as I adopt Aristotle's idea of virtue as an excellence of character that involves both the intellect and the emotions, and his idea of well-being or *eudaimonia* as the individual's HPG, without adopting all his assumptions about virtue or *eudaimonia*, such as that virtue is global or that the philosophical life is the most *eudaimonic* life. My claim that well-being as the individual's HPG entails a life of virtue should be understood to mean that it entails a life that exhibits virtuous dispositions at least in some spheres, and is motivated by the central moral principles and commitments in most other spheres.[2] As I argue in chapter 6, people who live a life that most of us would regard as morally good or decent overall are mixed: virtuous in some respects, principled but not virtuous in some, weak or akratic in yet others, inculpably mistaken in some, and self-deceived or blatantly unprincipled in still others. In other words, good people are far from perfectly good. For this and other reasons, a life of well-being as the HPG is also far from perfect.

---

[1] Which is not to say that virtue can't be seen as desirable on other grounds. For example, Linda Zagzebski argues that what makes virtue desirable is that it is possessed by admirable people—moral exemplars. See Linda Zagzebski, "The Admirable Life and the Desirable Life" (2006), 53–67.

[2] To clarify: virtues imply principles, but not conversely. On the former, see Rosalind Hursthouse, *On Virtue Ethics* (1999), chapter 1. In "Virtue and Eudaimonism" (1998), Julia Annas argues that in Stoicism, virtuous deliberation is often explained in terms of "formulating general rules," and that "Virtue is in ancient theories the locus of what we call morality" (40). See also Annas, *The Morality of Happiness* (hereafter *Happiness*) (1993), chapter 1 and p. 452.

Before proceeding with the description of my project, I need to say something about the vexed terminology in this area of scholarship. Which term should we use for the prudential good, the good that ancient philosophers call *eudaimonia*: happiness—or well-being? Some philosophers insist that the modern notion of happiness is inaccurate as a translation of *eudaimonia*. Richard Kraut, however, argues that those who reject happiness as the correct translation of *eudaimonia* misconstrue both the ancient idea of *eudaimonia* and the contemporary idea of happiness.[3] For it is not the case, as they believe, that happiness for us is only a positive psychological state, and *eudaimonia* for Aristotle is only a matter of meeting certain standards (Kraut, "Two Conceptions," 167–173). For him as for us, happiness is both a positive psychological state and a matter of meeting certain standards; the difference is only that Aristotle thinks that the standards in question are objective, whereas we think they are subjective, dependent entirely on the attitudes of the individual in question.

Nevertheless, this has not persuaded everyone. According to L.W. Sumner, one of the most influential writers in contemporary philosophy of happiness/well-being, we should not translate "*eudaimonia*" as "happiness" precisely because our notion of happiness is "thoroughly subjective," having no truck with objective values, whereas Aristotle's conception of *eudaimonia* is thoroughly objective, having no truck with subjective attitudes; according to Bernard Williams, we should not do so because "it makes sense now to say that you are happy one day, unhappy another, but *eudaimonia* was a matter of the shape of one's whole life."[4] Hence both propose translating "*eudaimonia*" as "well-being." But there is no consensus on this point. Some philosophers writing in the virtue ethical or ancient philosophy tradition, such as Rosalind Hursthouse and John Cooper, translate "*eudaimonia*" as "flourishing,"[5] whereas others, such as Julia Annas and Terence Irwin, translate it as "happiness."[6] In contemporary work on

---

[3] Richard Kraut, "Two Conceptions of Happiness" (hereafter "Two Conceptions") (1979), 167–197.
[4] L. W. Sumner, *Welfare, Happiness, and Ethics* (hereafter *Welfare*) (1996), 140; Bernard Williams, *Ethics and the Limits of Philosophy* (hereafter *Ethics*) (1985), 34.
[5] John Cooper, *Reason and Human Good in Aristotle* (hereafter *Human Good*) (1986); Hursthouse, *Virtue Ethics* (1999).
[6] See Annas, *Happiness* (1993), *Intelligent Virtue* (2011), and "Virtue and Eudaimonism" (1998), 53, in which Annas argues that "happiness" and not "well-being" is the correct translation of *eudaimonia*. See also Sarah Broadie, *Ethics with Aristotle* (1993); Terence Irwin, *Aristotle's First Principles* (1990), and *Nicomachean Ethics* (hereafter *NE*), trans. T. Irwin, 2nd ed. (1999); Richard Kraut, *Aristotle on the Human Good* (1991); Martha Nussbaum, "Who Is the Happy Warrior? Philosophy Poses Questions to Psychology" (hereafter "Happy Warrior") (2008), S81–S113; Nicholas White, *A Brief History of Happiness* (hereafter *History*) (2006); and Daniel C. Russell, *Happiness for Humans* (hereafter *History*) (2012).

well-being outside of this tradition, some philosophers, including Sumner and Daniel Haybron, use "happiness" to refer to a positive psychological disposition, and "well-being" to refer to a partly normative state of the individual's overall prudential good.[7] There is no consensus among psychologists either: Martin Seligman uses "*eudaimonia*," "authentic happiness," and "well-being" interchangeably; some use "happiness" and "well-being" interchangeably; and some simply talk about "subjective well-being" or "psychological well-being."[8]

Unsurprisingly, the lack of consensus in academic discussions reflects a similar lack in everyday language and thought. We wish happiness, not well-being or *eudaimonia*, to those we love, and we hope that our own lives will be happy. By this we rarely, if ever, mean that we wish or hope for nothing more than a sense of fulfillment; typically, we mean that we wish or hope for a sense of fulfillment in a worthwhile life. In some other contexts as well, the term "happiness" is the most natural one to use. Novels and movies can have happy or unhappy endings, but never endings of well-being or ill-being or flourishing. And there is an advantage to keeping our terminology as natural as possible: it makes for easier reading, and it keeps us philosophers tied to the everyday concerns about which we philosophize. In light of these disagreements, it seems that there is as much reason for choosing "happiness" as there is for choosing "well-being" or "flourishing" or "*eudaimonia*" to refer to the prudentially good life.[9] Nevertheless, given the state of academic discussion I can best avoid confusion by using "eudaimonia," "well-being," or "flourishing", depending on the context, for the prudentially good life. The terms "happiness" and "fulfillment" or "sense of fulfillment" I will use for the positive emotions, thoughts, and evaluations—whether conscious, subconscious, or unconscious—that are commonly regarded as part of such a life. I will call my own conception of the prudentially good life "*eudaimonia*" or

---

[7] James Griffin, *Well-Being: Its Meaning, Measurement, and Moral Importance* (hereafter *Well-Being*) (1986); Sumner, *Welfare* (1996); Daniel M. Haybron, *The Pursuit of Unhappiness: The Elusive Psychology of Well-Being* (hereafter *Unhappiness*) (2008).

[8] Martin E.P. Seligman, "Eudaemonia, The Good Life: A Talk with Martin Seligman" (http://www.edge.org/3rd_culture/seligman04/seligman_index.html); *Authentic Happiness* (2002); David Lykken, *Happiness* (1999); Jonathan Haidt, *The Happiness Hypothesis* (hereafter *Happiness Hypothesis*) (2006); Carol D. Ryff and Burton H. Singer, "Know Thyself and Become Who You Are: A Eudaimonic Approach to Psychological Well-Being" (2008), 13–39, at 9.

[9] The term, "prudential value," was coined by Griffin in *Well-Being*, and is now widely used to distinguish the self-interested value of a life from other dimensions of its value: moral, perfectionist, or aesthetic. Sumner develops these distinctions further, and Haybron still further.

"well-being as the highest prudential good (HPG)." Hopefully, this will prevent confusion.

There is also a terminological issue regarding the use of "subjective" and "objective" for theories of well-being. As already indicated, I divide theories into subjective and objective according to whether they exclude or include objective values in their accounts. But they are not always distinguished by this criterion. Sumner calls all theories that are partly dependent on the individual's point of view "subjective," even if these theories also regard certain objective values as essential. By doing so, he observes, we preserve the symmetry between prudential values and perceptual properties, which are regarded as subjective because they are partly dependent on the perspective of (normal) observers. Sumner suggests reserving the term "objective" for the (implausible) view that well-being is simply a matter of meeting certain objective standards, regardless of the individual's emotional condition or her evaluation of her life. Theories that hold that we are well-off to the extent that we function well, or to the extent that we perfect our powers, or to the extent that we are virtuous, or even to the extent that our lives are filled with pleasure and devoid of pain, regardless of our own perspective on our lives, are all examples of what Sumner calls objective theories of well-being.

On Sumner's characterization, however, even Aristotle's conception of *eudaimonia* turns out to be subjective—a distinctly odd result.[10] Moreover, given the many meanings of "subjective" ("experiential," "mental," "personal," "relative," "neither true nor false"), "subjective" is misleading as a name for the view I am defending. So I hereby appropriate the word "objective," with its favorable resonance ("Now let's be objective," "This view is objectively true," etc.), for theories that make objective worth essential to well-being, and reserve "subjective" for views that deny this. This choice also preserves symmetry with theories of perceptual properties, because theories that regard color (or, more generally, perceptual properties) and (human) value as partly dependent on the characteristic responses of normal human beings in normal circumstances are regarded by many philosophers as realistic or objective.[11] So understood,

---

[10] Earlier in his book, however, where he discusses the function argument, Sumner calls Aristotle's theory objective, because the argument identifies *eudaimonia* with good functioning and virtue.

[11] John McDowell, "Virtue and Reason" (1979), 331–350; "Values and Secondary Qualities" (1985), 110–129; David Wiggins, "Truth, and Truth as Predicated of Moral Judgments," in *Needs, Values, Truth: Essays in the Philosophy of Value"* (1987); and Geoffrey Sayre-McCord, "The Many Moral Realisms" (1986), 1–23. Maggie Little provides an excellent discussion of these and other works on moral realism in "Recent Work in Moral Realism: Non-Naturalism" (1994), 225–233.

the idea of objective well-being is perfectly compatible with the idea that objectively worthy lives can take many different shapes depending on the interests, opportunities, and abilities of the individual and, in fact, *must* take a shape that both suits the individual's own psychological nature and meets her standards to count as a life of well-being.

A theory of value objectivism or value realism that makes end values— values that we normally pursue only for their own sake, or as part of a larger value that we pursue only for its own sake—dependent on human needs, interests, reason, and emotions is clearly very different from a Platonic or Moorean objectivism, which holds that (human) values exist independently of us human beings, or that moral propositions "have truth value because they track certain independent facts which explain our use of moral concepts."[12] So although I will talk about normative facts and practical truths, I should not be taken to be referring to facts that exist independently of human nature or the circumstances of human existence. Normative facts are objective the way facts about health and fitness are objective. Some people are more comfortable talking about being responsive to the reasons there are than about being realistic about, or responsive to, objective values. If so, they are free to translate my talk of realism or objective values into their preferred terminology. So far as I can see, it makes no substantive difference to my argument.

As far as this book is concerned, any metaphysics of value that accepts the following three conditions qualifies as accepting the objectivity of values.

The first condition is that objectively (good) values must be compatible with true metaphysical and empirical beliefs and theories. Bad or "false" values are usually the result of false metaphysical or empirical beliefs or theories; or ignorance of, or blindness to, the relevant facts and true theories; or mistaken inferences from them. And even when these false values are not due to false metaphysical or empirical beliefs or theories, they are often rationalized by them. Examples abound: hostility to homosexuality on the grounds that homosexuality is unnatural, and the unnatural is bad; or (one of the oldest and still prevalent in many cultures) hostility towards

---

For a more recent defense of moral realism, see Joshua Gert, "Color Constancy and the Color/Value Analogy" (2010), 58–87.

[12] Christine Korsgaard, "Realism and Constructivism in Twentieth-Century Moral Philosophy" (2003), 99–122, at n. 3, 119. Korsgaard defends constructivism, which she characterizes as the view that moral concepts refer to solutions to the practical problems "faced by self-conscious rational beings." But she acknowledges that realism is compatible with constructivism if by moral facts we mean "the complex facts about the solutions to practical problems" (ibid., 118).

members of other races, countries, religions, or castes, on the grounds that they are defective as human beings or out to get the fully human members of one's own group. Such values are likely to crumble under a careful and honest consideration of a wide variety of perspectives and experiences. So the ability to pass the test of exposure to, and careful and honest consideration of, a wide variety of perspectives and experiences is a second condition of good values. The third condition is that values considered as character traits be "compossible," in the sense that the logical requirements of one not be contradicted by the logical requirements of another.[13] For example, if fairness, loyalty, justice, and loving kindness are all moral values, then it can't be the case that, *ceteris paribus*, fairness requires that we not favor our friends in grading exams *and* also that loyalty requires that we ought to favor our friends; or that justice requires that we ought to punish wrong doers *and* also that loving kindness requires that we turn the other cheek, and so on. But the logical compatibility of these character traits does not entail that their requirements can never conflict: traits that serve us well in the usual human environment can come into conflict with each other when the environment is disrupted, such as in war or famine, or even in less extreme situations of duress.

It might happen that even when all these conditions are met, disagreement persists about some values. My hunch is that in such cases disagreement shows one of two things:

(i) Some values are optional, but those who adopt or pursue them sometimes mistakenly believe that everyone is required to adopt or pursue them. Examples include art, cooking, technology, space travel, fighting for liberty, philanthropy, and so on. These are all objectively worthwhile pursuits, but unlike virtues such as justice, loyalty, generosity, and so on, they do not give everyone a reason to accord them an important place in their lives. For example, those who can't discriminate flavors, eat just to stay alive, and can do so without learning to cook have no reason to learn to cook; and those who are baffled by the workings of computers and iPhones, and don't need them in order to achieve their goals, have no reason to try to learn their workings. Everyone does, however, have reason to either have positive attitudes towards these values (love, approval,

---

[13.] I borrow the idea of compossibility from Hillel Steiner, "The Structure of a Set of Compossible Rights" (1977), 767–775.

tolerance) or, at least, no negative attitudes (hatred, disapproval, intolerance). Anyone who thinks that her or his own optional values are good and those of others bad or not as good is simply wrong. It is largely because many end values are optional that *eudaimonic* lives can take different shapes.

(ii) Another possible explanation for disagreement is that some values are indeterminate, in the sense that there are good reasons both for and against them, but people mistakenly think that there is decisive reason to opt for the one they prefer over the other. One example of an indeterminate value is raising extremely self-reliant, "free-range" (but somewhat less safe) kids in a city vs. raising extremely safe (but somewhat less self-reliant) kids.[14] Another is one's attitudes toward one's life conditions: should a person accept her decent, but far from ideal, circumstances with serenity and an eye on their positive elements, or risk a painful fight to change them for the sake of the ideal? Perhaps the right decision in each case is relative to the individual's temperament, abilities, and chances of success.

Some people believe that there are no objective values, and that all values are determined by one's society. For them, my thesis that well-being as the highest prudential good requires objective worth is a nonstarter. But it is not my task here to make a case for objective values; this has been done by others far more skillfully than I could, and if they haven't succeeded in convincing skeptics that there are objective values, there is no reason for me to think that I can. This book is meant for those who believe that there are at least some objective values, and that it is at least worth inquiring whether well-being requires such values.

1.2 What Are We Talking About?

The lack of a common language leads James Griffin to wonder if different philosophers are addressing "different fundamental notions"; he states that what they say about well-being and its cognates "will partly fix the subject they think important to elucidate as well as offer an elucidation of it."[15] Daniel Haybron complains that too many philosophers confuse well-being with the

---

[14.] Lenore Skenazy, *Free-Range Kids, How to Raise Safe, Self-Reliant Children (Without Going Nuts with Worry)* (2010). Skenazy became a heroine to some parents, and a monster to others, when she wrote that she allowed her 9-year-old son to ride the New York City subway alone.
[15.] Griffin, "Replies" (2000), 285.

best life for a human being, or the good life overall, notions that include ideals of human perfection and virtue. Griffin's suspicions and Haybron's complaint are well-founded: too often, we talk past each other as we defend our own views, and (purportedly) disagree or agree with others' views, blissfully unaware that we are talking about different things. Still, I don't think we are all *completely* confused. I think that Griffin's own distinction between the prudential value of a life, on the one hand, and its aesthetic or moral value, on the other (Griffin, *Well-Being,* 9), followed by Sumner's elaboration of this distinction in *Welfare, Happiness, and Ethics,* have helped a great deal to clarify the topic. Most contemporary philosophers writing on well-being agree with Sumner that in discussing well-being, they are addressing the prudential value of an individual's life, and that this value is subject-relative, in the sense that for someone to have well-being is to have a life that is going well for *her,* rather than only for others, or only by some aesthetic or perfectionist standard (Sumner, *Welfare,* 20–25). Moreover, if asked, I think most philosophers would agree that they are talking about the highest prudential value—the *summum bonum*—not a prudential value that makes life barely worth living, or merely a pretty good life. After all, when moral philosophers talk about virtue, they mean supreme moral goodness, not merely the absence of wickedness, or moral mediocrity; and when health and fitness experts talk about health and fitness, they mean the best physical condition, not merely the condition required for doing without a ventilator, or a so-so condition. Yet even the best in these categories—the *summum bonum,* virtue, and health and fitness—admit of degrees. It is possible to have the *summum bonum* even if one has gone through some painful struggles, to be virtuous even if one fails in some respects,, and to be healthy and fit even if one occasionally gets colds or sprains.

But how do we choose between the various conceptions or theories of the *summum bonum* on offer? The current state of the discussion offers no neutral concept of the *summum bonum*—the highest prudential good—that can serve as a standard for evaluating different conceptions of well-being. Fortunately, there is an old one ready to hand that we have only to dust off and polish: Aristotle's concept of the prudential good as the most final, self-sufficient, and most choiceworthy good. This concept is silent on the components of the *summum bonum.* It says nothing about virtue or self-development or knowledge or friendship—or even pleasure or happiness. All this makes it a good candidate for serving as a neutral standard of different conceptions of well-being, and allaying the worries just seen: namely, that we don't know what we are talking about, or that we are confusing well-being with a life of perfection. But there is one more requirement that this concept must satisfy to serve as a standard: it must be a standard that many people actually use for evaluating their lives, even if only implicitly, in the sense that they would recognize it as such when presented with it. If no one could do so, then the formal concept of the *summum bonum* or highest prudential good would be practically and theoretically useless. For if it played no role in anyone's life, what role could it play in one's philosophy of the prudential good?

My first task, then, will be to show that this concept of the highest prudential good is very much alive in ordinary thinking, and that any satisfactory conception of well-being must meet the conditions of the highest prudential good. Only such a conception can be "descriptively adequate"— that is, in tune with our core beliefs about our highest prudential good, as they figure in our everyday deliberations and explanations.[16] And only such a conception can be normatively adequate—that is, justify our passion for trying to understand and achieve the highest prudential good for ourselves, to create the conditions for achieving it for our children, to help those we love achieve it and, in general, to wish it to humankind. In chapter 3, I will explain why the main subjective theories of well-being cannot meet these conditions.

In the next section I will give an overview of some recent work on the topic of the relationship of virtue or morality to well-being.

1.3 Objective Theories of Well-Being

1.3.1 "Objective list" theories of well-being, as Derek Parfit has called them,[17] and Aristotelian and Stoic *eudaimonist* theories and their contemporary descendants, are among the best known objective theories of well-being. "Objective list" theories identify well-being with the possession of a list of human goods.[18] The following is a pretty standard list from Richard Arneson:

> A life that has lots of pleasure, especially when this comes by way of enjoyment of what is truly excellent, a life that includes sustained and deep

---

[16.] I borrow the term and the idea of "descriptive adequacy" from Sumner, *Welfare* (1996), 10–19.
[17.] Derek Parfit, *Reasons and Persons* (1984), 493–503.
[18.] Richard J. Arneson, "Human Flourishing versus Desire Satisfaction" (1999), 113–142. In *Well-Being* (1986), Griffin presents himself as, and has been widely interpreted as, offering an informed-desire account of well-being, although he also states on p. 33 that his view is not very different from the objective-list account. In his *Replies* he states that he made a mistake in calling his account an informed-desire account, because what he was really offering was an account of the objective constituents of well-being.

relationships of friendship and love, a life that includes significant achievement in art or culture or systematic scientific understanding, a life that includes significant and sustained meaningful and interesting work--these features of a life inherently make it a better one for the one who lives it.[19]

The objective list theorist appeals to intuition to include these or other items on the list of things that a life must have to count as prudentially good; depending on the theorist, then, the list can also include virtue. But in adding virtue to the list as just another ingredient of a life of well-being, along with knowledge, friendship, and so on, the objective list theorist makes himself vulnerable to the criticism that virtue can neither add very much to the self-interested value of a life, nor vice detract from it. The claim that virtue, or virtuous commitments, are an indispensable component of well-being can be made good only if it is shown to be deeply implicated in prudential goods such as knowledge of important things, or genuine friendship.

1.3.2 Most contemporary philosophers of well-being who take their inspiration from ancient ethics hold that well-being requires virtue, and that there is a necessary connection between the idea of the individual's well-being and the idea of her moral goodness as a person. Thus, Phillipa Foot argues that we have a conception of the human good, which she calls "deep happiness," on which the human good precludes wickedness and entails virtue.[20] In this sense, she states, the young German men who were executed for resisting the Nazis were happy (Foot, *Goodness*, 94–97). But there is another sense of happiness in which it seems true to say that happiness in this life "was not something possible for them," since their lives were cut short and they were deprived of the enjoyment of the goods of this world (ibid., 95). Finally, a third sense of "happiness" is present in the statement of the doctor who said of his patient that he was " 'perfectly happy all day picking up leaves'." Happiness, Foot concludes, "is a protean concept, appearing now in one way and now in another" (97). I agree with Foot's distinctions, and her conclusion that happiness can mean different things in different contexts. But an argument is needed to persuade skeptics that the idea of deep happiness is coherent and that it plays a significant role in people's lives. This is what I aim to supply in chapter 2.

---

[19] Arneson, "Liberal Neutrality on the Good: An Autopsy" (2003), 191–218 (http://philosophyfaculty.ucsd.edu/faculty/rarneson/neutrality.pdf, 22, accessed July 8, 2011).
[20] Phillipa Foot, *Natural Goodness* (hereafter *Goodness*) (2001), chapter 6.

Hursthouse's aim is both more and less ambitious than Foot's. It is more ambitious in actually making a persuasive case that virtue is "the only reliable bet" for flourishing (well-being).[21] It is less ambitious in holding that virtue is not necessary for flourishing. Under certain circumstances, Hursthouse argues, a thoroughly immoral person can flourish. But this conclusion is unwarranted on her own conception of flourishing as a life that not only is lived with "zest and enthusiasm," but that also contains "the sort of happiness worth having" (*Ethics*, 9–10), the sort we would wish to our children (ibid., 185). More attention to her own conception of flourishing would have led Hursthouse to argue for the stronger conclusion that although some wicked people may *feel* happy, they cannot flourish, cannot have *eudaimonia*, because their happiness is not worth having.

Another account that owes its inspiration to Aristotle is Richard Kraut's developmental account, according to which well-being consists of the enjoyable exercise of our cognitive, emotional, sensory, social, and physical powers.[22] If we start with widely held intuitions about what is good for us, Kraut states, and ask why it is good for us, we'll see that it either constitutes or promotes the healthy and enjoyable exercise of our powers (*Well-Being*, 135–141). This applies to virtue as well, including justice. Justice is good for us because it makes us members of a mutually trusting, cooperating, and caring community; the unjust defector might gain more material goods, but he would lose the communal emotional bond (ibid., 193–196). Understanding what justice calls for and being a just person also calls for "considerable thought," and can be "a welcome component of one's life as a thoughtful person" (ibid.,195).

This developmental account is certainly part of the overall explanation for why what is good for us is good for us. The question that remains, however, is why someone who is just toward, and has an emotional bond with, members of his own community should be just to members of other communities—other races, other nationalities, other religions—if his injustice profits him materially, and he feels no remorse or guilt. On Kraut's account, he is justified in being unjust towards members of other communities, so long as being unjust doesn't interfere with his enjoyable exercise of his intellectual, emotional, and practical powers.

One major problem facing any theory that seeks to show that well-being requires virtue (or the related thesis that rational self-interest requires

---

[21] Hursthouse, *Virtue Ethics* (1999), 172.
[22] Kraut, *What Is Good and Why: The Ethics of Well-Being* (hereafter *Well-Being*) (2007), 137.

morality) is that we are a small group species, but morality requires us to transcend our group-ism and treat all human beings morally. Another major problem is that our own selves—our points of view, our values, our desires—often seem far more real to us than other people's points of view, values, or desires, even when those other people are members of our own small group. Yet morality requires that we recognize the equal reality of other people. If well-being is understood entirely in psychological terms, it is unlikely to provide every moral agent with a reason (justification) to cultivate other-regarding virtue. Such a reason can come only from a conception of well-being that incorporates the idea of virtue.

The most sustained recent defense of such a conception is Daniel C. Russell's *Happiness* (2012). Russell's approach to, and treatment of, this issue are both close to, and importantly different from, mine. (Unfortunately, I came across Russell's book only after I had finished the major revisions on mine, so I will not have as much to say about it as I would have liked). The main substantive difference between us is that Russell thinks that it is hard to choose between the Aristotelian thesis that virtue is necessary, but not sufficient, for eudaimonia, and the Stoic thesis that virtue is both necessary and sufficient, whereas I think that there is no hope for the second, stronger thesis. This negative view is not shared by Annas or Lawrence Becker, who defend the Stoic view in recent work.[23] It must be admitted that this view has surprising popular appeal: we thrill to portraits of heroes who find their good in living a life of virtue, indifferent to the vagaries of fortune, facing torture and death in the service of a noble cause with equanimity, and making up for the shortness of their lives with their splendor. But finding fictional portrayals of stoical heroes thrilling is not the same as finding the attempt to live like one thrilling. As I'll argue, the claim that a life of well-being is identical with a life of virtue has highly counterintuitive consequences, implying as it does that no loss, no matter how tragic by our ordinary understanding, can affect our prudential good, unless it be the loss of virtue. It thereby sunders the connection with ordinary conceptions of well-being, and fails to be descriptively adequate.

---

[23] Lawrence Becker, *A New Stoicism* (1999), hereafter *Stoicism*; Annas, *Happiness* (1993); Annas, "Aristotle on Virtue and Happiness" (1989), 7–22 (repr. 1999), 35–55, "Virtue Ethics: What Kind of Naturalism?" (2005), 11–29. In *Intelligent Virtue* Annas stops short of arguing for the Stoic position, stating merely that this can be done only after showing that "there is a latent incoherence in thinking of happiness as made up both of living virtuously and of items such as money and status, which belong with life's circumstances rather than with the living of it" (167–168).

1.4. A Morality Fit for Well-being, a Well-being Fit for Morality

1.4.1 Since the central question of my book is whether morality—moral virtues, principles, acts—plays a necessary role in well-being, I need a conception of morality that allows for this possibility while also clearly passing the test of descriptive and normative adequacy. Simply identifying well-being with a virtuous life, or counterintuitively weakening virtue's demands to ensure that they never conflict with what looks like well-being, fails both tests of adequacy for both well-being and virtue, and amounts to admitting that there is no good argument for the alleged connection between them. An argument with teeth must show that morality is necessary for well-being using conceptions of morality and of well-being that are descriptively and normatively adequate. In particular, its conception of morality must make room for genuinely other-regarding virtues, and its conception of well-being must make room, in Hursthouse's felicitous phrase, for the "smile factor." I will argue that a conception of well-being that meets the formal constraints of the highest prudential good and the Aristotelian conception of virtue as an enduring, deep-seated intellectual-emotional disposition to think, feel, choose, and act "at the right times, about the right things, towards the right people, for the right end, and in the right way"[24]—and to take pleasure in so doing—can best meet these demands.

The claim is sometimes made that the corpus of ancient Greek ethics does not make the sharp distinction between moral and non-moral reasons often found in modern ethics, being concerned, rather, with the larger question of how to live one's life. Hence, this claim has it, Greek ethics has no truck with the notion of duty or obligation as a special moral notion.[25] This point is true in the sense that Greek ethics doesn't identify morality with other-regarding duties or virtues, and doesn't regard the agent's well-being as a non-moral issue. At the same time, however, it recognizes that it is the other-regarding virtues that pose the real challenge to the *eudaimonist* thesis, for it seems that we can be virtuous in relation to ourselves, or in intellectual and creative/productive matters, without being virtuous in relation to others. Even Aristotle, who doesn't take up this challenge, acknowledges in passing that it is possible to be virtuous in one's own affairs without being virtuous (just) in relation to others (*NE*

[24.] Aristotle, *NE* (1999), Bk. II, 1106b21–24.
[25.] Williams, *Ethics* (1985), chapters 1 and 10.

129b31–1130a14). (This, of course, is an astonishing concession, given other passages in which he claims that the virtues are global and united.) When Glaucon and Adeimantus challenge Socrates to show them that virtue is necessary for *eudaimonia*, it is on the virtue of justice—giving others their due—that they focus.

There is another sense in which the moral versus non-moral distinction *is* relevant to Greek ethics: it regards reasons of virtue as distinct from, and not to be weighed on the same scale as, reasons of utility or pleasure. Thus, the courageous individual does not ask himself if it's rational for him to act courageously on this occasion, given that it will make him late for the show, wet his shoes, and maybe even cause him to sweat. For him, as for us now, the claims of courage override or "silence," as John McDowell would say,[26] the claims of entertainment, convenience, and personal hygiene. (Sometimes cleanliness is *not* next to godliness.)

1.4.2 Some people dismiss the idea that other-regarding virtues are essential for well-being as so obviously contrary to the evidence that, they believe, it can only be a symptom of wishful thinking, the wish to see the good rewarded and the wicked suffer. This sort of wishful thinking—the "belief in a just world"—has been called a "fundamental delusion" by some psychologists.[27] The charge is true if the belief in question is the jejune idea that the Virtuous Person always gets the Prince or Princess and the Vicious the Toad, or that the Virtuous never suffer nor the Vicious ever enjoy anything. But as we shall see, neither disjunct is entailed by the claim that well-being as the HPG requires virtue.

Part of the reason that it seems obvious to some people that other-regarding virtues cannot be required for well-being is their conception of well-being. A case in point is Stephen M. Cahn's one-paragraph "refutation by counterexample" of the *eudaimonist* thesis.[28] The counterexample features a "happy immoralist," whom Cahn describes as follows:

Fred's life has been devoted to achieving three aims: fame, wealth, and a reputation for probity. He has no interest whatever in friends or truth. Indeed, he is treacherous and thoroughly dishonest. Nevertheless, he has attained his three goals and is, in fact, a rich celebrity renowned for his supposed

---

[26] McDowell, "Virtue and Reason" (1979), 50–76. In *Happiness* (1983), 121–124, Annas argues that there are enough similarities between ancient concerns about virtue and modern concerns about morality to justify thinking that ancient concerns are about morality.

[27] Melvin Lerner, *The Belief in a Just World: A Fundamental Delusion* (1980), cited in Marilyn Friedman, "On Being Bad and Living Well: Virtue and the Good Life," unpublished ms.

[28] Steven M. Cahn, "The Happy Immoralist" (2004), 1.

integrity. His acquiring a good name while acting unscrupulously is a tribute to his audacity, cunning, and luck. Now he rests self-satisfied, basking in renown, delighting in luxuries, and relishing praise for his reputed commitment to the highest moral standards.

There are many good reasons to think that this particular portrait of a "happy immoralist" lacks psychological credibility,[29] but my concern here is with Cahn's assumption that *eudaimonia* is nothing more than an assortment of positive psychological states. There is a venerable tradition of anti-*eudaimonists* defining *eudaimonia* thus—and then triumphantly dismissing the *eudaimonist* claim that well-being requires virtue in a page or less. Thus Kant, who in *Groundwork of the Metaphysic of Morals* takes it for granted that well-being for the ancients, as for him, consists entirely in a positive mental state.[30] Kant also assumes that the virtues of the ancients are just affairs of temperament, that genuine virtue consists of the "strength of will" to obey the imperatives of a "Pure Practical Reason," and that duty and rational motivation can have no truck with self-interest and emotional motivation, those denizens of the natural, non-rational realm.[31] With these assumptions in place, it needs hardly any argument to show that any meeting of well-being and virtue is purely coincidental.

But even Aristotle would have dismissed the *eudaimonist* claim if he had defined either *eudaimonia* or virtue as Kant does. He would also have dismissed the *eudaimonist* claim if he had subscribed to an ascetic morality that sees our natural desires and pleasures as sources of sin (as some religious moralities do); or to a morality that regards moral goodness as consisting of self-sacrifice, preferably painful (a view that is widespread in ordinary thinking); or to the view that moral goodness consists of acting from, and only from, the impersonal point of view (a view espoused by some consequentialists). In relegating pleasure, joy, self-interest, or the personal point of view to a lower, non-moral, or even immoral, realm, these theories all but tell us that we must choose between moral goodness and well-being. The problem with this is not that people *cannot* choose the former over the latter, but that they cannot choose it consistently without resentment, frustration, or misery. That they *can* choose it satisfies what Owen Flanagan calls the Principle of Minimal Psychological Realism

---

[29] See chapter 7 in this volume and Jeffrie G. Murphy, "The Unhappy Immoralist" (2004), 11–13.
[30] Immanuel Kant, *Groundwork* (1785), chapter 1, trans. H.J. Paton, in *The Moral Law* (1948).
[31] This is true of Kant in the *Groundwork*, but in some later works he softens his stand on the emotions. See Section 1.4.3.

(PMPR): "Make sure when constructing a moral theory or projecting a moral ideal that the character, decision processing, and behavior pre-scribed are possible... for creatures like us."[32] But that they can choose it only unhappily satisfies what I call the Ogden Nash Lament:

O Duty,
Why hast thou not the visage of a sweetie or a cutie?
....
Why glitter thy spectacles so ominously?
Why art thou clad so abominously?
Why art thou so different from Venus?
And why do thou and I have so few interests mutually in common between us?[33]

A moral ideal that hopes to attract adherents must be more than mini-mally realistic. One lesson to draw from the discussion so far is that the issue of the role of morality in well-being cannot be settled independently of our conception of morality or of well-being. Another lesson is that a relevant—and interesting—questioning of the neo-Aristotelian thesis that *eudaimonia* entails a life of virtue must do one of two things: (i) show that *eudaimonia* does not entail virtue even when *eudaimonia* is conceived of as the individual's highest prudential good and virtue is conceived of as an integrated intellectual and emotional disposition to think, feel, and choose the right thing for the right reasons; or (ii) reject one or both of these ideas as implausible or incoherent. But although there have been many criticisms of the Aristotelian conception of virtue, few have been directed at the claim that virtue is an integrated intellectual and emotional disposition to do the right thing for the right reasons, a disposition that includes practical wisdom.[34] The main criticisms have been directed at

---

[32] Owen O. Flanagan, Jr., *Varieties of Moral Personality: Ethics and Psychological Realism* (1991), 32.

[33] Ogden Nash, from "Kind of an Ode to Duty" (1995).

[34] Two prominent examples of philosophers who have questioned the need for practical wisdom are Julia Driver, *Uneasy Virtue* (2001, reprinted 2007) and Michael Slote, *Morality from Motives* (2001). Driver argues that a virtue is "a character trait that produces more good (in the actual world) than not systematically," and that moral virtue is a trait that systematically results in good consequences for others in the agent's usual environment (82). Such a trait does not require practical wisdom, hence practical wisdom is not essential to consequentialist virtue. But even traits like good-heartedness or sympathy can be misdirected without practical wisdom; hence they would produce more good consequences with it. Slote argues that practical wisdom, understood as a faculty that both chooses the means and specifies the ends, is unnecessary, because the virtuous agent's virtue tells her what she needs to do without deliberating about it. But this a priori ruling out of the need for deliberation, whatever the circumstances, assumes, I think, a world far simpler and more transparent than the one we live in.

virtue-globalism: the thesis that if you have a virtue in one domain of your life, you must have it in all of them. As we will see, however, a successful criticism of virtue-globalism makes the thesis that virtue is required for *eudaimonia* or well-being more, not less, plausible. In particular, it allows a more plausible interpretation of the thesis that virtue is the primary element in *eudaimonia*. Again, although there have been detailed arguments to show that the claim that *eudaimonia* requires a virtuous life is implausible, none of them has employed the notion of *eudaimonia* as the highest prudential good, a good that is most complete, self-sufficient, and most choiceworthy for a human being. Nor have any of the arguments attempted to show that this idea of the individual's own highest good is implausible or otherwise problematic. Of course, if "the most complete, self-sufficient, and most choiceworthy good for a human being" is defined in moral terms, then the thesis that *eudaimonia* entails a life of virtue becomes true by definition. But this, as we'll see, is not the only way to forge a conceptual connection between a virtuous life and well-being.

1.4.3 The project of showing that a virtuous life is necessary for well-being gains support from the thought that a rational morality must, at the very least, not be in constant conflict with the agent's own good. Hence, a morality that equates moral goodness with self-sacrifice, or that is completely indifferent to the agent's self-interest, lacks rational backing. This serves as a constraint on an acceptable conception of morality, a constraint that the conceptions we have just considered fail to satisfy. In this connection, it is worth noting that even those theories that reject, with one hand, the idea that a rational morality cannot be indifferent to the agent's well-being, seem compelled to pay tribute to this idea with the other by making the agent's well-being the reward of virtue. Thus, Kant's theory, ascetic theories, and common sense morality all hold out hope for "true happiness" or well-being for the virtuous or dutiful in the hereafter—even as they urge us not to act from the motive of achieving well-being. Kant's concession on this point is especially telling. As is well-known, in the *Groundwork* Kant casts scorn on moralists who define moral character partly in psychological terms and make *eudaimonia* the supreme good (and (part) justification) of morality. Yet in *Critique of Practical Reason*, he posits a hereafter expressly for the sake of satisfying what he regards as a need of Pure Practical Reason: the need to believe that the complete good—perfect virtue with perfect happiness—can be realized.[35] In *Religion Within*

---

[35] *Critique of Practical Reason* (1788), trans. Mary J. Gregor, 2nd ed. (1996), 113–114.

the Limits of Reason Alone Kant goes even further, arguing that if "the firm resolve to do better in the future.... encouraged by good progress" doesn't "beget a joyous frame of mind," a person can never be "certain of having really attained a love for the good, that is, of having incorporated it into his maxim."[36] The most radical departure from the *Groundwork* doctrine, however, comes when he attributes a non-instrumental moral worth to feelings, stating that benevolent feelings are part of a "beautiful moral whole" which is "required for its own sake."[37]

As doubt about the ontological status of the hereafter has grown and the here and now has become more urgent, the intellectual stock of ascetic moralities has fallen, and reconciling morality with the agent's well-being in this life has once again become a more important task. Feeling the rational pressure of this demand, most contemporary consequentialists distinguish between motivation and justification, and argue that the best way to maximize the good is to act on our everyday, non-moral motivations to benefit those we know and care about, including ourselves.[38] Common sense morality also proclaims, cheerfully and frequently, if inconsistently, that we "owe it to ourselves" to further our own (morally permissible) interests.

Like *eudaimonist* virtue ethics, rational choice theories, which first appear around the same time as *eudaimonist* theories, also seek to show that morality is required by the agent's own rational interests (and justified by that fact).[39] Yet the two kinds of theories have grown side-by-side with barely a nod of recognition to each other. This is largely due to their very different conceptions of the agent's rational interests (her prudential good), and of morality. Rational choice theories start with mutually disinterested agents—agents who take no interest in each other's interests—and purport to show that even such agents can, under certain circumstances, come to see that they will do better to become moral and take an interest in each other's interests. One influential version of such a theory is David Gauthier's neo-Hobbesian contractarianism, according

---

[36] *Religion Within the Limits of Reason Alone* (1793), Bk. One 19, 20, trans. Theodore M. Greene and Hoyt H. Hudson (New York: Harper and Brothers, 1934/1960).

[37] *The Doctrine of Virtue.* Part 2 of *The Metaphysic of Morals.* (1797), trans. Mary J. Gregor, 2nd ed. (1996), 485.

[38] Consequentialists as diverse as J.J.C. Smart and Peter Railton defend versions of this view. See Smart, "An Outline of Utilitarianism," hereafter "Utilitarianism," in Smart and B. Williams, *Utilitarianism: For and Against* (1973), 3–74, and Railton, "Alienation, Consequentialism, and the Demands of Morality" (1984), 134–171.

[39] Glaucon posits that morality rests on a mutually beneficial contract in Plato's *Republic*, Bk. II.

to which morality, conceived of as the disposition of constrained maximization with other constrained maximizers, beats the disposition of indiscriminate straightforward maximization.[40] In other words, on this theory, those who have internalized the principle of keeping their agreements with others who have also internalized this principle do better, overall, than those who are disposed to cheat. In contrast to *eudaimonist* virtue ethics, however, moral dispositions on this theory are entirely instrumental to an independently defined self-interest to which notions of objective worth are irrelevant. Moreover, contractarianism has a very restricted view of who has moral standing, namely, only those who can enter into mutually beneficial cooperative relationships and those they have an interest in protecting.

David Schmidtz's non-contractarian rational choice theory does not have these limitations. Schmidtz argues that even if we start with an instrumental conception of rationality, our psychology will lead most of us to become reflectively rational, that is, disposed to care about the nature of our ends and not only about the effectiveness of our means to our ends. This will lead most of us to be motivated to care about something other than survival, because mere survival is not worth caring about.[41] We will develop the self-regard and integrity that are essential to personal morality, and most of us will also develop the other-regard—respect and concern—that is essential to interpersonal morality (*Rational Choice*).

So far this is quite congenial to a *eudaimonist* virtue ethics. It ceases to be congenial only when Schmidtz claims that even a Mafia assassin can be reflectively rational, so long as he has self-regard and integrity, and respect and concern for his fellow assassins (*Rational Choice*, 233). The assassin still violates collective rationality and the interpersonal strand of morality towards people outside his community, and so he still falls seriously short of being fully reflectively rational. But as in Kraut's theory, this fact does not give him sufficient reason to become more moral. Such a reason can come only from a concern for, or a fear of, his larger community.

Rational choice theory makes at least two important contributions to the attempt to show that the agent's own good requires morality. One contribution is showing the importance of external constraints. Those who see no reason of self-interest for being moral when they can get away with their immorality need to be given external reasons. The other contribution is

---

[40.] David Gauthier, *Morals By Agreement* (1986).
[41.] David Schmidtz, *Rational Choice and Moral Agency* (hereafter *Rational Choice*) (1995), chapters 1–3.

showing that *some* morality toward *some* people is instrumentally advantageous in most circumstances even if we start out caring about little beyond survival or a narrowly defined self-interest. But the output of rational choice theory is necessarily limited by its input. With its richer conception of self-interest understood as *eudaimonia*, and of morality understood as virtue, *eudaimonist* virtue ethics aims to reach the richer conclusion that living virtuously is essential to *eudaimonia*.[42] This aim is facilitated by the fact that both *eudaimonia* and virtue are understood partly in terms of certain emotional dispositions. Hence they enjoy a natural fit that is missing from the conceptions of self-interest and morality in rational choice theories.

1.5. Well-being: Happiness in an Objectively Worthwhile Life

Part I: Well-Being. The main argument of my book can be stated in the following five propositions:

(i) Well-being as the HPG consists of happiness in an objectively worthwhile life.

(ii) Someone who leads such a life must be characteristically autonomous and reality-oriented, that is, disposed to think for herself and seek truth or understanding about important aspects of her own life and human life in general, and disposed to act on her understanding when circumstances permit.

(iii) To the extent that someone with these traits succeeds in achieving understanding and acting on it when circumstances permit, she is realistic.

(iv) To the extent that she is realistic, she is virtuous.

(v) Hence well-being as the HPG requires virtue.

But even the HPG comes in degrees, because happiness and objective worth come in degrees (1.2 above). The life of someone who is largely autonomous and reality-oriented has some objective worth even if she is mistaken about some fundamental human values, a worth it would not have if she lacked all autonomy and reality-orientation. But to the extent

---

[42] I will not be talking about the complicated issue of the moral standing of animals, but there is no reason why virtue ethics cannot recognize their standing as moral patients as well as other moral theories can.

that she has these traits, *and* is informed about fundamental human values and disposed to pursue or honor them in her actions, she is realistic, and insofar as she is realistic, she is virtuous.

In identifying well-being as the HPG with happiness in an objectively worthwhile *life,* I mean to distinguish my view from the traditional *eudaimonist* view that identifies *eudaimonia* with a certain sort of *activity.* Well-being as the HPG consists of happy, worthwhile activities as well as periods of happy non-activity, pure receptivity. It is true, as I argue in chapter 2, that who we are and what we do matters more to well-being as the HPG than what happens to us, but what happens to us and what is given to us by nature and other people is also important. Joy in the beauty of nature, pleasure in the health of our bodies, appreciation of others' achievements, delight in being the object of love—all these are part of our well-being. Indeed, the fact that these are partly constitutive of our well-being is indispensable to a full explanation of our nature as agents. If our well-being was unaffected by the beauty of nature, there would be no landscape artists or gardeners; if it was unaffected by others' achievements, we would probably be incapable of taking joy in our own achievements; and if it was unaffected by others' love of us, we would be incapable of loving them.[43]

In chapter 2, I explicate the concept of the HPG as the most final, self-sufficient, and most choiceworthy good, and argue that only well-being conceived of as happiness in a worthwhile human life qualifies as such a good. Both this concept of the HPG and this conception of well-being are widely-held and psychologically defensible notions. In other words, both meet the demand for descriptive adequacy. They also meet the demand for normative adequacy, because they justify our caring for our own well-being and wishing it to others. Widespread, too, is the idea that being realistic (autonomous, reality-oriented, and informed) about the important features of one's own life and human life in general is a prudential value that is necessary for a fully worthwhile life. I conclude the chapter by addressing some common criticisms of objective conceptions of well-being, and arguing that they do not apply to the conception I defend.

In chapter 3 I discuss the main subjective conceptions of well-being: hedonism, desire-satisfaction, authentic life-satisfaction, individual nature-fulfillment, and value-based life-satisfaction (VBLS).

[43.] Harry F. Harlow's experiments with monkeys show the importance of the loving touch for the well-being, even normal development, of baby monkeys and, by extrapolation, baby humans. See Harlow, "The Nature of Love" (1958), 673–685 (http://psychclassics.yorku.ca/Harlow/love.htm, accessed March 4, 2013).

I argue that none of them is descriptively or normatively adequate, because their requirements can be met even by someone who spends his life on Nozick's experience machine, or in counting blades of grass. Subjectivists about well-being face the following dilemma: if they reject the idea that objective worth is essential to well-being, their theories have highly counterintuitive consequences and cannot meet the constraints of descriptive or normative adequacy; but if they seek to make their theories plausible, they must accept the necessity of objective worth, and their accounts cease to be purely subjective. In this chapter, I also respond to the subjectivist challenge that objectivist theories give short shrift to the individual's own point of view or her individual nature, or that they confuse the prudential value of a life with other dimensions of value.

Part II: Autonomy, Realism, and Virtue. In chapter 4 I argue that autonomy and reality-orientation understood as character traits are prudential values that are also conditions of objective worth and, thus, of well-being as the HPG. An autonomous and reality-oriented individual seeks self-understanding and understanding of others, but there is no guarantee that she will succeed; indeed, she might be badly mistaken in these respects. By her own standards, then, she would regard her life as sadly lacking in worth and well-being. And she would be right, because objective worth requires that we be in touch with the important features of our own lives and human life in general. To the extent that we meet this requirement, we are realistic, and realism, I argue, entails a life of the central virtues. In short, well-being as the HPG requires happiness in an objectively worthwhile life, such a life requires realism, realism entails a life of virtue, hence well-being as the HPG entails a life of virtue. If I'm successful, my theory will have grounded virtue in elements that are uncontroversially (more cautiously, less controversially) regarded as elements of well-being, and shown that a virtuous life is not only a means to, or mere icing on, the cake of our prudential good, but part of the cake itself. And this is not, as some critics think, a mere terminological difference from theories that see virtue and well-being as two independent aims or states of individuals.[44] Contrary to some subjectivists, then, there is no insuperable conceptual barrier between the prudential and the moral.[45]

---

[44] White, *History* (2006), 139–140, argues that the difference between *eudaimonist* and non-*eudaimonist* views seems to be merely terminological, because like the latter, *eudaimonist* theories also cannot do away with conflict between virtue and other requirements of well-being.
[45] In *Welfare* (1986), Sumner argues that there is such a barrier, and in *The Examined Life* (1989), chapter 2, Robert Nozick suggests that there might be.

Moreover, unlike purely subjective conceptions of well-being, the thesis that realism is an objective prudential value can explain why we regard those whose lives completely lack objective worth with horror or pity, even if they themselves feel positive about their lives.

My claim that a realistic life is necessary for well-being is open to two challenges. One challenge comes from common sense, which says that my view flies in the face of an obvious truth, namely, that it is possible to know too much for your own happiness. Since happiness is one of the two central components of well-being, it follows that it is possible to know too much for your own well-being. The other challenge, which has recently gained currency among psychologists and philosophers, comes from the claim that people with mild illusions about themselves tend to be happier, nicer, mentally healthier, and more productive than highly realistic people. So realism is not only contrary to happiness, it is also, apparently, contrary to objective worth. If these challenges succeed, my thesis is eviscerated. I take on these criticisms in chapter 5, contending that, properly understood, being realistic really is good for us, even if, on a particular occasion, acting realistically proves to be disastrous.

Part III: Well-Being and Virtue. In chapter 6 I argue that the Aristotelian conception of virtue as an integrated intellectual-emotional disposition is, with some qualifications, a psychologically realistic and plausible conception of moral excellence, the height of moral achievement. It is also best suited to the project of showing that a virtuous life is necessary for *eudaimonia* both constitutively and instrumentally. It is not my task to show what makes a trait a virtue, but the thesis that virtue is necessary for *eudaimonia* entails that only traits that are characteristically compatible with its possessor's *eudaimonia* can be virtues, and that traits that by their very nature are incompatible with the agent's *eudaimonia* cannot be virtues.[46] It does not follow, however, that every virtuous *act* is compatible with the agent's *eudaimonia*.

Acceptance of the Aristotelian conception of virtue as an integrated intellectual-emotional disposition does not commit me to the idea that virtue is global. Hence it also does not commit me to the idea that the virtues are globally united or reciprocal. Globalism holds that if an individual has a virtue in one domain of his life, he must have it across the board, and the unity or reciprocity thesis holds that if he has one virtue, he must have all.

---

[46] "Characteristically," because in the midst of thieves, aggressors, cheaters, or tyrants, virtuous traits can be turned into weapons against their possessors.

I argue that even the most virtuous person is not virtuous in every area of his life, but that in the areas in which he is virtuous, he must have all the relevant virtues. In short, the relevant virtues are united within these areas, not across the board. Nevertheless, even in areas in which he is virtuous, he is not perfectly virtuous. For virtue requires recognizing and responding in a variety of appropriate ways, as Christine Swanton puts it, to both the "demands of the self and the demands of the world," and the demands are many and complex.[47] Perfect virtue and perfect *eudaimonia* serve as yardsticks and ideals, however abstract, and however implicitly grasped, of moral excellence and the highest prudential good, respectively, ideals that we might live up to in rare, splendid, periods of our lives, but that we can only approximate to a greater or lesser degree the rest of the time.[48] So even the most virtuous person is not perfectly *eudaimonic*. Recognizing these facts has important consequences for how we conduct ourselves in the world: how we evaluate and feel about ourselves and others, what we expect of ourselves and others, and how we act and react. In turn, how we conduct ourselves has important consequences for *eudaimonia*.

Some critics of globalism argue that character is fragmented, in that virtue and the other character traits are local, that is, confined to possibly only one kind of situation. So if I am right that virtue is partly constitutive of *eudaimonia*, it follows that *eudaimonia* also is fragmented. I argue that the nature of virtuous motivation and practical wisdom, as well as the nature of virtue acquisition, show that virtue cannot be fragmented. And although social and cognitive psychology have revealed new barriers to rationality and virtue, the barriers are not insuperable. Hence some virtue is still possible to us.

In chapter 7 I defend my claim that well-being as the highest prudential good entails a life of virtue against a variety of challenges, both internal and external. Some of the external challenges miss their mark because they assume a different conception of virtue, or of *eudaimonia,* from mine. An important objection, however, is that someone's life can be objectively worthwhile by virtue of some important intellectual, aesthetic, or other kind of achievement, and still be devoid not only of other-regarding virtue, but even of other-regarding moral decency. I argue that someone who has the capacity for other-regarding moral virtue, but is still devoid of it, is to

---

[47] Christine Swanton, *Virtue Ethics: A Pluralistic View* (hereafter *Pluralistic View*) (2003).
[48] Neither ideal is, in Broadie's words, "an explicit, comprehensive, substantial vision," a Grand End (*Ethics with Aristotle*, 1993), 198. Hursthouse, *Virtue Ethics* (1999), 136–139, calls the idea of such a vision a "Platonic fantasy". White, *History* (2006), 173, also points out that we don't have "*a completely and consistently articulated* concept of happiness [well-being]."

that extent impoverished, even if he has other worthwhile achievements and the virtues required for those achievements. But some highly productive people's capacities for understanding other people and, thus, having other-regarding moral goodness might be minimal *because* they have these unusual productive capacities. All they might be capable of doing is abiding by other-regarding moral principles without really understanding why. Their virtue might be limited to their creative or productive lives. My claim that objective worth requires other-regarding moral goodness does not apply to them, or to anyone who lacks the relevant capacity.

Some criticisms arise from the very structure of Aristotelian and neo-Aristototelian *eudaimonism*. One criticism is that the thesis that *eudaimonia* requires both virtue and external goods is internally unstable, and should be replaced by the stronger Stoic thesis that virtue is both necessary and sufficient for well-being. I defend the Aristotelian thesis against the charge of instability, and argue that the Stoic thesis, while making for a "neater" theory, assumes an implausible view of human psychology, and makes a mystery of both virtue and *eudaimonia*. Another criticism is that the Aristotelian primacy of virtue thesis is highly counterintuitive, and should be replaced by the weaker thesis that virtue plays no essential role in well-being. This criticism is justified on some interpretations of the role of virtue in Aristotelian *eudaimonism*, but these interpretations are not forced on us by the primacy of virtue thesis.

I conclude in chapter 8 by defusing skepticism about the thesis that well-being as the HPG entails a life of virtue. I do this by questioning certain claims often made on behalf of virtue, such as the claim that the more virtuous *must* have more HPG than the somewhat less virtuous, regardless of their circumstances. This would be true, I argue, only if virtue was both necessary and sufficient for well-being as the HPG. But I reject the sufficiency thesis. I also reject the idea that the wicked *must* suffer pain and conflict rather than simply an absence of the HPG. If these claims were true, vice and akrasia would be less prevalent. But if we keep in mind that the HPG has both a psychological and an objective normative component, and that both virtue and the HPG come in degrees, we can see that none of these claims follow from the thesis that the HPG entails virtue. My thesis will no doubt strike some readers as far too weak to be satisfying. A stronger thesis, however, one that satisfies our longing for perfection, fails to apply to us, the imperfect and divided products of evolution.

CHAPTER 2 | Well-Being as the Highest Prudential Good

"The habit of being happy enables one to be freed, or largely freed, from the dominance of outward conditions."

—ROBERT LOUIS STEVENSON

"What man actually needs is...the striving and struggling for a worthwhile goal, a freely chosen task."

—VIKTOR FRANKL, *Man's Search for Meaning.*

2.1. The Concept of the Highest Prudential Good

2.1.1 My aim in this chapter is twofold: first, to show that Aristotle's concept of the highest (prudential) good captures important elements in many, if not most, people's ideal of well-being; and second, to endorse a widespread conception of well-being that meets the formal constraints of this concept. The result, I hope to show, is a conception of well-being that is internally coherent, intuitively plausible, and highly attractive. Thus it satisfies both the descriptive and the normative requirements of an adequate conception of well-being.

There is no one accepted interpretation of Aristotle's concept of the highest prudential good, but my aim is not interpretive; it is to take what I think is true from this account, and ignore or modify the rest. What is uncontroversial is that Aristotle is inquiring into the agent's own good, not the good of others, or the agent's overall goodness. Moral goodness, or virtue, enters the discussion only as part of his *conception* or *theory* of the highest prudential good, not as part of his basic *concept* of the highest prudential good.

Aristotle starts by arguing that if there is a highest prudential good for a human being, it must be most final (or most complete), self-sufficient, and most choiceworthy (Aristotle, *NE*, I.7). There are many things that we choose both for themselves and for the sake of other things, such as friendship and health. Friendship and health are inherently desirable, but each also serves a further purpose: for example, friendship affords us the assurance of help in times of need, and health enables us to do our work well. In turn, having such assurance and being able to do our work well are themselves both inherently desirable and means to further ends. At some point, though, both in our deliberations and in our pursuits, we reach an ultimate end, an end that is desirable only for itself. If this were not the case, desire would be "empty and futile"—and we know, Aristotle implies, that it isn't empty and futile (ibid., 1094a 18–22).

This, of course, isn't enough to establish that there must be only one ultimate end rather than several. But if the highest prudential good (HPG) is a certain kind of life—and it is—then it makes little sense to suppose, at the most abstract or formal level of description, that there might be more than one such end. What, then, are the formal features of a life that can count as the HPG? It is a life that is most final because we desire it for itself and only for itself, self-sufficient because with it we lack nothing, and most choiceworthy because it is not one good among many (ibid., 1097a15–1097b20). For if it were one good among many, the addition of another good would make it better, and this new resultant good would be the most choiceworthy good. Hence, the HPG is an inclusive, not exclusive or dominant, end.[1]

We can now see that these three features of the highest prudential good stand in a relationship of mutual entailment. It is because the HPG is most final, encompassing everything desirable for its own sake, that it is self-sufficient; it is because the HPG is self-sufficient that it is most choiceworthy; and it is because the HPG is most choiceworthy that it is most final.

---

[1] This distinction was first drawn by W.F.R. Hardie in "The Final Good in Aristotle's *Ethics*" (1965), 277–295 (reprinted in J.M.E. Moravcsik, ed., *Aristotle: A Collection of Critical Essays* (1967)), and in Hardie, *Aristotle's Ethical Theory* (1968), chapter 2. Hardie argues that Aristotle's explicit view is that *eudaimonia* is a dominant good, but that occasionally he sees, correctly, that it is an inclusive good. In the Introduction to her *Essays on Aristotle's Ethics* (1980), Amélie Rorty provides an excellent discussion of the issue, including the somewhat different meanings of "dominant" and "inclusive" in the literature, and an excellent argument for the inclusive end interpretation (16–24). Cooper, *Human Good* (1986), 97–99 and Irwin, trans. *NE* (1999) also agree with the inclusive end interpretation, whereas Kraut, *Aristotle on the Human Good* (1991) defends the dominant good interpretation. Regardless of which interpretation is correct, I think that the more plausible view in its own right is the inclusivist view.

There seems to be nothing in this idea of the highest prudential good that is alien to the modern mind. It is natural to think in terms of the best kind of life for ourselves, and such thinking starts at an early age. Children often say things like "this is what I've wanted all my life" and talk about what they would like to have or be when they grow up, imagining this state of being grown up as their entire—fulfilling—future. It is also natural to regard what we see as the ideal life for ourselves as the final end, the end that provides the ultimate explanation and justification for all our particular goals, actions, and desires. The idea that the individual's highest prudential good is her most final, most choiceworthy, and self-sufficient good is, moreover, the common stuff of fiction. The story comes to a satisfactory close when the protagonist finally achieves her most important goal, the one that gives her "all that her heart could desire," allowing her to live happily (that is, have well-being) ever after. Of course, we adults know (even if we keep forgetting) that "true happiness" (well-being) is not something we are assured forever with the possession of some external good; we know that it is largely a matter of the way we live our lives. But "happily ever after" captures a desire that everyone capable of the highest prudential good can recognize. No wonder, then, that it reappears in so many different religious conceptions of eternal bliss in the hereafter— the Christian heaven, the Muslim Paradise, the Hindu *moksha*, and the Buddhist nirvana.[2]

The yearning for a complete good—a life so desirable that nothing added to it can make it better—has a phenomenological basis. Many of us have known moments in which we feel complete, as though life's promise has been fulfilled and all our desires satisfied. They are moments in which we feel simultaneously that if we died then, we'd have nothing to regret— and also, with utter clarity, that life is supremely worth living for its own sake. When we project this sense of completeness over our entire lives, we have the emotional equivalent of a good that is an ultimate, encompassing end for all our choices.

At this point, some might question Aristotle on his claim that the HPG is the *most* final good—a good that we desire *only* for itself—because surely it is possible to desire the positive emotions that are partly constitutive of

---

[2] According to the Buddhist scholar, Walpola Rahula, nirvana isn't quite the same as happiness, but it is difficult to say what it is since it is so different from any earthly experience, and our language has evolved to describe earthly experience (*What the Buddha Taught: Revised and Expanded*, 1974). Suffice it to say that nirvana is absence of all negative mental states—such as suffering, anxiety, restlessness, and so on—and akin to positive mental states such as tranquility, joy, contentment. To achieve nirvana is to achieve the "Ultimate Truth."

the HPG as a means to survival, or as a means to living a better life. For example, if in despair our thoughts turn to suicide, we can find it in ourselves to try to overcome the despair and seek happiness both for its own sake and in order to keep living. Again, if we find ourselves being mean and crabby out of a deep dissatisfaction with life, we can find it in ourselves to try to overcome the dissatisfaction and be happy both for its own sake and in order to become better people. As both Kant and Nietzsche recognize, moral goodness can be aided by happiness. These facts in themselves, however, only show that happiness is not the most final good, and not that the HPG is not the most final good.

Another claim that Aristotle makes is more questionable, namely, that everyone seeks the HPG. He forgets misery-lovers, as well as people who don't want to make the effort to seek the HPG, and people who don't seek it because they feel guilty about seeking it. This oversight does not, however, affect his concept of *eudaimonia*.

2.1.2 After stating that everyone regards *eudaimonia* as the HPG, Aristotle next argues that *eudaimonia* must be secure or stable, because "we intuitively believe that the good is something of our own and hard to take from us" (*NE* 1095b 25). A good that was otherwise equally worth choosing, but easily lost, would surely not be as choiceworthy as a good that was hard to lose. Other things being equal, if offered a choice between them on a platter, why would anyone choose the good that was easily lost? There *are* some goods that are inherently transient, such as sunsets, romantic evenings, performance art, or Andy Goldsworth's transient art, and, arguably, their value depends, to some extent, on their transience.[3] An eternal sunset would lose its special charm, and an endless performance would be exhausting both for the performers and the audience. But *eudaimonia* is neither inherently transient, nor less valuable for not being so. Indeed, quite the opposite: those who desire it or possess it want to possess it as long as possible, because a life with it is better for them than a life without. So it would no more make sense to think that a *eudaimonic* life would be better if it was short-lived than to think that a healthy life would be better if it was short-lived. As the highest prudential good, a *eudaimonic* life must be a life that is not easily lost.

If *eudaimonia* is "something of our own and hard to take from us," then it cannot be largely a matter of what happens to us, but a matter of what we do, and of what we do with what happens to us—that is, of our attitudes

---

[3] Thanks to William Glod for raising this question.

to good and bad fortune, our character traits and personality. Moreover, if our well-being were not to an important extent dependent on our attitudes, or if our attitudes were not to an important extent under our own control, we could not regard well-being as something to *pursue* or *aspire to,* but only as something to *wish for.* But it is both something to aspire to and something to wish for. Hence it must depend to a large extent on the kind of selves we have, on the way we live in this world—the way we function—intellectually and emotionally.

So far, then, there is nothing controversial in the concept of the highest prudential good. This concept of the highest prudential good also stands the test of explanatory robustness: it explains why *eudaimonia* can be so hard to keep, why we expend so much effort trying to achieve it or keep it, and why wishing it to those we love is an expression of love. For all these reasons, a satisfactory *conception* of *eudaimonia* or well-being must meet the formal constraints of the highest prudential good.

2.2 Happiness as Partly Constitutive of *Eudaimonia*/Well-Being

2.2.1 Happiness as a long-term psychological state is a central part of well-being on nearly everyone's conception of well-being, whether subjective or objective, and most accounts of happiness regard pleasure as an important part of happiness. Aristotle argues that pleasure is crucial to *eudaimonia*, for all men "weave pleasure into their ideal of...[*eudaimonia*]" (*NE* VII.13 1153b 14–15). In particular, "[p]erceiving that we are alive is pleasant in itself. For life is by nature a good, and it is pleasant to perceive that something good is present in us" (1170b 1–2).[4] This kind of pleasure is what is now sometimes called "attitudinal" pleasure, the attitude of being pleased at or by something. But sensory pleasures, including the appetitive pleasures of food, drink, and sex, also play an important part in a life that is *eudaimonic* when we enjoy them in the right way, that is, the way connoisseurs and cooks do, discriminating flavors (*NE* 1118a 27ff), aroma, bouquet, structure, and textures. In contrast, the glutton enjoys only the sensation of food going down his throat and glutting his

---

[4] There is a scholarly bias in favor of discussing Aristotle's conception of *eudaimonia* almost entirely with reference to the function argument, excluding all reference to pleasure, other than the pleasure of virtuous activity. In his "Two Conceptions" (1979), Kraut corrects this bias by reminding us of the passages just quoted.

belly (ibid., 1119a 20). Although Aristotle doesn't talk about sexual pleasure, we can extrapolate: sexual pleasure is part of a *eudaimonic* life when it involves our conceptual and imaginative abilities, rather than simply the relief of sexual tension.[5] Indeed, even purely passive pleasures like those of a massage, or sleep, are important, both for the sheer experience, and for their restorative value.

Here, again, the Aristotelian view is quite commonsensical and widely shared. The importance of pleasure, including appetitive pleasure, is widely recognized across many different cultures. The ancient Indian writer, Vatsayana, wrote an entire book—*Kamasutra*—on, among other things, sexual pleasure as an important part of well-being. Even Islam, which denies the pleasures of wine to Muslims here on earth, makes them an important part of the attractions of life for devout Muslim men in the Islamic heaven.[6] But everyone also agrees that a life that revolves around appetitive or purely passive pleasures cannot be a happy life, let alone a *eudaimonic* life. Happiness requires the disposition to enjoy life, to be and feel engaged with life, to look forward to the next hour and next day. And whereas the disposition to be pleased is part of the disposition to enjoy and be engaged with life, it is not identical with it.

Happiness also requires a sense of purpose or meaning, a sense that our activities are worthwhile. A happy life for a human being has to be, at least, a life of purposeful activity, a life in which we set and pursue goals that we find both enjoyable and meaningful. In Nietzsche's more colorful language, "Formula of my happiness: a Yes, a No, a straight line, a *goal*..."[7] And "If we possess our *why* of life we can put up with almost any *how*."[8] Indeed, the compelling pull of a sense of meaning explains why some people are willing to renounce all worldly goods, or even their lives, in the service of a cause they regard as meaningful.[9]

---

[5] See my discussion in "Carnal Wisdom and Sexual Virtue," ed. R. Halwani (2007), 134–146.

[6] "They are comfortably seated on couches arranged in rows; we pair them with beautiful-eyed maidens," *The Qu'ran*, trans. M.A.S. Abdel Haleem (2008), 52:20. "There they shall pass from hand to hand a (wine) cup which does not lead to any idle talk or sin" (52:23). "There will be maidens restraining their glances, untouched beforehand by man or jinn" (55:56). Thanks to Irfan Khawaja for pointing me to these passages.

[7] Nietzsche, *Twilight of the Idols*, hereafter *Twilight*, trans. R.J. Hollingdale (1968), Maxim 44, p. 37.

[8] Ibid., Maxim 12, p. 33. Nietzsche goes on to declare that "Man does *not* strive after happiness; only the Englishman does that." Here he seems to have the Benthamite notion of happiness as pleasure. The earlier statement, then, is either about a more sophisticated notion of happiness or about well-being.

[9] According to Viktor Frankl, *Man's Search for Meaning: An Introduction to Logotherapy*, 3rd ed. (1984), the search for meaning is "the primary motivational force in man" (104). It is, at any rate,

The importance of finding one's life both enjoyable and meaningful is well recognized by therapists and counselors. In particular, they understand that exercising our agency, being initiators and goal-setters and not just passive consumers of pleasant experiences, is central to a sense of meaning because it is an expression of our "effectance motive," the need to feel competent and in control of our lives.[10]

A sense of meaning and enjoyment of life are not, of course, unrelated to each other. A sense of meaning is one of the chief sources of enjoyment of life, and enjoyment of life is one of the chief sources of a sense of meaning. But it is possible for someone who finds her life largely enjoyable to judge it as meaningless (perhaps because of unrealistic ideals). Conversely, it is possible for someone who finds her life meaningful to find little enjoyment in it (perhaps because of repeated failures; or a naturally depressive temperament; or a lack of fit between her interests, abilities, or temperament on the one hand, and her activities on the other). This divergence is borne out by some empirical studies, in which people who evaluate their lives as satisfactory (and, thus, meaningful) by their own standards nevertheless also acknowledge being anxious or sad (Haybron, *Unhappiness*, 84–86). Only someone who finds her life both enjoyable and meaningful will have a sense of her life overall, or an aspect thereof, as happy, deeply fulfilling—a sense that it is complete and leaves nothing to be desired (which is not to say that she will cease to desire, a state of affairs she would surely find highly undesirable). Although one can stay alive out of fear of death, or a punishing God, or a sense of obligation to family or country, it is this kind of happiness that makes one feel that life is worth living for its own sake. It is also part of what people have in mind when they say that eternal happiness for the blessed in heaven is the highest good, and what parents wish for when they wish happiness to their children.

A happy person, a person who finds his life both meaningful and enjoyable, is emotionally fulfilled. He has a sense of fulfillment as an ongoing,

---

most people will agree, a powerful motivational force, both for good and for bad. See Seligman, *Flourish: A Visionary New Understanding of Happiness and Well-being* (hereafter *Flourish*) (2011); *Authentic Happiness* (2002); and Carol D. Ryff and Burton H. Singer, "Know Thyself and Become Who You Are: A Eudaimonic Approach to Psychological Well-Being" (2008), 13–39 (http://ioa126.medsch.wisc.edu/midus/findings/pdfs/692.pdf, accessed April 2013.) Ryff and Singer report that some studies of older women show that those who had a sense of purpose in life, felt that they were growing, and had good relationships, had "better neuroendocrine regulation," "lower inflammatory markers," and even better HDL cholesterol.

[10] The term was coined by the psychologist, Robert White in 1959. Cited in Haidt, *Happiness Hypothesis* (2006), 220.

dispositional feature of his life or a certain period of his life. Happiness, in this long-term sense, is a steady undercurrent of one's consciousness that colors one's experience of life rather than simply a frequent recurrence of feelings of enjoyment or meaningfulness. In this respect, happiness is like love. To love someone is to be disposed to think about and respond to her in certain ways: to be glad that she exists, to have one's attention drawn by her, to share her joys and sorrows, to wish her well, and most of all, perhaps, to delight in her.[11] Episodic feelings of love without the disposition to love do not add up to love; similarly, episodic feelings of happiness without the disposition to be happy do not add up to happiness. Happiness, in Haybron's words, is a *"psychic affirmation"* of one's life, or, in more pronounced forms, *"psychic flourishing"* (*Unhappiness*, 182). A happy person feels "fully at home" in his life, rather than defensive or alienated; he is *engaged* with his life, rather than passive or disengaged; and he *endorses* his life as "worth pursuing enthusiastically" (ibid., 122, 127).[12] Haybron points out that someone who has episodic feelings of happiness, but also a propensity to be easily irritated, depressed, stressed-out, and so on, is not really very happy (136–138). What is missing, I would say, is the disposition to enjoy life or find it meaningful. Happiness in the dispositional sense inclines us to "take greater pleasure in things," and to be "slower and less likely to become anxious or fearful, or to be angered or saddened by events" (139). Or if we do tend to become angry easily, it does not spoil our happy mood, because it is like a summer shower that disappears almost as quickly as it appears.[13]

A life with the highest prudential good, then, must be a life of happiness, a life we find both enjoyable and meaningful, with only occasional intrusions of sadness, sorrow, disappointment, dissatisfaction, pain, depression, or ennui.[14] The disposition to be happy can tide us over rough times, when life offers little that is joyful or meaningful, and provide a buffer from deep unhappiness, allowing us to feel that something better is within our reach.

2.2.2 If the highest prudential good is largely up to us, and happiness is central to this good, then happiness also must be largely up to us. Haidt is

---

[11.] I argue for the last claim in "Love" (2003), 42–69.

[12.] Haybron does not explicitly include a sense of meaning in his conception of happiness, but his claim that a happy person endorses his life as worth pursuing enthusiastically might come to the same thing.

[13.] Thanks to Michael Lacewing for bringing up this possibility.

[14.] Yet even some of these normally undesirable emotions can be happiness-constituting or happiness-promoting in some contexts. Think, for example, of frightening movies and sad dramas, sought out for being frightening and sad, respectively. The same is true of physical pains. In

right to state that "happiness comes from between," that is, from both our attitudes and our external circumstances, because without the essentials of life, caring relationships, and work that can engage us, we cannot be happy (ibid., chapter 10). Nevertheless, it is safe to say that so long as we are not utterly deprived of these external goods, our happiness depends more on who we are than on these goods. This is one of the strongest points of agreement, cutting across cultures, historical eras, academic disciplines, and religions. It is also a common theme in the psychological, self-help, religious, and philosophical literature on well-being.[15] The thought common to all of them is that without the right attitudes we cannot enjoy even the most propitious circumstances, whereas with the right attitudes we can overcome most adversities. For example, someone who is prone to focus on what he lacks, no matter how trivial, rather than on what he possesses, both fails to enjoy what he has and fails to reach the future he yearns for—for when the future arrives bearing the desired goods, his focus shifts to what little he lacks. He simultaneously lacks "mindfulness" about the present and a long-range perspective on his life.[16] When the glass is three-quarters full, it's the empty quarter that draws his gaze and crystallizes his emotions and thoughts. Prone to counting his disappointments rather than his blessings, he is devastated when ill fortune strikes. Without the right attitudes, then, he has neither the resources to enjoy his blessings, nor the resources to handle adversity. Something similar is true of someone who cannot distinguish between the important and the unimportant, or between the now and the future. He sweats the small stuff, treating every setback as a matter of life and death, thereby dying many times.[17]

Unhappiness, Haybron uses this phenomenon of "hedonic inversion," in which pains become pleasurable and pleasures painful, as an argument against the hedonistic theory of happiness (71–72).

[15.] This view is shared by the ancient *eudaimonist* philosophers, and by many contemporary psychologists. In *Flourish* (2011), Seligman argues that we cannot have well-being or flourishing without support from our strengths—our positive human qualities—of which he identifies twenty-four. Cognitive psychotherapy, started by Aaron Beck, enables people to overcome depression by retraining their thoughts and feelings to be more realistic. In *The Reflective Life: Living Wisely With Our Limits* (2008), Valerie Tiberius provides a very good discussion of the importance of perspective, optimism, self-awareness, and what she calls "attentional flexibility" for living a good life. Although she doesn't equate her conception of a good life with a life of well-being, the traits she identifies seem necessary for at least the conception of well-being I defend here.

[16.] Mindfulness in the sense of giving full attention to the present moment, without making any evaluative judgments, is an essential part of Buddhist philosophy and meditative practice. All I mean by it here is full appreciation of what is good about one's life in the present.

[17.] The basketball coach, Dean Smith, is claimed to have said: "If you treat every situation as a life and death matter, you'll die a lot of times."

Immersed in the here and now, he lacks the perspective that allows a wiser person to see that "this too shall pass."

If *eudaimonia* is largely a matter of our attitudes, then it cannot be a life devoted to the pursuit of honor (or, for that matter, wealth or power), depending as honor does "more on those who honor than on the one honored."[18] Moreover, such a life is easily lost. The story of paramedic Robert O'Donnell offers a particularly poignant example of someone who lost his life after he became inordinately dependent on the adulation of others for his happiness. O'Donnell volunteered to save two-year old Jessica McClure from the well she had fallen into, risking his own life in a gruesomely frightening rescue.[19] He became a hero, appearing on network television and being interviewed by the press. He was given a part in a made-for-TV movie about the rescue, but the networks cut the part without notifying him. After months in the spotlight, he suddenly disappeared from the news, and started slipping into a depression. He never recovered. His marriage ended in a divorce, he was fired—or resigned—from his job amid suspicions of drug use, and eight years later he took his own life.

By contrast, someone who seeks happiness primarily in his own activities, who counts his blessings instead of bemoaning his losses, who sees things in perspective, distinguishing between the important and the unimportant, has the resources to win in most everyday circumstances, and to survive even in many extraordinary ones. It is this individual who is self-sufficient, not the individual blessed with the goods of fortune but impoverished in his outlook.

These claims are supported both by common experience and by evidence from psychological research. Mihaly Csikszentmihalyi presents persuasive evidence that people can find happiness, even "flow"—a state of enjoyable absorption in which our feelings, wishes, and thoughts are in harmony, and in which time seems to fly—in a wide variety of activities, so long as they present just the right level of challenge for our skills, and provide immediate feedback.[20] Cleaning house, for example, can be as

---

[18] Cf. David Hume, "our regard to a character with others seems to arise only from a care of preserving a character with ourselves," in *Enquiry Concerning the Principles of Morals*, Section IX, I ([1751], 1983), 77.

[19] See Lisa Belkin, "Death on the CNN Curve," *The New York Times Magazine*, July 23, 1995 (http://byliner.com/lisa-belkin/stories/death-on-the-cnn-curve, accessed April 2013), and Patrick Rogers, "Well of Darkness," May 15, 1995, People.com (http://www.people.com/people/archive/article/0,,20105787,00.html, accessed April 2013).

[20] Mihaly Csikszentmihalyi, *Flow: The Psychology of Optimal Experience* (1990).

satisfying, engaging, and meaningful to the engaged cleaner as proving theorems can be to the lover of mathematics, or operating with complete focus and precision can be to the surgeon. In a study of people in different occupations, the psychologist Amy Wrzesniewski finds that those who approach their jobs as vocations by considering their contribution to the purpose of the organization and to their own lives find flow even in work that, to most of us, would be quite off-putting, such as janitorial work in a hospital.[21]

I acknowledged earlier that the right attitudes are not proof against unhappiness, that external circumstances can make happiness impossible. Nevertheless, even in such circumstances, our attitudes can shield us from misery. Boethius' *Consolation of Philosophy* is eternal testimony to this claim. At the height of his fortune, Boethius is betrayed by those he trusts and imprisoned for treason. While awaiting his execution, he is at first overcome by despair. But then Lady Philosophy appears to him, reminds him of the great fortune he has enjoyed till then, and chides him for his unhappiness over losing it now. She reminds him that fortune is fickle and that it is in his power to be *eudaimon*. The result is his *Consolation of Philosophy*. In our own times, as we know, people have survived grave injustice, including severe torture, or the destruction of everything and everyone they cared for, without letting it make them permanently bitter or resentful. Elie Wiesel lost both his parents and a sister in the Holocaust by the age of sixteen, but survived to begin life anew.[22] Less well-known, and in a way more dramatically illustrative of the fact that, to a large extent, it is up to us not to let ourselves be destroyed, is the story of Admiral James D. Stockdale, who survived unimaginable torture and indignities in a North Vietnamese POW camp with the help of Epictetus' *Enchiridion*.[23] Epictetus helped him to see that the greatest harm was not a broken back, but betrayal of his cause and comrades and the breakdown of his agency (Sherman, *Stoic Warriors*, 6). The evidence that it is, to an amazing extent, up to us not to be miserable is powerful and valuable, even if not everyone can be as heroic as Stockdale.

---

[21] Cited in Haidt, *Happiness Hypothesis* (2006), 222.

[22] His book, *Night* (1985) expresses the road he took from despair to hope to life again.

[23] See Nancy Sherman, *Stoic Warriors: The Ancient Philosophy behind the Military Mind*, hereafter *Stoic Warriors* (2005).

[24] *Cicero on the Emotions, Tusculan Disputations 3 and 4*, trans. Margaret Graver (2002), at 3:35.

My use of these examples of extraordinary heroism is not meant to suggest that those of us who may not be as heroic are doomed to ill-being. Fortunately, most of us will never be so severely tested, hence we will never be called upon to show such heroism. What we need are simply the positive attitudes and strengths necessary for dealing with the vagaries of everyday life. And these are possible for nearly everyone.

My use of these examples is also not meant to deny that even the most heroic person has limits. With the well-known exceptions of Socrates and the Stoics, almost everyone agrees that no one is completely invulnerable to circumstance. As a Stoic, Cicero tried not to give in to the grief he felt over the death of his beloved daughter, Tullia, but found himself rejecting Stoic teachings instead. "It is not within our power to forget or gloss over circumstances which we believe to be evil...They tear at us, buffet us, goad us, scorch us, stifle us—and you tell us to forget about them?"[24] To the extent that happiness requires external goods, and to the extent that these are dependent on good fortune, happiness is also dependent on good fortune. Hence it can be undermined or destroyed by great misfortune. And since *eudaimonia* requires happiness, *eudaimonia* too is vulnerable. The *eudaimonic* person, though self-possessed and independent, is not impervious to the loss of his objects of love. Many great misfortunes, Aristotle acknowledges, can tarnish or even rob us of *eudaimonia* by robbing us of happiness. Moreover, I argue in chapter 7, this is how it *should* be.

In this section I have argued that a life that meets the constraints of the HPG must be happy, that is, both enjoyable and meaningful to the one who lives it, and that it must be largely a matter of our own attitudes and actions rather than of external goods like fame or wealth. I will now argue that it must also be a life in which our happiness is based on a realistic evaluation of, and response to, the important facts of our own life and human life in general. There are good reasons why this idea is a recurring theme in philosophy and psychology, as well as in fiction and religion.

2.3 Realism as Partly Constitutive of *Eudaimonia*/Well-Being

2.3.1 It is important to most of us that we actually achieve our goals, and not just that we have the pleasurable but illusory *experience* of achieving them, that the people we care about actually fare well, and not just

---

[24] *Cicero on the Emotions, Tusculan Disputations 3 and 4*, trans. Margaret Graver (2002), at 3:35.

that we deludedly *believe* that they do, and so on. This is one of the main reasons why, when presented with Robert Nozick's experience machine thought-experiment, students overwhelmingly reject the illusion of perfect happiness on the experience machine for the reality of imperfect happiness off the machine.[25] The importance of having a sense of fulfillment that is rooted in the actual conditions of our life also explains why it makes sense to think of a man who is confident in the loyalty of his unfaithful friends as an "unhappy man." He is "unhappy" because he is living in a "fool's paradise." His confidence is unjustified and his wish for true friends unful-filled, even though he is ignorant of these facts. If he learned the truth, he would feel hurt and betrayed, and rightly judge that period of his life to have been sadly lacking. His well-being requires that his happiness be a response to his circumstances and his needs, tendencies, traits, or attitudes.

But what about those who prefer to live in a fool's paradise? Do they have any reason to change their preferences? Like everyone else, they have instrumental reasons for not living in a fool's paradise. For one, a sense of fulfillment based on illusion is precarious, since the truth has a way of revealing itself in unexpected and unexpectedly unpleasant ways. For another, ignorance about ourselves—our own needs, tendencies, traits, abilities, attitudes, and relationships—can lead us to pursue goals we are ill-suited to pursue well or happily.[26]

There is also a conceptual reason for being informed about these and other important facts of our lives. To the extent that we are ignorant of important features of our circumstances, or of our actions, goals, charac-ter, or relationships, our positive feelings and self-evaluations and, thus, our well-being, are rooted not in the lives we actually lead, but in a fiction. Here again we have an analogy with love: to love someone for who he is,

---

[25] Nozick discusses this thought experiment in *Anarchy, State, and Utopia* (1974), 42–45, and in *The Examined Life* (1989), 104–108. I have repeated this thought experiment with students semester after semester. No matter how attractive I make the machine, I can never persuade more than 5% of undergraduates or 10% of graduate students to sign up for it (I note the difference in percentages without comment). In other words, only a small minority of students see no reason to be in touch with reality even if their experiences and mental states can be considerably improved in virtual reality. Informal surveys of small groups of middle-aged adults produced no takers for the machine. By contrast, when I did the experience machine thought experiment with a small group of elderly women in a retirement home, a large number opted for the machine. The attachment to reality, like the attachment to life, can be affected by the quality of one's life and one's future prospects.

[26] Valerie Tiberius and Alicia Hall also make this point in "Normative Theory and Psychological Research," hereafter "Normative Theory" (May 2010), 212–225. Haybron (*Unhappiness*, 2008) has a particularly insightful discussion of the importance of choosing goals and activities that fit our emotional natures.

one must know who he is. To the extent that I am ignorant of who he is, the object of my love is not he but my fantasy of him. Knowing him as he actually is a condition of my loving him for himself. Likewise, knowing myself and my life as it actually is a condition of my positive evaluation of my life being veridical. To the extent that I am ignorant or deluded about my character or the circumstances of my life, my evaluation of my life as going well for me is unfounded, my happiness is based on an illusion, and my apparent well-being is only apparent.

What makes these facts important and why? A plausible answer is: they play a causally or explanatorily central role in our individual lives as members of a human society, such that without them the shape and structure of our lives would be unrecognizably different. But we can't be informed about them without also being informed about the general features of human life that are expressed in true empirical generalizations and theories. Some of these general features, such as the ability for thinking logically and tracking the truth, practical rationality in thought and action, and relationships of love, work, or play, have a central role in the life of everyone capable of well-being as the HPG.[27] Other features, such as the ability for sleuthing, making movies, or doing high-level mathematics, are important only in some lives. Hence understanding ourselves involves understanding both what is central to (nearly) all human lives and thus to our own, and what is peculiarly central to our own lives. It is in light of such understanding that well-being as the highest prudential good requires that we find our lives happy and fulfilling.

In turn, such understanding requires a stance of openness to important facts about ourselves and others, and a readiness to draw the implications of what we learn, integrate them with the rest of our beliefs, values, and motivations, weed out inconsistencies, and live accordingly. In other words, such understanding requires reality-orientation. Reality-orientation does not guarantee that we will always be successful in grasping a situation, or drawing the right conclusions from what we do grasp. In other words, it doesn't guarantee understanding or truth. But its complete absence does guarantee, as I argue in chapter 4, if not the absence of all truth, at least the absence of understanding.

2.3.2 Since reality-orientation involves an attempt to understand important facts about ourselves and our social world, it must also involve

---

[27.] Cf. Martha Nussbaum's list of eight features that she suggests all human beings who are fully human share in "Non-Relative Virtues" (1993), 242–269. These features, she argues, form the common core around which different societies construct somewhat different conceptions of human nature..

an attempt to think for ourselves, that is, to be independent-minded, autonomous. Autonomy is sometimes taken to mean free will or freedom of action. I mean by it simply the disposition to think independently and live (so far as circumstances allow) by one's independent judgments in important areas of our lives, rather than to adopt the going values and beliefs merely because they are the going values and beliefs. My life counts as going well for me only if it goes well for me from my own point of view, my own standards. In an important sense, a life lived in imitation of others, or in blind deference to a code, is not really my own life, and an evaluation of it as going well by their standards is not really my own evaluation. The highest prudential good for me has to suit my nature as an individual and a human being; living contrary to my nature is a recipe for unhappiness and failure. Autonomy—independence of mind and the disposition to live by one's independent judgments—is, thus, another conceptual requirement of well-being. But as I argue later, not all judgments a person makes on her own are autonomous in the relevant sense, nor is reliance on the testimony or guidance of others necessarily incompatible with being autonomous.

A familiar criticism at this point is that my conception of well-being promises to be highly parochial, because it implies that members of strongly communal or anti-individualistic cultures cannot have well-being as the HPG. But if by a strongly communal society is meant a society in which people are compelled to live by a narrow and rigid code, isn't it true that they don't have well-being as the HPG? Is living by a rigid code, without trying to understand why, without discovering who they are, without any self-direction, really the most choiceworthy good for human beings? It is certainly possible for some people in such societies to be happy, but well-being is more than just happiness.

The idea that reality-orientation and autonomy are necessary for an objectively worthy life is supported indirectly by the justifications often given by oppressors for their oppression of certain groups or individuals: namely, that those whom they enslave or otherwise oppress are inherently slavish or in the grip of illusion, lacking the very capacity for autonomy or reality-orientation, and, thus, the very capacity for understanding themselves and living inherently worthy lives.[28] The only worth their

---

[28] No doubt in most cases this belief rests on several thick layers of self-deception, as shown by the fact that oppressors are strongly inclined to shut their eyes to evidence showing that the slavishness of their victims, to the extent that it exists, is not inherent, but learned as a self-protective response to oppression. The point, however, is that oppressors feel compelled to cite lack of autonomy and realism as a justification for their oppression.

lives can have, according to these oppressors, is instrumental (serving well the ends of their superiors) or derivative (acting according to the instructions of their superiors). Moreover, oppressors will often add, those they oppress need to be ruled for their own good. Such arguments have been used by defenders of slavery from Aristotle to the Romans to the Arabs to the Americans of the erstwhile slaveholding south. They have also been used (and still are being used in many parts of the world) to justify the subordination of women. In *The Subjection of Women,* Mill notes that the chief rationalization men use to deny women equal liberty is that women by nature lack the ability for self-direction.[29] Aristotle also grants only a secondary virtue to women, the virtue of being receptive to the reason of virtuous males. And the ayatollahs and secular tyrants of the modern world who demand blind obedience from their subjects do so on the grounds that these subjects are incapable of recognizing or pursuing the true and the good on their own.

Thus, like those who *respect* the right of people to direct their own lives as they see fit on the ground of their capacities for autonomy and reality-orientation, those who *deny* it to certain groups, or certain members of their own groups, also see the capacity for autonomy and reality-orientation as essential for leading a fully worthwhile life. What they refuse to acknowledge is that their victims have the requisite capacity. *Their* worth, oppressors often claim, is secondary, lying in following the direction of their superiors, or of the religious or political code prescribed by their superiors.

There are some exceptions to my claim that the capacities for, and exercise of, reality-orientation and autonomy are valorized everywhere. Some religions might regard following the strictures of their faith without trying to understand them to be the most worthwhile life for a human being. Even here, however, the thought is that such independence of mind and attempt to understand what matters in life are worthless because we don't have the capacity to gain the requisite understanding, and not that they would be worthless even if we had the capacity. After all, the being of highest worth, God, is depicted as supremely reality-oriented and autonomous.

Even in societies that disvalue reality-orientation and autonomy, however, it is not the case that *no one* can have any autonomy, reality-orientation, or self-knowledge. In every society some people just are more self-directed, more questioning, more truth-seeking, than the average. As a character in

---

[29] For a thorough and still relevant review and critique of such justifications, see John Stuart Mill, *The Subjection of Women* (1988).

Memoirs of a Geisha tells Chiyo, the heroine, some people—people like Chiyo—are like water, which "changes shape and flows around things, and finds the secret paths no one else has thought about—the tiny hole through the roof or the bottom of a box."[30] These traits are a source of pride and happiness to Chiyo, but they also bring her into conflict with others, and the conflict is a source of unhappiness until she finds allies. In a society that imposes a rigid, narrow code on people, well-being requires greater luck in achieving happiness and being realistic than in a society that allows or encourages autonomy, reality-orientation, and self-knowledge.

Nevertheless, for reasons I give in chapter 6, regardless of the nature of our society, reality-orientation and autonomy do not guarantee complete realism—that is, complete practical understanding of the human world and the pursuit of goals that are both worthwhile for a human being and suited to our individual abilities and interests. Hence the life we forge by our own lights is not necessarily a *eudaimon* life.

2.4 Objective Worth as Partly Constitutive of *Eudaimonia*

The highest prudential good must be a life worthy of us as human beings and as the particular individuals we are. This is a conceptual require-ment of the most choiceworthy good. Moreover, insofar as we are reality-oriented, we want not only to *believe* that our lives are objectively worthwhile, but to actually *have* objectively worthwhile lives—that is, worthwhile for creatures with our needs, interests, and capacities—including the capacity for asking what sort of life counts as worthwhile. In wishing for well-being as the HPG, we wish for a life in which, as Susan Wolf puts it, "subjective attraction meets objective attractiveness."[31] One of the reasons the students in my class-room experiment gave for not

---

[30.] Arthur Golden, *Memoirs of a Geisha* (1997/1999), 125. The novel is set in the early to mid-20th century Kyoto.

[31.] See Susan Wolf, "Happiness and Meaning: Two Aspects of the Good Life" (Winter 1997), 207–225, and *Meaning in Life and Why it Matters* (2012). Wolf argues that happiness and meaning are both part of the good life, and that "Meaning arises when subjective attraction meets objective attractiveness," and we actively engage with the objectively attractive thing ("Happiness and Meaning," 211). What she calls "meaning" includes what I call "sense of meaning" as well as what I call "objective worth," and what she calls the "good life" is what I call "well-being." Since she regards both meaning and happiness as essential to the good life/well-being, our basic conceptions of well-being are similar. In *Meaning in Life*, however, Wolf's focus is meaning, not well-being or the good life. Further, whereas Wolf distinguishes between reasons of meaning on the one hand, and moral and egoistic reasons, on the other, I make no such a priori distinctions. On my view, moral reasons can be reasons of meaning as well as reasons of self-interest.

wanting a life of perfect but illusory happiness on Nozick's experience machine is that they can't be "truly happy" without doing something worthwhile with their lives, without making a positive difference in the world. Without this, their lives are incomplete, lacking in something that matters to them. If they were to discover late in their lives that their lives had been worthless, they themselves would judge their lives as lacking in the most choiceworthy good for a human being.

The view that the highest prudential good requires objective worth is widespread among philosophers of different persuasions. Joseph Raz defines well-being as the success of a person's life from his own point of view, where his success is not only—or even always—a matter of *achieving* his goals, but also of *acting well* in the pursuit of objectively worthy goals, whether or not he actually achieves them.[32] In the same vein, Nozick argues that the individual's positive emotions and evaluations of his life constitute well-being (which he calls "happiness") only if they are made in response to a life that truly *is* valuable, or that the individual has good reason to *believe* is valuable, "in whatever dimensions he considers most important and whatever dimensions *are* most important" (*Examined Life* 113). If someone's evaluations of his life were "egregiously unjustified and false, we would not call him [truly] happy" (*Examined Life* 111).

The pull of the thought that a life of well-being is a worthwhile life does not leave even a hard-bitten act-utilitarian like J.J.C. Smart unaffected. For try as he might, Smart cannot bring himself to say that a life in which we spend most of our time hooked to pleasure-producing electrodes is a life of well-being. He argues that "as we are now, we just do not want to become electrode operators. We want other things, perhaps to write a book or get into a cricket team."[33] "Happiness" [well-being], he continues, is a partly evaluative word, and most of us do not approve of a life in which we spend most of our time as electrode operators (22). This is why, according to Smart, John Stuart Mill declares that intellectual pleasures are higher than the pleasures of pushpin, and that it is "better to be Socrates dissatisfied

---

[32] Joseph Raz, *The Morality of Freedom* (1986), 289, 297–299 (hereafter *Freedom*). In *Ethics in the Public Domain* (1994), he defines well-being as "(1) whole-hearted and (2) successful pursuit of (3) valuable (4) activities" (3). Raz argues that people pursue the goals they do because they regard them as having independent value (i.e., value that is independent of their desiring it). Hence, if they turn out to be wrong in their beliefs, they themselves will regard their lives as lacking in well-being (*Freedom*, 299, 308). I differ from Raz on this point only in holding that this is true only of reality-oriented people, not everyone. Cynics, immoralists, opportunists, and the akratic recognize that their goals do not have independent value.

[33] J.J.C. Smart, "An Outline of a System of Utilitarian Ethics" (1973), 20.

than a fool satisfied": Mill approves of the former kinds of pleasures, and disapproves of the latter (ibid.,15, 22). But Smart omits Mill's own explanation for his approval: Mill's explanation is that Socrates' pleasures are truly *worthy* of a human being, befitting the sense of dignity that all human beings possess to a greater or lesser degree.[34] Mill's reasons for rejecting the satisfactions of a fool, then, are akin to Aristotle's reasons for dismissing the life of "gratification" of "grazing animals" as unfit for human beings (*NE*, I.5).

The idea that a life of well-being must not only be happy but also objectively worthwhile—and happy largely because it is objectively worthwhile—is central to the appeal of religious views that equate well-being with a joyful or peaceful state of existence achieved and preserved through the pursuit of the truly worthwhile. And when we ask what counts as truly worthwhile, the answer often given is: that which accords with our nature, our humanity, and the nature of the world or, more perspicuously, that which is appropriately responsive to what matters in human life. The ancient philosophers of the West are famous for holding this view, but the view appears in other cultures and philosophies as well. Thus, for example, the Buddha tells us that the Eightfold Path of right thinking and living that "opens the eyes" to our own nature and the nature of the world is also the path that destroys suffering and leads to peace of mind. C.S. Lewis forges an even stronger connection between being in touch with reality, on the one hand, and well-being, on the other, when he states that heaven and joy are reality, and hell illusion, a "shutting up of the creature within the dungeon of its own mind."[35]

To be sure, many of the metaphysical beliefs associated with these ideas are comforting illusions or, at best, vague ideas without much empirical or rational support. And ironically, for many people belief in them is due not simply to a desire for living a worthwhile life, but also to a desire to escape from this imperfect empirical reality with its bumps and bruises into the illusion of a smoother, more comforting reality beyond space and time.

---

[34] It is probably false to say that *all* human beings have a sense of dignity, but Mill's point stands even if only most do. The important point is that those who are capable of well-being as the HPG possess a sense of dignity. Cf. David Hume, "[I]nward peace of mind, consciousness of integrity, a satisfactory review of our own conduct...are circumstances very requisite to happiness, and will be cherished and cultivated by every honest man, who feels the importance of them" (*Enquiry Concerning the Principles of Morals* (1983), 82).

[35] C.S. Lewis, *The Great Divorce* (1946), 69.

The point remains, however, that the idea of living in accord with what matters in human life is still part of the ideal of well-being as the HPG. And the illusory metaphysical beliefs often go hand-in-hand with many true beliefs about what really matters in this life.

To conclude: well-being as the HPG entails that we live objectively worthwhile lives, and this in turn entails being realistic about certain empirical and normative facts. Realism in this full empirical-normative sense consists of being in touch with important facts about oneself and others, and living accordingly. Realism is, therefore, an objective value that is partly constitutive of the prudential value of our lives. In the next section I address some objections to the idea that well-being requires objective worth.

2.5. A Problem with Objective Worth?

One criticism commonly levied at objective theories is that they are paternalistic, requiring that we impose our own values on others if we want to promote their well-being.[36] It is important to remember, however, that a conception of well-being in itself does not tell us to promote other people's well-being, let alone to promote *our* conception of their well-being; the prescription to promote others' well-being can come only from a substantive theory of ethics or politics, and a sensible ethics and politics must be alive to the dangers of busybodyism. Additionally, even if one is in a position to promote others' well-being, an obvious non-paternalistic way of doing so is to support them (as Kant puts it) in their permissible ends, instead of (self-defeatingly) imposing one's own values on them— self-defeatingly, because for these values to benefit them, they must find them attractive and admirable enough to integrate them into their valuational and motivational system. Pursuing good values kicking and screaming, so to speak, does nothing for their well-being.

Another criticism of objective theories is that they are elitist. This charge is harder to understand but easier to rebut. Is the thought here that objective well-being requires extraordinary ability, but subjective well-being is open to all comers? If so, the worry seems unfounded. The conception of objective

---

[36.] Todd Kashdan, et al., "Reconsidering Happiness: The Costs of Distinguishing Between Hedonics And Eudaimonia" (2008), 219–233, at 227. In "Well-Being" (2010), 403–432, Tiberius and Plakias reject this criticism, but in "Normative Theory and Psychological Research: Hedonism, Eudaimonism, and Why it Matters" (hereafter "Normative Theory") (May 2010), 212–225, Tiberius and Hall accept it, calling it "a troubling implication of a theory of well-being" (213).

well-being that I defend requires us to be reality-oriented and autonomous, but the ability for reality-orientation and autonomy is an ability that all normal people have. True, not everyone has this ability to the same extent, whether because of innate features or because of upbringing. But this is also true of happiness: some people are born with a happy personality—a high genetic happiness set-point—some with a melancholic or grouchy one.[37] Some people are brought up by happy people in circumstances that promote happiness, others by unhappy people in circumstances that promote unhappiness. Yet these would be poor reasons for excluding happiness from a conception of well-being. It may be that the view that well-being requires objective worth is just plain false. But that is a different criticism, which I address in chapter 3.

Objective theories have also been criticized for ignoring the subjectivity of well-being, the fact that my good must be my good from my perspective. But what sort of objective theory do critics have in mind? Tiberius and Hall define objective theories as those "that claim that there are at least some components of well-being whose status as components of well-being does not depend on people's attitudes toward them"(*op. cit,* 213). Presumably, this means that you would be better off with these components even if you found them hateful. A striking example is the objective list theory, which states that "certain things are good or bad for us, whether or not we want to have the good things, or to avoid the bad things."[38]

The objective list theory can certainly be faulted for ignoring the subjectivity of well-being. But a theory that doesn't share in this fault doesn't cease to be objective. On my theory, there is an asymmetry between objectively bad and objectively good values: objectively bad values are partly constitutive of our ill-being, whether or not we want to avoid them,

---

[37] David Lykken and Auke Tellegen, psychologists at the University of Minnesota, studied 1,500 pairs of twins (732 monozygotic and 765 dizygotic), and concluded that our basic level of happiness—happiness "set point"—depends largely on our emotional genetic blueprint. This is the level of happiness we tend to be at under normal circumstances, and that we return to after a spike from good news or a dip from bad news. See David Lykken, *Happiness* (1999), chapter 2. Lykken emphasizes, however, that there is much we ourselves can do to live below or above our set point.

[38] See Derek Parfit, *Reasons and Persons* (1984), 499, where he lists "moral goodness, rational activity, the development of one's abilities, having children and being a good parent, knowledge, and the awareness of true beauty" as necessary parts of well-being. In "Subjective Well-Being" (2009), Erik Angner, describes Nussbaum's Aristotelian theory in "Happy Warrior" (2008) as an objective list theory because it identifies *eudaimonia* with a list of virtuous activities. However, on the Aristotelian view of virtue, virtuous activities—both those that are from virtue and those that are motivated rightly but not from virtue—cannot be pried apart from the agent's positive attitude towards them. Hence it is not possible to say of this view that virtuous activities are good for you regardless of your attitude towards them.

whereas objectively good values are partly constitutive of our well-being only if we have certain pro-attitudes towards them. This is true both of objective values that are necessary for a worthwhile life, such as certain character traits, and of objective values that are optional, such as math or romantic love. Well-being requires that we internalize the traits necessary for a worthwhile life, and pursue those worthwhile optional goals, of the many available to us, that suit our particular natures. Our activities must engage our interests and passions to be fulfilling and, indeed, to be our "own," both expressive of, and suited to, our individual natures. In this emphasis on individuality, my conception of well-being is more Millian than Aristotelian. In our post-Darwinian age, a defensible conception of well-being must be responsive, as Mill's was, not only to the fact that we human beings are mostly alike, but also to the fact that we are very different in our tastes, talents, and abilities. These differences, combined with differences in our social situations, make all the difference to the sorts of lives different individuals need for their own fulfillment. Hence my conception of well-being as happiness in an objectively worthwhile life escapes the objection from subjectivity.

2.6 Conclusion

I have argued that the ancient concept of the highest prudential good, and a conception of well-being that meets its formal constraints, capture important elements in our ordinary thinking about our own prudential good. The highest prudential good is a good that is most final, self-sufficient, and most choiceworthy, and well-being meets these conditions and the condition of subjectivity only if it is defined as happiness in an objectively worthwhile life. My conception of objective worth as requiring that one be characteristically realistic (reality-oriented, autonomous, and informed) is neither paternalistic nor elitist.

In chapter 3 I discuss subjective theories of well-being. The main problem with them, I argue, is that if we take them at their word that objective worth is irrelevant to well-being, then their conception of well-being lacks the importance we give to it in our actual lives, an importance that alone justifies the intellectual firepower directed at analyzing and understanding it. To meet the normative demand, theories of well-being have to recognize objective worth as partly constitutive of well-being. My discussion will focus on L.W. Sumner's "authentic happiness" account of well-being, as his is the best worked-out and most influential

account of well-being, as his is the best worked-out and most influential subjectivist account, but I will also consider the other main subjectivist accounts: hedonism, informed desire-satisfaction, Haybron's individual nature-fulfillment, and Tiberius, Plakias, and Hall's value-based life-satisfaction (VBLS).

CHAPTER 3 | Well-Being: From Subjectivity to Objectivity

"Ever' man wants life to be a fine thing, and a easy. 'Tis fine, boy, powerful fine, but 'tain't easy."

—MARJORIE KINNAN RAWLINGS, *The Yearling*

3.1 Hedonism and Desire-Satisfaction

3.1.1 The hallmark of subjectivist theories, as noted in chapter 1, is their sharp dichotomy between a life's prudential value, on the one hand, and its moral or perfectionist value, on the other. The dichotomy is based on the assumption that an individual's objective goodness—her virtue, or her perfection (full or high development) in some valued sphere of human life, such as the intellectual, artistic, productive, or physical spheres—is neither necessary nor sufficient for her prudential good. I will discuss the five most influential of these theories in order to prepare the way for my conception of well-being as the highest prudential good (HPG). The rejection of objective values, I will show, leads even the most sophisticated subjectivist theory to be descriptively or normatively inadequate to our everyday conception of well-being. Moreover, to make their theories descriptively and normatively adequate, the more sophisticated theories adopt standards of authenticity or good functioning that their own premises bar them from adopting.

Two well-known subjective theories of well-being are classical hedonism and desire-satisfaction. According to classical hedonism, well-being consists of happiness, and happiness of pleasure; thus, well-being consists of pleasure. According to the desire-satisfaction theory, well-being consists of the satisfaction or realization of (informed) desire. Both theories seem plausible on their face. Life would be drab indeed without pleasure, and when we feel or reflect that things are going well, the feeling or reflection is infused with pleasure. Again, a life in which our desires were continually frustrated is no one's idea of a desirable life, and whatever else a life of well-being might be, surely it is a desirable life. Conversely, if our desires are satisfied, there seems nothing left wanting as far as our well-being is concerned. Yet an analysis of these theories reveals insuperable problems with each. As many critics have pointed out, hedonism ignores the individual's own values and preferences, whereas the desire-satisfaction theory ignores the individual's positive experiences and emotional states, all of which are crucial features of a life that is good for us.

Although all forms of hedonism equate well-being with pleasure, their conceptions of pleasure differ: internalist hedonism claims that pleasure is a particular sensation or feeling common to all pleasurable experiences; externalist hedonism claims that pleasure is any kind of positive (satisfying, pleasing, etc.) experience; and attitudinal hedonism claims that pleasure is the propositional attitude of being pleased, happy, cheerful, or glad about a state of affairs or event. Unfortunately, the internalist and externalist forms of hedonism ignore the fact that among the things that constitute our well-being are states of the world, not only mental states, let alone only pleasurable mental states.[1] It is important to most of us that our positive mental states reflect the actual conditions of our lives, including the state of people and things (projects, institutions, our society, the world) that matter to us. Moreover, it matters to us that our objects of love and concern prosper even if we are unaware of this fact, indeed, even if we must remain unaware of it. This is why, for example, parents provide for their children after their deaths, even though they will (necessarily) not be around to see their children enjoying their largesse. It might be thought that parents provide for their children because they take pleasure in the thought of their children enjoying their largesse. That parents take such pleasure is true; it doesn't follow, however, that it is for the sake of this pleasure that parents provide for their children. There are cheaper ways for parents to get this pleasure, such as fantasizing that the pittance they are bestowing on their children is actually a largesse, or that their children don't need a largesse because they will all win "Who Wants to Become a Millionaire?" contests. More importantly, they wouldn't take pleasure in the thought of their children enjoying their largesse if they didn't have any love or concern for their children. A satisfactory theory of well-being must

---

[1] The first two kinds of hedonism are thoroughly discussed and criticized by James Griffin, *Well-Being* (1986), chapter 1, and Sumner, *Welfare* (1996), chapter 4, among others.

leave room for the rich diversity of human concerns, not exclude them by definition, as internalist and externalist hedonisms do. In particular, it must recognize that states of the world matter to well-being.

Fred Feldman's attitudinal hedonism avoids these problems by identifying pleasure with the propositional attitude of being pleased (or being happy, approving, and so on) about a state of affairs or event.[2] Intrinsic attitudinal pleasure in x is the sole source and bearer of prudential value. Joy, delight, gladness, contentment, satisfaction can all be analyzed into intrinsic attitudinal pleasure. Even sensory and emotional pains and pleasures are nothing but forms of intrinsic attitudinal pleasure. But this seems highly implausible. A person can be pleased that dialysis is saving his life, without finding dialysis at all pleasurable. Conversely, he can find his fourth drink of the evening extremely pleasurable, without being pleased that he is drinking his fourth drink. Furthermore, babies (and many animals) can have sensory and emotional pains and pleasures without having any attitude towards them. Perhaps the deepest problem with Feldman's thesis is that one can take intrinsic attitudinal pleasure in one's own unhappiness, even one's suffering, if one believes that one deserves to be unhappy or suffering. But it's odd to regard this condition of life as prudentially valuable, or no less valuable than being pleased that one's life is happy.

3.1.2 The desire-satisfaction theory makes the opposite mistake from the hedonist theory by equating well-being with desire satisfaction, and desire satisfaction with the occurrence of certain states of affairs (thus, my desire that it snow tonight is satisfied if it snows tonight). Thereby it equates well-being with the occurrence of certain states of affairs, ignoring the fact that central to our well-being is some sort of positive experience or emotion. As a result, the desire theory has some highly counterintuitive consequences. Suppose, for example, that I'm miserable because I've been told that my estranged but beloved daughter has died, when all I wanted was for her to live and to flourish. In fact, however, I've been told a lie, and she is very much alive and flourishing. According to the desire theory, regardless of my emotional condition, I am actually doing well, because my desire for my daughter to live and flourish has been satisfied. The desire theorist could respond that my desire not to be given false tragic news about my daughter has been frustrated, and that is what explains my misery. But in the nature of the case, I don't know that this desire has been

---

[2] See Fred Feldman, *Pleasure and the Good Life: Concerning the Nature, Varieties, and Plausibility of Hedonism* (2004), and "Replies" (2007), 439–450. Haybron also criticizes attitudinal hedonism in *Unhappiness* (2008), chapter 4.

frustrated, so it cannot be the cause of my negative emotional state. The straightforward explanation of my misery is that I take the tragic news to be true, and my misery is inherently bad because of the negative feelings and evaluations it involves. It is neither the result, nor a manifestation, of desire-frustration (just as, in the case of Feldman's attitudinal hedonism, misery is not a manifestation of the attitude of being displeased that *p*).

The desire theory also implies that we are made no better off by pleasant surprises. Suppose that I'm bored stiff with my job as an accountant, but one day a friend in the comedy business asks me to help him write a skit. I agree reluctantly, but then discover that I'm good at comedic writing and really enjoy it. According to the desire theory, this does not make me any better off because I never desired to write the skit or to get enjoyment from it. The desire theorist could respond that enjoyable activities make me better off even when I don't have a *specific* desire for them because, like most human beings, I have a *general* desire to get enjoyment from my activities. It is certainly true that most of us have such a general desire, although it is hard to say which (if either) comes first, the general desire or experiences of enjoyment. But not everyone has this general desire. There *are* people with dour personalities, people who disapprove of all pleasures and enjoyments. Yet even they might be taken by surprise and find themselves enjoying an experience. But the desire-theory must insist that the enjoyment is no part of their well-being because they did not desire it.

The problems with the simple desire-satisfaction theory are not obviated by the less simple informed desire-satisfaction theory, according to which well-being lies in the satisfaction of informed desires, desires formed, as Griffin puts it, through an "appreciation of the nature of the objects of desire" (*Well-Being*, 15). For there is still the possibility that what we *think* will make us well-off—a trip to Rome, marriage to the man or woman of our dreams—will actually make us worse off. This possibility, in Sumner's words, is inherent in the prospectivity of desire—that is, in the fact that "my preferences about the future always represent my view now of how things will go then" (*Welfare*, 131). Satisfaction of informed or rational desires is often a source of well-being, but it is neither necessary nor sufficient for well-being. Hence it cannot be identical to well-being.

A possible reply is that informed desires are desires that are informed all the way through, that is, informed even about the desires we will have if they are satisfied.[3] If their satisfaction leads us to desire that they had never been satisfied, then our original desires were not informed. Conversely, if

---

[3] Erik Angner, "Subjective Well-Being: When, and Why, It Matters" (2012).

an uninformed desire is frustrated, it does not necessarily detract from our well-being. In the skit example, if I had known that I would enjoy writing skits and come to desire doing so after trying my hand at one, I would never have been reluctant to write a skit. My reluctance was uninformed, hence the frustration of my desire not to write the skit did not detract from my well-being.

The informed desire-satisfaction theory, then, does somewhat better than the simple version of the theory, but like the simple version, its insistence that enjoyment or pleasure play no constitutive role in well-being is both inherently counterintuitive and counterintuitive in its implications. The chief of these is that it is compelled to say of those who want to be, and are, miserable and suffering, that they have well-being.

Both hedonism and the desire-theory fail to be descriptively adequate to our ordinary notion of well-being, as this operates in our pre-reflective judgments and deliberations, and in our psychological explanations (Sumner, 10–12). For Sumner, this ordinary notion incorporates both the experiential aspect of well-being emphasized by the hedonist theory, and the state-of-the-world aspect emphasized by the desire theory. A satisfactory theory of well-being must take both aspects of well-being into account.

3.2 Sumner's Subjective Conception of Well-Being

Sumner attempts to do just this by arguing that well-being is subjective, and that its subjectivity entails that well-being must be a function both of our mental states and of certain states of the world. This novel and subtle view requires some unpacking. Sumner correctly distinguishes *subjectivity* from *subject-relativity*. It should be uncontroversial that well-being is subject-relative or perspectival. To say that someone's life is going well is to say that it is going well for *her*, rather than in itself or for others (*Welfare,* 20). Subject-relativity is "one of the deepest features of the language of welfare [well-being]," where well-being is understood as the prudential value of a life, as distinct from its ethical, perfectionist, or aesthetic value. When we assess the moral value of someone's life, we look not (only) at its value for her, but (also) at its value for others.[4] When we assess

_____

[4] Sumner identifies morality with other-regarding morality, but even if we take a broader view of morality, one of the chief challenges to the thesis that virtue is necessary for well-being comes, as I noted in chapter 1, from the other-regarding virtues or the other-regarding aspect of morality, including justice and honesty.

the perfectionist value of someone's life—the extent to which the agent has developed her powers or capacities—we assess it from the perspective of her membership in the human species. But subject-relativity is part of the language of well-being, part of what we mean when we talk about someone's life as going well for her.

The subject-relativity of well-being does not, however, entail subjectivity. To say that well-being is subjective is to say that an individual's well-being depends, ultimately, on her sense of satisfaction in her life when she regards it from her own point of view, that is, from the point of view constituted by her values, attitudes, interests, and so on (ibid., 38–40). But it is perfectly possible for someone to accept the subject-relativity of well-being without accepting its subjectivity.[5] Thus, someone who rejects the importance of subjectivity altogether (in Sumner's terminology, an objectivist) may hold that a life goes well for an individual when, for example, it meets his basic needs, or exemplifies the fulfillment of his function or nature as an individual of a certain kind, regardless of the individual's own priorities and values.[6] That well-being is partly or entirely dependent on the individual's attitudes is a further, substantive claim that must be argued for.

Sumner first argues for the weaker thesis that it is a necessary condition of well-being that an individual's attitudes towards his life be positive, for this provides the best interpretation or explanation of the subject-relativity of well-being, of why our concept of well-being is the concept of someone's life going well *for him* (38, 41). If an individual's own attitudes had *no* bearing on how he was faring, it would be hard to see why we thought of his well-being in subject-relative terms.

[5.] For example, Stephen Darwall argues that "a person's good is constituted, not by what that person values, prefers, or wants (or should value), but by what one (perhaps she) should want insofar as one cares about her." See *Welfare and Rational Care* (2004), 4. Presumably what one should want for a person one cares for is what is actually good for her. On my objectivist conception, however, what matters to well-being is both objective worth and the individual's own attitudes.

[6.] In *Welfare* (1986), Sumner discusses the needs view defended by David Braybrooke and others (53–60), and the function or teleological view defended by Aristotle and environmental ethicists Robin Attfield and Paul Taylor (69–80). Attfield and Taylor extend the Aristotelian teleological principle to all living things. Sumner's central criticism of the function theory is that it makes an illicit move from someone functioning well to his having well-being (78–79). Sumner suggests that, on this view, it is possible, implausibly, for someone's life to be going well for her even if her life is filled with pain and frustration. As an interpretation of Aristotle's view in the *NE*, however, this criticism is tendentious, since many philosophers argue that Aristotle regards pleasurable activity and external goods as essential to *eudaimonia*. I return to this issue in chapter 7.

This seems right. What is controversial is Sumner's thesis that well-being is *entirely* subjective, in the sense that objective values play no essential role in it; they play a role only if the individual endorses them. Well-being, he argues, consists of authentic happiness, understood as a sense of life-satisfaction that is underwritten by an authentic endorsement of one's life, that is, an endorsement that is both empirically informed and autonomous (160, 167). Sumner sees the authenticity requirement as following from the subjective nature of well-being, rather than from notions of human worth or dignity. That is to say, an individual's authentic endorsement of his life as going well for him is both necessary and sufficient for his life really going well for him. But why must well-being, be entirely subjective? Because, Sumner argues, there are insuperable problems with the claim that objective valves play an essential role in well-being. I shall start by showing that Sumner's arguments against objective standards do not work. Then I shall argue that, contrary to his claim, the requirement of authenticity does not follow from the subjective nature of well-being, that it is actually an objective value in subjective garb. Hence, in opening the door to authenticity, Sumner has unwittingly opened the door to an objectivity requirement: the requirement that the life conditions an individual finds fulfilling and endorses really *be* valuable. At the same time, however, the constraints imposed by Sumner's conception of authenticity are so weak that they can be satisfied even by someone who wishes to stay hooked to the experience machine for his entire life.

3.3 The (Im)Possibility of Objective Standards

Sumner holds that a thoroughgoing subjectivism about well-being is the only game in town, because there can be no objective standard for well-being. Such a standard cannot be prudential, he argues, because it is circular to say that the objective requirement for well-being (the prudential value of a life) is that the life be truly prudentially valuable (*Welfare*, 164–165). But neither can the standard be moral or perfectionist, for we can imagine someone who is a paragon of virtue, or who has perfected his central human capacities to an exemplary extent, failing to find much satisfaction in his ethical or perfectionist excellences (ibid., 20–25, 164–165). Think of the honest, just, and generous man who fails to realize his dreams, loses his wife to his dazzling neighbor, and his wealth to his counterfeit friends. Or the lonely genius, who dies never having known the simple pleasures of hanging out with drinking buddies or the intimacy of romantic love.

From the fact that virtue and perfection do not guarantee well-being, Sumner concludes that there is a conceptual gulf between prudential values, on the one hand, and moral or perfectionist values, on the other, and hence that well-being is entirely subjective. Those who value morality or human perfection enough to see it as part of their well-being will measure their well-being partly by moral or perfectionist standards; those who do not, will not. The individual's own priorities determine what makes her life better for her; there are no objective constraints on prudential values (93).

These arguments, however, are too quick. No doubt it is circular to say, "Alpha's life is prudentially valuable because it is prudentially valuable." But there is no reason to think that we cannot say something more informative about the prudential standard Alpha's life must meet to be prudentially valuable. Using a prudential standard for measuring well-being is no more circular than using a moral standard for measuring the moral value of a life, or using weights for measuring the weight of a bag of potatoes. Indeed, what else could we use to measure the prudential value of a life if not a prudential standard? If, as I argued in chapter 2, objective worth is a prudential good, then it can also be a prudential standard of the prudential value of a person's life.

Sumner's second argument, namely, that we cannot use moral or perfectionist standards to measure well-being because even a paragon of morality or human perfection may fail to have well-being, merely shows that virtue or perfection are not *sufficient* for happiness, not that they are not *necessary*.[7] Hence, Sumner's arguments do not support his conclusion that there are logical or conceptual barriers to thinking that prudential standards can be (partly) objective. The idea that all prudential values must be subjective creates an artificial and indefensible conceptual gulf between prudential values on the one hand, and moral and perfectionist values on the other. In principle, then, given my argument in chapter 2 that objective worth is partly constitutive of a life of well-being as the HPG, if it could be shown that virtue and perfection are entailed by objective worth, they could also serve as standards of well-being as the highest prudential good.

---

[7] As we saw in chapter 1, in *The Examined Life* (1989), Nozick suggests that well-being entails evaluating one's life as good in the dimensions that one regards as "most important" and that "are most important," and that morality is one of these dimensions (113). But in the very next sentence he undercuts his suggestion by making the same (mistaken) objection to this claim as Sumner: namely, that a moral person need not be happy.

But Sumner also has an epistemological objection to the claim that there are objective standards for well-being: if the individual's own (authentic) point of view on her life does not determine her well-being, he asks rhetorically, who is to decide which goals or ways of life really are prudentially valuable? "The enlightened elite? Mill's 'competent judges'? Philosopher kings?" (164). But this is a problem only if we assume that well-being does not require any objective values. Since this has not been shown, then, if objective standards are relevant to well-being, anyone who knows what they are can judge which ways of life are prudentially valuable.

Sumner's next objection is that, even if we had good answers to all these questions, an objective standard of value "seems objectionably dogmatic in imposing a standard discount rate on people's self-assessed happiness" (165). (Although Sumner says "happiness" here, the rest of the passage makes it clear that he actually means "authentic happiness" or "well-being.") There is "no right answer to the question of how to respond to shifts in personal values or standards" (165). Once again, however, if there is an objective standard of value, then there is a right answer—or, more precisely, a range of right answers (since objective standards don't necessarily yield singular answers). And if there are right answers, then there is nothing dogmatic about saying that a person who has pursued false values should discount his earlier assessment of his well-being when his values change for the better. How much he should discount them depends on how bad his earlier values were and why he held them. Some relevant questions are: Did these values harm him seriously or was his pursuit of them just a minor waste of time? Did he enjoy himself spending his days shooting pool instead of attending classes, or did he do it just to appear cool? If he enjoyed himself, then there is at least some redeeming value to his frivolity; if he did it just to appear cool, then his values were bad for him twice over. Likewise, if there is an objective standard of well-being, then it can't be "presumptuous," as Sumner complains, to say of someone whose central goals are worthless that his life is not going well for him, even if he judges otherwise (166). It would, of course, normally be presumptuous to tell him so. But it would also normally be presumptuous to tell an irrational person that she lacks an important human perfection or a cowardly person that she lacks moral fiber, even though it would not be presumptuous to make these judgments *tout court*. We can apply objective standards to others without announcing our views to them—or to anyone.

It is safe to conclude, then, that Sumner's objections to objective prudential standards do not succeed in demolishing them. Moreover, as I argue below, Sumner's subjective conception of well-being as authentic happiness is an unfit candidate for the highest prudential good. The problem lies in Sumner's content-free conception of authenticity, a conception that allows even a life of servility or pretence to count as authentic. A content-free conception of authenticity is, indeed, fine for some purposes. It suffices for defining the capacity for governing oneself and being a responsible agent. But a plausible conception of well-being as the highest prudential good requires a substantive conception of authenticity, authenticity as a character trait.

3.4 Well-Being as Authentic Happiness

3.4.1 Happiness, for Sumner, consists of a sense of satisfaction in the conditions of one's life (the affective component), and an actual or hypothetical endorsement of these conditions in light of one's values (the evaluative component) (145–146). By contrast, authentic happiness or well-being is life-satisfaction that is underwritten by an authentic endorsement of one's life (i.e., an endorsement that is both empirically informed and autonomous) (160, 167). It must be informed to ensure that the life one endorses truly is one's own life, and it must be autonomous to ensure that the values that constitute the standpoint from which one assesses one's well-being truly are one's own (160). As Sumner explains, "If a subject's endorsement of some particular (perceived) condition depends on a factual mistake, or results from illusion or deception, then it is not an accurate reflection of her own underlying values. And if those values have been engineered or manipulated by others then they are not truly hers" (174).

The epistemic or information requirement raises the question of how much and which information an authentically happy individual must have. Clearly no one has the complete truth about the empirical conditions of her life. Sumner rejects both the truth or reality test, and the justifiability test, as "presumptuously dogmatic" (159). The reality test stipulates that our positive assessment of our lives not be based on factual error about the relevant conditions of our lives; the justifiability test weakens this to read that it not be based "on any false beliefs that were *unreasonable* under the circumstances" (159). Both requirements, however, presume to "dictate to individuals how much their deviations from an ideal epistemic standpoint should matter to them" (159). These requirements are dogmatic because in fact we do *not* always revise our assessment of our happiness as authentic on the discovery of error in our beliefs. Our ordinary notion of well-being is sensitive to this fact, and our philosophical theories should be too. Sumner's answer to the question of how much information the individual must have in order for her judgment of her happiness to be authentic is: whichever information "would make a difference to a subject's affective response to her life, given her priorities" (160).

He illustrates this thesis with the example of a woman who is happy with her lover, but discovers after they have parted ways that he was unfaithful and self-serving. In light of her new information, she is likely to conclude that although she felt happy before she discovered his deception, her happiness was not *authentic* (i.e., she lacked well-being in that period of her life (160–161). But it is also possible that she will conclude that her lover's infidelity and deception are not important to her, and so her happiness *was* authentic: "'*C'est la vie*; at least he was charming and we had a lot of fun'" (161). To protest that she ought to care about his infidelity enough to declare that her happiness with him was inauthentic would be "presumptuously dogmatic" (159). Authentic happiness—well-being—requires an informed response to one's life only insofar as the information makes a difference to that response. We should treat people's self-assessments as authoritative unless we have reason to believe that they don't reflect their own values.

I have no strong reason to disagree with Sumner's analysis of this case, at least if I suppose that a belief in her lover's stellar character was no part of the basis of this woman's relationship with him, and her discovery of his faithlessness was no part of her reason for ending it. It does not follow, however, as Sumner believes, that there are no objective criteria for deciding when authentic happiness does require information about the facts of our lives. A general unconcern with the moral character of the people deeply involved in our lives, I will argue, is incompatible with well-being as the HPG.

3.4.2 The next stage in Sumner's argument concerns autonomy. An informed positive assessment of one's life, he argues, is not sufficient for guaranteeing the authenticity of an individual's happiness, because a person's preferences and evaluations may have been distorted by social conditioning or deprived circumstances. In other words, her preferences and evaluations may not be, in a sense to be explained, her own. As Amartya Sen puts it in a much-cited passage:

A person who has had a life of misfortune, with very little opportunities, and rather little hope, may be more easily reconciled to deprivations than others reared in more fortunate and affluent circumstances. The hopeless beggar, the precarious landless labourer, the dominated housewife...may all take pleasures in small mercies, and manage to suppress intense suffering for the necessity of continuing survival....[8]

A common reaction to such cases is that people in such circumstances who say—and feel—that they are well off cannot just be taken at their word, because they cannot see where their true good lies. But this route is not available to a thoroughgoing subjectivist. On what grounds, then, can a subjectivist like Sumner say that, for example, we shouldn't take the dominated housewife at her word? Sumner's grounds are that her evaluation of her life is *heteronomous* (166). Autonomous judgments, values, and goals are those that are in some sense one's own. Building on two standard accounts of autonomy, the hierarchical and the historical, Sumner argues that what makes them one's own is that one endorses them or identifies with them after a process of critical reflection (or would identify with them if one went through such a process), and that this process itself is conducted in the light of a person's own standards (167–170).[9] Values that would not survive critical reflection, or even those that would but are adopted in the light of standards that are not one's own, cannot be thought of as autonomous. In turn, standards that count as "one's own" are those acquired through normal or nonmanipulative processes of socialization (i.e., processes that enable a person to reflect on the most fundamental standards and values he will use in his practical deliberations and evaluations in the course of his life). Manipulative processes of socialization, by contrast, are those that tend to undermine a person's ability to reflect critically on the values being inculcated (170). For example, someone who is brought up to believe that, as a female, her rational powers are inferior to those of men, and that her womanhood requires that she defer to her husband in all important matters in their lives together, has been subjected to a manipulative process of socialization. Since these beliefs serve as her basic, unquestioned regulative standards in her choice of goals and actions, if she fails to acquire the ability to reflect on them, her deliberations and judgments about specific norms, goals, or actions— no matter how thoughtful and independent within the boundaries of her unexamined standards—will be heteronomous, and her life-satisfaction inauthentic.

[8.] Amartya Sen, *On Ethics and Economics* (1987), 45–46; quoted in Sumner, ibid., 66.
[9.] The hierarchical account of autonomy goes back to Harry Frankfurt, "Freedom of the Will and the Concept of a Person" (1971), 5–20, and the "historical" account to John Christman, "Autonomy and Personal History" (1991), 1–24.

3.4.3 Sumner intends autonomy to be a condition of true subjectivity or selfhood, and not an objective value. But does he succeed in his intention? A woman who has internalized the view that she lacks the ability to think for herself in important matters just because she is a woman, that she is inferior to men in these matters, certainly lacks autonomy in a substantive, normative sense. But does not the fact that she has internalized these views, that they have become part of her identity, mean that these views are her own in a perfectly straightforward sense? She values certain ways of being and not others, she sees the world through these values, she wills to act or not in certain ways because of these values, she feels joy, shame, pride, or disappointment in accord with these values. In a perfectly straightforward sense, the problem is not that these basic values or standards are *not* her own, *but that they are*. And this is a problem because they are demeaning and thereby (on my view) bad for her.

It is true that the capacity for critically reflecting on our values is an important human capacity, necessary for self-knowledge as well as for self-evaluation. It is also true that in critically reflecting on our values, and endorsing or rejecting them, we play an active part in making our identities. And so it is plausible to say that the values we identify with are more our own if we endorse them after critical reflection in light of our alternatives (or would endorse them if we were to reflect on them). In other words, they are more our own if we (hypothetically or actually) accept them after such reflection. But why should this extra step matter so much? Why isn't it good enough to internalize our values through habituation and acculturation? Someone who thinks of well-being as happiness in an objectively worthwhile life has an easy answer to this question: being able to endorse our values after critical reflection is important because the ability for doing so is necessary for functioning well as a human being and for leading an objectively worthwhile life. Someone whose upbringing has severely compromised her ability for such reflection has had her ability for functioning well and leading an objectively worthwhile life compromised. It seems that Sumner also is implicitly moved by these considerations about the value of critical reflection in human life. In requiring the ability for such reflection, he brings objective normative concerns into his theory and robs it of its purely subjective status. Thus he opens the door to other objective notions of well-being.[10]

---

[10] Haybron also criticizes Sumner for using an objective standard, but on the grounds that Sumner would label as heteronomous a person's acceptance of manipulatively acquired values even after the person had been exposed to the facts and reflected on these values (*Unhappiness*, 2008,

At the same time, however, as I argue in the next section, Sumner's value-subjectivism weakens his conception of autonomy so much that its requirements can be met even by someone who doesn't like thinking for herself and rarely makes the effort to do so.

3.5 Autonomous Heteronomy

Let's consider the oppressed woman further. This woman gets the opportunity to learn about the oppression of women and other, more open, ways of life. She attends consciousness-raising classes, and goes through a period of critical reflection on her long-held belief that her rational powers are inferior to those of men. At the end of this period, however, she comes full circle and endorses her life of submission as satisfying because it gives her what she most needs for her well-being: financial security and social status. Her submission may consist only in going along with her husband's decisions even when she judges them to be wrong, or—and Sumner's account leaves this open—even in abdicating her judgment of right and wrong because she does not like the responsibility of thinking for herself about these things.[11] Her autonomy is exercised only in the (actually or hypothetically) continually renewed second-order choice to refrain from making her own judgments and first-order choices in large areas of her life. He decides who her friends should be, which movies she may watch or which books she may read, how they should spend their money, how she should behave at home and in society, and so on. By hypothesis, in these central areas of human life she lives unreflectively and uncritically accepts her husband's choices and values. In effect, she says, "I'm not interested in thinking for myself and having values of my own in these areas. It is enough for me that I have financial security and social status." She autonomously decides to live heteronomously in these central areas of her life.

On Sumner's view, even her life of abject servility counts as autonomous simply because she periodically renews her informed and autonomous endorsement of her life of servility (182).

To take another example: imagine someone so lazy that he has no desire to do anything that requires effort. He has inherited a tidy sum of money,

---

190). I think this is a misinterpretation, as the example of Sumner's housewife that I discuss below shows.

[11] Cf. the case of the servile wife in Thomas E. Hill, Jr., "Servility and Self-Respect" (1991), 4–18.

so he doesn't need to work to survive. He eats out of cartons, drinks out of cans, and spends the day being pleasantly regaled by sitcoms. Every now and then he feels somewhat bored, but is too lazy to bestir himself. Then he discovers the Experience Machine Center, where people can sign up for a lifetime of a variety of positive experiences at an affordable cost. The only condition is that they be unhooked every month to renew their decision to be kept on the machine—or not. He considers the situation and the alternatives open to him, and decides to sign up. "Life enough," he thinks, "to have the *experience* of living a challenging, exciting, enjoyable, and worthwhile life in which I make my own decisions over central areas of my life. Why should I bother to actually *live* a challenging life and, possibly, hurt or harm myself?"

Sumner's view implies that this is sufficient to render his decisions and his life autonomous and informed. Since he is also happy on the experience machine, the lazy fellow meets Sumner's requirements for authentic happiness or well-being. Most of us would say, however, that even if such a life can be called happy, it can only barely be called *authentically* happy. For *what* the lazy fellow endorses is a life in which he is neither autonomous nor informed. Indeed, even if he is unhooked every day to renew his decision, he can barely be said to be *living* a life.

At this point, like other defenders of content-free conceptions of autonomy, Sumner could respond that, in autonomously choosing to live a certain way, he bestows autonomy on that way of life. But is autonomy the kind of thing we can bestow on a way of life, regardless of the actions and attitudes that constitute that way of life? No more, it seems, than liberty. If I freely (that is, in liberty) sell myself into slavery, I do not thereby convert slavery into a state of liberty. Even if I am given the liberty to choose liberty every month, I do not cease to be a slave during the time I am not at liberty to choose. Similarly, the lazy fellow does not cease to be heteronomous during the time he is hooked to the machine. To claim that whatever we choose is autonomous so long as we choose it autonomously is to make the autonomous choice of heteronomy logically impossible. But this is no more impossible than is the free choice to give up one's freedom. The claim that whatever life we choose autonomously is autonomous also has other implausible implications. It entails that the subservient housewife's life, in which she abdicates her decision-making powers in many important areas of her life, is no less autonomous than it would have been had she chosen to not abdicate them. Likewise, it entails that the lazy fellow's life in a virtual reality, in which he periodically makes one decision, is no less autonomous than it would have been had he chosen to live in the world, making many autonomous decisions every day.

Sumner has defended his view by arguing that my objections conflate two different conceptions of autonomy: autonomy in the sense of reflectively choosing between alternatives on the basis of values that are truly one's own, and autonomy in the sense of making one's own decisions about one's life or some aspect thereof.[12] This difference is illustrated by a patient who autonomously waives his right to make his own medical decisions about certain aspects of his treatment. This patient, says Sumner, "continues to be autonomous over that part of his...life" in the first sense, although not in the second.[13] But are there really two senses of autonomy in play? Let us assume that the patient charges his doctors and family members to base their decisions on his values, and they do so. Then it is true that he (indirectly, through his doctors and family members) chooses between alternatives on the basis of values that are truly his own. But is it true that in this scenario he does not (indirectly) make his own decisions? By charging his doctors and family members to make decisions that will serve his ends, and to do so within the constraints of his values, the patient in effect controls the two most important components of the decision: the goal and the means. Hence, insofar as he chooses between alternatives on the basis of values that are truly his own, he also makes his own decisions, albeit indirectly. The converse is also true: if the patient doesn't make his own treatment decisions even indirectly, he doesn't choose between alternatives on the basis of his own values. Let us suppose that the alternatives facing the patient are the moderate risk of death or the certainty of life in a wheelchair, and he has no idea what he values more: independence, even at the risk of death, or life, even though in a wheelchair. Sometimes the risk of death seems worthwhile for the sake of independence; sometimes life, albeit in a wheelchair. So he autonomously decides to let his doctors and family choose for him. He also can't decide on the means they may use to achieve whatever goal they decide on: a very painful procedure with a short recovery time, or a moderately painful procedure with a long recovery time. By his own choice, the patient plays no role in the decisions made for his treatment. Equally, it should be clear, he doesn't choose between alternatives on the basis of his values. In short, without making one's own decisions, directly or indirectly, one cannot live by one's own

---

[12] Email correspondence, April 24, 1997.
[13] Ibid., February 24, 1998.

values, and without living by one's own values, directly or indirectly, one cannot make one's own decisions. The distinction is a distinction without a difference.

This is even more evident in the case of the slothful fellow and the subservient housewife. To be sure, these individuals are more autonomous than they would have been if they hadn't even exercised second-order autonomy periodically. But they lack robust autonomy, autonomy as a character trait, because they fail to live by their own independent thinking in important areas of their lives. In allowing such minimally autonomous agents to count as no less autonomous than substantively autonomous agents, Sumner's conception of autonomy fails dramatically in descriptive adequacy.

Someone might question whether Sumner's view really can allow a life of servility, or a life on the experience machine, to count as autonomous, on the grounds that no one who chooses such a life can retain his capacity for making autonomous choices, as required by Sumner's theory.[14] But even if a person is unlikely to retain his capacity for making autonomous choices under such circumstances, it is not impossible for him to do so, as Sumner himself acknowledges (182). Indeed, I do not see why it is even unlikely. If someone chooses a virtual existence because his fundamental standards dictate achieving life-satisfaction with the least amount of effort and pain, then his standards, affective responses, and desires are in perfect harmony, and there is no reason why he should lose his capacity to reflect on his alternatives—an effortlessly satisfying virtual life vs. an effort-full, less satisfying real life—in light of his standards. He might lose his motivation to do this reflection when he is unhooked since, by hypothesis, he has complete life-satisfaction in virtual reality, and living a life worthy of him as a human being is not something he cares about. But if he is forced to reflect on his alternatives, and endorses his machine existence, he counts as living autonomously on Sumner's conception of autonomy.

A similar analysis applies to the subservient housewife on the hypothesis that she has complete life-satisfaction and that living a life worthy of her as a human being is not something she cares about. Let us suppose that the provenance of her periodic reflection on her alternatives is the attempt by family and friends to get her to become more independent, more her own person. They create vivid portraits of the joys of such an

---

[14] This suggestion is due to Theo van Willigenburg.

existence. But all their efforts result in her choosing, over and over, her life of subservience to her husband. Then she counts as living autonomously on Sumner's conception of autonomy.

3.6 Informed Ignorance

3.6.1 As this discussion suggests, Sumner's epistemic condition for authenticity also faces problems. This condition, it will be recalled, requires merely that we be in touch with the empirical conditions of our lives, *in those sectors, and only those sectors, that matter to us*. The man on the experience machine, lost in a world of make-believe, counts as living a life in touch with the empirical conditions of his life so long as he is unhooked periodically to choose between this world and the real world. Or consider the young man discussed by Sumner. This young man has been raised in a religious community that forbids any teaching of modern science, but later enters a university and gains access to the forbidden knowledge (170). He goes through "a period of doubt and indecision," but ultimately "decides to reaffirm his commitment" to his community's beliefs and way of life.[15] He does so, let us say, not because he believes that his community's way of life is morally better or that modern science is wrong, but because life in the outside world, with its rapid changes and countless choices, leaves him feeling confused and unhappy. He needs and values the safe, predictable, close-knit nature of his community; this is where he feels at home, where his senses expand and his mind is at peace. But since his community restricts knowledge of the outside world, rejects modern science, and demands obedience to its metaphysical and moral beliefs, this young man must act in conformity to these beliefs, even though he doesn't accept most of them. So far, so good—at least for Sumner's epistemic condition, if not for the young man. The problem for Sumner's epistemic condition arises from the fact that, if acting against his own views creates cognitive dissonance for the young man, he is free to deceive himself into believing that his own views are false, and his community's true. For Sumner's epistemic condition for authenticity requires only, as noted above, that we stay in touch with (certain) empirical conditions of our lives, and his own or the community's metaphysical

---

[15.] Sumner uses this example to convince us that this young man's commitment is made autonomously (170). But it can equally be used to show that his commitment and subsequent way of life meet Sumner's epistemic requirement for well-being.

and moral values are not empirical conditions of the young man's life. Commonsensically, however, someone who deceives himself about the metaphysical and moral values he lives by is far from authentic. Once again, then, Sumner's conception of authenticity is far from descriptively adequate.

Other examples of lives that would count as informed and autonomous enough for authenticity on Sumner's view readily come to mind: a Don Quixote who devotes himself to ideals that he suspects are chimerical, but who is unbothered by that possibility because what he values most is the sense of meaning or comradeship or glory that living for these ideals brings him; or a fanatical terrorist or Nazi who chooses a life of blind obedience to an ideology for the sake of a sense of purpose and avoiding the effort to think for himself, unbothered by the possibility that his objects of devotion might be hollow (Albert Speer is on record as saying that it was a relief not to have to think for himself).[16] So long as Don Quixote and the fanatical terrorist periodically face the fact that their ideals might be mistaken and then renew their reflective endorsement of their ideals—preferring a sense of meaning, or the relief and security of being directed by another, to the alternatives—their well-being counts as authentic. Again, we needn't suppose, incoherently, that they engage in their reevaluations because they are committed to facing reality and thinking for themselves. All we need suppose is that circumstances lead them to reevaluate their lives periodically: perhaps children run after Don Quixote when he appears in their town, jeering at him for tilting at windmills, or perhaps the fanatical terrorist's parents plead with him to give up his foolish devotion to his cause, and so on.

We must conclude, then, that Sumner's view of authenticity is compatible with a great deal of ignorance and self-deception about matters metaphysical and moral, and a great deal of servility, conformity, and blind obedience. These traits and ways of life are incompatible with authenticity on his view only if a person does not (actually or hypothetically) periodically endorse them after critical reflection (158–163 and 170–171). Consequently, Sumner's view of authentic happiness is perfectly compatible with a life

---

[16.] See Jonathan Glover, *Humanity: A Moral History of the Twentieth Century* (1999), 361. The 2003 Pakistani-French-German film, *Khamosh Pani* ("Silent Waters"), provides another example in the young, sweet, but feckless Saleem who, for the sake of gaining a sense of purpose, abandons his mother and girlfriend to join General Zia's extremists in promoting the cause of an intolerant and fanatical Islam in the late 1970s.

spent mostly in make-believe or self-deception, or under the direction of others.[17]

3.6.2 Earlier in this chapter I argued that Sumner's view that our values are autonomous, i.e., our own, only if we reflectively endorse them is unjustified, because internalized values are our own in a perfectly straightforward sense, and that the real motivation for this view is recognition of the fact that the capacity for critical reflection is necessary for functioning well and leading an objectively worthwhile life. But the examples I have considered show that this requirement of reflection and endorsement is also too weak, because it is easily satisfied by self-deceived, deluded, or subservient people. Indeed, since authenticity requires only hypothetical endorsement of one's values, it can be satisfied without any reflection at all. Hence the lazy man's life counts as authentic *without any actual reflection*, so long as he *would* have decided to live hooked to the machine *had* he reflectively considered the matter, and would have renewed his decision to stay on it had he reflectively reconsidered the question. More realistically (and therefore more problematically), the dominated housewife's life counts as authentic *without any actual reflection*, so long as she *would* have decided on this life *had* she reflectively considered the matter and would have renewed her decision to remain dominated had she reflectively reconsidered the question.

---

[17] In a later article, however ("Is Virtue Its Own Reward?" (1998), 18–36), Sumner does seem to argue that self-deception about metaphysical and moral values is incompatible with authentic well-being. His argument goes as follows: if (a) an authentic sense of self-worth is an important component of well-being, and if (b) the sense of self-worth of evil people is necessarily inauthentic, requiring self-deception or heteronomy, then (c) only good people can have an authentic sense of self-worth and, hence, only they can have well-being. In support of (b) Sumner cites empirical evidence that some evil people become and remain evil only by deceiving themselves about the humanity of their victims, or being indoctrinated into evil such that they cannot reflect on their wicked values (34–35). They need to deceive themselves about their victims' humanity because a clear-eyed perception of their victims' humanity would be incompatible with a sense of self-worth. If we could establish that this is true of all evil people, Sumner states, then we could justifiably conclude that no evil person has an authentic sense of self-worth.

Note, however, that Sumner has gone beyond subjectivism in arguing that evil folks' self-deception about their victims' humanity renders their sense of self-worth inauthentic. For "humanity" is a normative, and not an empirical, feature of people. Sumner might argue that evil people's self-deception (or ignorance) about their victims' humanity rests on their self-deception (or ignorance) about their victims' empirical features. But whereas this might explain most evil people's evil, it doesn't explain everyone's (and also doesn't explain all acts of immorality by the average person). Some evil people are aware of their victims' humanity, but unmoved by it and unashamed about their own indifference. Their sense of self-worth is rooted in their consciousness of their own power, rather than the worth of their lives. On the subjectivist view, such people have authentic self-worth and well-being. On the objectivist view, however, the fact that their sense of self-worth is so thoroughly unjustified is enough to render it inauthentic.

3.7 Authentic Happiness vs. the Highest Prudential Good

3.7.1 Sumner's conception of authentic happiness, then, is a poor candidate for being the highest prudential good. Someone who has the highest prudential good has fulfillment in a life that is worthwhile and that she recognizes as worthwhile; as such, her life is supremely enviable. But there is nothing enviable about the people we have considered. An individual who happily accepts her life of subservience to her husband in ignorance of her own abilities and alternatives evokes sympathy. But an individual who accepts her life of subservience after she has realized her own abilities and become aware of more self-sufficient ways of life, merely because she doesn't like the responsibility of thinking for herself, evokes pity. "You knew better," we are inclined to say. The same applies to a Don Quixote or fanatical terrorist who reduce their lives to an exercise in absurdity or futility for the sake of a sense of purpose, or for the sake of avoiding the effort to think for themselves, with little concern for the merit of their ideals.

The pity and horror such lives evoke are connected to the thought that the individuals in question are willingly wasting or misusing their lives. Like wasted wealth, a wasted life is a life ill-spent, having little or no "purchase" on any real value for its owner. Even if the subservient housewife does great good to her family by allowing herself to be used as a mere tool, and even if she takes great satisfaction in her role, her life is a waste from the prudential point of view, for she never really creates a life of her own, a life in which she is her own end. In "happily" wasting her life, she fails to understand or care about her own highest prudential good, because she fails to understand or care about leading a worthwhile life. If she thinks she is leading a worthwhile life in being used largely as a tool for her family's good, she is either making a fundamental mistake about her own nature as a human being, or else confusing the notion of an objectively worthwhile life with the notion of a useful or psychologically satisfying one.

My view that these lives are wasted should not, however, be taken to imply that no one can choose any of them rationally. As I acknowledged in chapter 2, someone whose circumstances promise only a life of unending, meaningless pain or misery could rationally choose the experience machine as an escape from his fate, just as he could rationally choose suicide as an escape from his fate. A sense of happiness based on illusion can trump real misery and meaninglessness. Likewise, my criticism of the "happily" subservient wife should not be taken to imply that there are no circumstances under which the choice of subservience is not rational. Subservience might, for example, be preferable to severe physical abuse.

Regardless of how rational such choices might be, however, the lives in question lack well-being understood as the highest prudential good.

3.7.2 One lesson to draw from the problems with Sumner's conception of authenticity is that a plausible conception of authenticity and of the highest prudential good cannot be indifferent to how much control, or how much contact with reality, an individual has in important areas of her life. The "important" here is key. Someone who is well-informed about her Twitter fans or the intimate details of her friends' sex lives, but not about her own or her friends' characters, needs, or abilities, is someone who is woefully out of touch with her life. This remains true even if, in addition to this stock of information, she knows by heart the names of all the current celebrities, and the styles of all fifty pairs of her Manolo sandals. The plea that knowing her own or her friends' characters or abilities is not high on her list of priorities does not defeat the claim that she is woefully ignorant, because character and ability are central to one's particular life as a human being.

Again, someone who can make up his own mind about what to eat, but uncritically mouths the opinions of significant others about politics, society, and culture, counts as highly heteronomous, even if he autonomously endorses his conformity to others on these matters. The plea that he has neither the time nor the competence to form his own opinions in these areas does not defeat this claim; for someone who lacks the time or the competence to form his own opinions about such things is free to have no opinions about them. The problematic feature of his attitude is that he feels he must be in line with the opinions of those who "count," whatever or whoever they are. He lives secondhand, and doesn't care that he lives secondhand.

Consider, by contrast, someone who is well aware of her own and her friends' abilities, needs, and character, but ignorant of the details of her friends' sex lives or the make and color of her sandals. Despite her pockets of ignorance, it would be odd to describe her as being out of touch with her life, because she is in touch with the things that are central to it. Again, consider an actor who, after due consideration of others' views, makes up his own mind about what counts as good acting or good moviemaking, and suspends judgment about issues that he does not have the competence, time, or inclination to form a considered opinion about (such as, for example, the benefits or harms of foreign aid). His actions and attitudes show him to be the very model of an autonomous person, someone who knows what is required for making up his own mind and who does make up his own mind about many things that are central to his life.

People who are heteronomous in, and out of touch with, important aspects of their lives, seem to lack robust selves. Insofar as they are heteronomous, they lack *their own* point of view on their lives and the world, and insofar as they are out of touch with important aspects of their lives, they lack a point of view on *their lives*. Consequently, they seem to skim the surface of life. Hence, although it is possible for them to be satisfied with their lives, their satisfaction is superficial. The highest prudential good must be a life that is truly an individual's own, and it is her own only if she is autonomous and informed in important areas of her life, including her character and abilities. In turn, being informed about herself and others requires an understanding of such general facts as what is typically harmful or beneficial, painful or pleasurable, and rewarding or aversive for human beings. For although no one is just an instance of the type, "human being," neither is anyone sui generis, and understanding herself and those she cares about requires understanding human nature.[18] Moreover, whether or not someone regards these things as important, they are causally connected in deep and pervasive ways with whatever she does regard as important. Hence she cannot be either well-informed or autonomous without being well-informed and autonomous in these important areas of her life.

In the next section I discuss a different kind of subjective theory, Haybron's individual nature-fulfillment theory.

3.8 Well-Being as Individual Nature Fulfillment

Haybron's chief aim in *Pursuit of Unhappiness* is to provide an account of happiness rather than well-being, but he does also sketch an original conception of well-being as individual nature-fulfillment or self-fulfillment. In defending the nature-fulfillment conception of well-being, Haybron harks back to the *eudaimonist* view. His is a very modern *eudaimonism*, however, for unlike traditional *eudaimonism*, the nature or self whose fulfillment concerns Haybron is not human nature, or both human and individual nature, but rather, individual nature alone (chapter 9). Individual nature-fulfillment, he argues, consists of both life-satisfaction (the fulfillment of

---

[18.] Including, to some extent, abnormal human nature, such as autistic or psychopathic natures, since these are but the extreme end of spectra on which we all occupy a position. See Temple Grandin, *Thinking in Pictures and Other Reports From My Life with Autism* (2006).

our rational individual natures) and of happiness (the fulfillment of our emotional natures).[19]

I have already introduced the reader to Haybron's conception of happiness in chapter 2, but an amplification of it prior to discussing his conception of well-being will be useful. Haybron rejects Sumner's life-satisfaction conception of happiness for a variety of reasons, the two main ones being (i) that life-satisfaction reports are notoriously unstable, changing with mood, context, and completely irrelevant factors such as the weather, and (ii) that life-satisfaction reports often diverge from our emotional states, which have a better claim to being constitutive of happiness or unhappiness than life-satisfaction or dissatisfaction.[20] Haybron argues at great length, and with great eloquence, that happiness is neither just an experience, nor just a feeling, but an emotional disposition made up of positive moods and emotions, and mood-propensities to have these moods and emotions (ibid., chapters 6 and 7). As such, happiness is "a state of one's being" (139). A happy person *"confronts the world in a different way from the unhappy."* Happiness consists of psychic affirmation or, in "more pronounced forms...*psychic flourishing*" (111). A happy life is a life that is emotionally fulfilled; happiness is a favorable, long-term emotional response to one's life, and a central component of well-being.

After this, however, it comes as a surprise when Haybron states that even the brainwashed, or Rawls' grass-blade counter, or "someone whose brain is pathologically stuck on 'happy'," can be happy (though not flourishing) (185–186). It is a surprise because one would have thought that such people do not really have the depth to affirm their lives. Can a grass-blade counter, or someone who is happy no matter what her circumstances, be seen as confronting the world, or responding to his life? Even if the former counts all the grass blades in the world, he'll find precious little of the world on them. And someone "whose brain is pathologically stuck on 'happy'" is, by definition, not responding to the circumstances of his life, since if he were, his happiness would not be pathological.

Let us, however, grant that such people are happy. Is Haybron entitled to claim, as he does, that although such people can be happy, they cannot have well-being, because their happiness is not authentic? Haybron builds

---

[19] Fulfillment of our rational natures requires, among other things, living according to our reflective judgments of what is important (*Unhappiness*, 193–196).

[20] Haybron himself calls his view of happiness and of well-being objective, because emotional fulfillment, which is partly constitutive of well-being, requires living a life that suits one's nature, even if what one desires or endorses lies elsewhere. In my taxonomy, however, his view is still subjective because it rejects objective worth as a constituent of well-being.

on Sumner's conception of authenticity, arguing that authentic happiness requires (among other things) "proper functioning, at least within broad limits," and that the "richer, more complex" one's way of life, the greater the authenticity of one's happiness, because "such ways of living more fully express one's nature." Rawls' grass-counter's happiness doesn't express "his nature, his individuality," because it lacks "the richness of an ordinary human life" (186). Likewise, "someone whose brain is pathologically stuck on 'happy'...is not credibly viewed as authentically happy." His "happiness is more like that of the soma eater." The same is true, in varying degrees, of the brainwashed, the manipulated, the deceived, and so on; their responses to their lives are either not their *own* responses to their lives, expressing their own nature, or not their responses to their *own lives*. Well-being requires authentic happiness.

But what allows Haybron to use notions such as "the richness of an ordinary human life" and "proper functioning" after jettisoning the idea that well-being has anything to do with *human* nature-fulfillment, or *human* functioning, in favor of an account of well-being as individual nature fulfillment? He might answer that his appeal to these notions is entirely epistemic: most human beings wouldn't be fulfilled by counting blades of grass because most of their capacities would be left unrealized, hence we can safely conclude that the grass-counter's nature also remains unfulfilled. But what if this is false? Someone with highly limited capacities might be able to fully exercise them in counting blades of grass—or the pebbles in a jar. So if he is also happy (and Haybron states that a grass counter can be happy), there is no reason to think that he can't have well-being, on Haybron's conception of well-being. Yet it remains true that the life of such a person lacks the richness of an ordinary human life, and that this is a tragedy.[21]

A covert appeal to proper human functioning appears again in Haybron's declaration that the brainwashed or manipulated cannot have well-being because their happiness is not their own response to their lives, not an expression of their own nature. As with Sumner, what really motivates Haybron here is a normative discomfort with regarding brainwashed or manipulated people's responses to their lives as authentic, a discomfort to which he is not entitled, given his value subjectivism. For in a purely descriptive sense, the responses of these people *are* their own, in that they

---

[21] For similar arguments against Haybron's conception of well-being, see Russell and Mark Le Bar, "Well-Being and Eudaimonia: A Reply to Haybron" (forthcoming), and Russell, *Happiness* (2012), 45–64.

come from their internalized values or preferences, from the natures they have acquired. And so long as they are not deceived about their circumstances, their responses are to their own lives. Like Sumner, Haybron also illegitimately makes well-being conditional on a normal, healthy human life, and opens the door to objective accounts of well-being.

3.9 Value-Based Life-Satisfaction

Tiberius, Hall, and Plakias define well-being as life-satisfaction according to "appropriate values," that is, values that are in accord with the individual's informed goals and interests, and with her affective nature.[22] In their view, "when life-satisfaction judgments are informed and grounded in appropriate values, then these judgments are made from a perspective that is authoritative for a person's well-being" (Tiberius and Hall, *Normative Theory*, 220). In its emphasis on individual sovereignty, their theory is akin to Sumner's; in its emphasis on values that accord with the individual's nature, their theory is akin to Haybron's. Yet their theory differs from both in rejecting the idea that happiness is essential to well-being; according to them, well-being depends entirely on the individual's "appropriate" values. They agree that most people value happiness, and that if someone's values lead to misery, that usually shows that those values are inappropriate for her (ibid., 218–219), because values "require affective engagement" (Tiberius and Plakias, *Well-Being*, 426). But this is only usually, not necessarily, the case. If someone values unhappiness, and unhappiness suits his nature (let us say that his mind dwells on the melancholy; he tends to see the dark lining around every silver cloud; if feelings of happiness intrude involuntarily into his consciousness, he feels uncomfortable and instantly seeks to compensate by remembering occasions for misery; and so on), then his well-being is compatible with being unhappy. Even "serious depression" is compatible with a person's well-being if she does not value her own "happiness, enjoyment, positive affect, or mental health" (ibid., 426). On the other extreme, if someone values only pleasure, and pleasure suits his nature, then she can have well-being even on Nozick's experience machine (Tiberius and Hall, "Normative Theory," 221).

Tiberius, Hall, and Plakias are right to point out that some people, however rare, do not value happiness; tortured artists and the unhappy Wittgenstein, who (putatively) claimed on his deathbed that he'd "had a

---

[22] See Tiberius and Hall, "Normative Theory" (2010); Tiberius and Plakias, "Well-Being" (2010).

wonderful life," might be evidence, and misery lovers certainly are. But they don't explain how someone can *appropriately* value unhappiness if appropriate values require "affective engagement," and "affective engagement" means "positive affective engagement." More importantly, they don't explain why we should regard the lives of tortured but wonderful people as lives of well-being rather than simply as unhappy lives of great worth. If the only pleasure and joy someone's life contains are the pleasure and joy of achievement or of virtuous activity, if it is filled with psychic pain or misery from all the other usual sources of well-being, it seems to be sorely lacking in something important, something the possession of which would make it better for him. This is why people who are doomed to unhappiness because of a native depression or melancholy seek help— or escape in suicide. Wittgenstein, evidently, was such a person, several times contemplating suicide to escape his unhappiness. This fact alone is a *reductio* of the claim that he had well-being. At the very least, someone who has well-being must *like* living; indeed, he above all people must love and desire his life, because well-being is something enviable.[23] If he is so unhappy that life becomes a burden to him and he wants to die, what he has on the usual understanding is ill-being. The same is true of people who turn to drugs to relieve their depression or melancholy and find themselves saddled with "uplift anxiety" and a sense of loss—loss of their identity.[24] The failure of the drugs to produce the desired effect—positive emotions and moods without any undercutting anxiety—leaves such people caught between a rock and a hard place. Highly gifted but bipolar people who shun drugs that could alleviate their depression or melancholy because they find that these drugs rob them of their creative inspiration are in the same unfortunate position.[25] Happiness, in the sense of long-term emotional fulfillment and the disposition to enjoy life, to welcome it, to affirm it, is at the core of our everyday concept of well-being; claiming that we can have well-being even if we are unhappy—depressed, melancholic, anxious, and so on—is to rob the concept of the meaning it has in everyday life as well as in the long tradition of philosophical accounts of well-being.

[23.] Aristotle claims that the happy man above all people must love and desire his life, because he sees that his life is most desirable (*NE* 1170a 26–29). Thus, the happy person's love of his life is based on a perception of the objective desirability of his life. But even someone who wrongly thinks that her life is objectively desirable and who enjoys living should love her life.

[24.] On uplift anxiety, see Haybron, *Unhappiness*, 183.

[25.] See Kay Redfield Jamison, *Touched with Fire: Manic-Depressive Illness and the Artistic Temperament* (1993). In most cases, however, according to Jamison, the right drug at the right dose actually helps bipolar people become both happier and more productive.

The normativity of well-being also poses a problem for the value-based life-satisfaction (VBLS) theory of Tiberius, Hall and Plakias. Tiberius and Hall argue that their theory offers an advantage that some have thought to be the province of objective theories of well-being alone: it can show why well-being is normative for us, that is, why it is worth pursuing, why we should pursue some values and not others, and why we should care about other people's well-being—indeed, not only care about it, but use it as a basis for public policy and decisions about how resources "should be distributed" ("Normative Theory," 214). Their general argument for thinking that their theory meets these normative demands is that "[t]he fact that appropriate values are an ideal to aspire to means that when we wish someone a life that lives up to their values, we are wishing for something necessarily worthwhile" (220). But what is appropriate for an individual and worthwhile to him on VBLS can be quite inappropriate and worthless objectively speaking. People's well-being on VBLS can lie in the pursuit of pleasure to the exclusion of everything else, or in controlling others, or in servile obedience to another, and so on. Hence, from a third-person point of view there is reason to hope that they will *not* have a life that "lives up to their values," and that they will *not* get any of our resources to help them do it.

Tiberius and Hall state that they can accommodate the *eudaimonist* idea that functioning well is important for well-being "because people *value* functioning" (221). They favorably compare the life of stressed-out Jim working long hours with irritating co-workers on developing an AIDS vaccine with the life of easygoing Will who, on inheriting some wealth, has given up his career as a physician to paint mediocre paintings (222). Will, they claim, has more pleasure, but it is Jim who is functioning well and who has well-being. But on their theory Will lacks well-being only if he values functioning well more than he values his leisure and painting. If he doesn't, then there is no reason to deny that he may have more well-being than Jim. VBLS doesn't allow Tiberius, Hall, or Plakias to argue that everyone *should* value functioning well. Nor does it allow them to argue that people *should* not adapt to severe injustice or gross material deprivation, or that the life-satisfaction of someone who adapts to severe injustice does not necessarily show that she is well-off, because if she knew that her values would be better served without such injustice, she would resent the injustice and judge her life as not going well (221). For it is entirely possible that what this person values most is following in the footsteps of her forebears and gracefully accepting the injustice visited on her as karma, or God's will.

In such a case, VBLS entails that if she has life-satisfaction, is not misinformed about her circumstances, and has values that are appropriate to her nature, she has well-being, and as much well-being as someone who fulfills these conditions *and* lives in conditions of justice. For on a subjectivist theory, our attitudes towards injustice or poor functioning need have no more importance for well-being than our attitudes towards, say, ice cream.

Adaptation to injustice or poor functioning is contrary to well-being for objective theories because it is contrary to living well as a human being. But, like other subjectivist theories, VBLS rejects the idea that living well as a human being has anything to do with well-being, without actually successfully weaning itself from this idea. Consequently, like other subjectivist theories, it cannot satisfy the formal requirements of well-being as the highest prudential good, or show why we should wish well-being to those who seek it in ignoble or pathetic ways of life.

3.10 Conclusion

Subjectivist theories of well-being are both descriptively and normatively inadequate to our ordinary notion of well-being. To gain plausibility for their views, some subjectivists appeal to proper functioning, or informed reflective endorsement of one's life by one's own standards, as necessary conditions for well-being. But these appeals are not only incompatible with their subjectivism, they are also, when combined with subjectivism about values, too weak to rule out pathetic, servile, or barely human lives as lives of well-being. Furthermore, their objections to objectivist theories—most importantly, that such theories can neither explain the subject-relativity of well-being nor bridge the alleged conceptual barrier between well-being and objective standards—do not work against my conception of well-being as happiness in an objectively worthwhile life.

In chapters 4 and 5 I will fill out my conceptions of autonomy and realism as admirable character traits that are also prudential values and objective standards of a worthwhile life.

PART TWO | Autonomy, Realism, and Virtue

CHAPTER 4 | Autonomy and Reality-Orientation

"I am autonomous if I rule me, and no one else rules I."

—JOEL FEINBERG.

"Who in the world am I? Ah, that's the great puzzle."

—LEWIS CARROLL, *Alice in Wonderland.*

4.1 Introduction

An autonomous person is self-governing. Joel Feinberg expresses the idea at the heart of autonomy when he quips: "I am autonomous if I rule me, and no one else rules I."[1] And I rule myself if and only if my own judgments (evaluations, decisions) characteristically govern my plans and actions. For my judgments reflect my habitual emotions, desires, and values, and these largely *are* my self. As we have seen, however, not all actions or ways of being, even those that have been critically endorsed by the agent in light of her own standards, are autonomous in the robust sense, the sense that is incompatible with being servile, blindly obedient, or conformist.

Feinberg offers a vivid portrait of the autonomous person as supremely self-possessed: he or she is " 'his own man,' or 'her own woman' "; he has a distinct identity; "his tastes, opinions, ideals, goals, values, and preferences are all autonomously his," that is, when he alters his convictions, he does so "for reasons of his own ... without guilt or anxiety"; he plays an ever-increasing role in his own creation from childhood to maturity, even though at every step he is the product of his earlier self and his environment; he has integrity; he controls himself rather than

---

[1] Joel Feinberg, "The Idea of a Free Man" (1980), 3–29, at 21.

being controlled by others; he is self-reliant and has initiative; and he takes responsibility for his actions and his character.[2]

This portrait is clearly an idealization: no one is "his own man" in all "his tastes, opinions, ideals, goals, values, and preferences," if only because no one has the time or ability to form his own opinions or tastes, or make his own decisions, in every domain of life. As Robert C. Roberts and W. Jay Wood put it, "[f]or even the most creative person...the intellectual [and practical] life is a network of deep dependencies."[3] But Feinberg's portrait of the autonomous person captures the basic orientation of such a person, and explains why he is seen as noble and proud. By contrast, a thoroughly conformist, servile, or blindly obedient person's life is ignoble or, at best, pathetic. Even if, in obedience to some benevolent authority figure, what he does accords with the genuinely worthwhile, if and to the extent that he does it blindly or mindlessly, the worth of his actions does not accrue to him and he does not live a life of his own.

Those who hold that being servile, blindly obedient, or conformist is just as autonomous as being independent and self-reliant, imply, oxymoronically, that the character and actions of an independent, self-reliant individual are no more self-governing than those of an individual who willingly goes through life imitating others or doing their bidding, so long as his character and actions meet the formal conditions of content-neutral autonomy. As I pointed out in chapter 3.5, however, if this view were true, it would be impossible to autonomously endorse heteronomy, because the autonomous endorsement of any value, V, would transform it into an autonomous value. But just as there is no contradiction in saying that P can freely (that is, in liberty) consent to slavery, or that Q can rationally and honestly conclude that dishonesty is the best policy, there is no contradiction in saying that R can autonomously choose heteronomy. If freely consenting to slavery bestowed liberty on P's subsequent actions, or honestly concluding that he should be dishonest bestowed honesty on Q's policy of dishonesty, or autonomously choosing heteronomy bestowed autonomy on R's subsequent decisions, P could not become a slave, Q could not act dishonestly, and R could not choose heteronomously—contrary to the hypothesis in each case.

It is worth noting that much of the disagreement over autonomy stems from not realizing that we need different conceptions of autonomy to serve

---

[2] Feinberg, "Autonomy," *Harm to Self: The Moral Limits of the Criminal Law* (1986), 27–51.
[3] Roberts and Wood, *Intellectual Virtue: An Essay in Regulative Epistemology* (2007), 261.

different purposes: no single conception of autonomy can do everything it is often pressed to do, any more than a single conception of well-being can do everything it is often pressed to do. Central to all content-neutral conceptions of autonomy is the thought that our freedom and responsibility as agents lies in our ability to reflect upon and revise our first-order desires, attitudes, and values. Hence on these theories it is perfectly coherent to say not only that we can autonomously *adopt* servile or conformist desires, but also that we can autonomously *live* servile or conformist lives, so long as we retain the ability to reflect on and endorse the choice to be thus.[4] One or another of the extant content-neutral conceptions of autonomy, or a combination thereof, may well suffice for defining the conditions of freedom and responsibility or of social and political status; it is at least true that we cannot be absolved of responsibility for our actions, deprived of our rights, freed of our obligations, or subjected to paternalistic government interventions simply because we have chosen a life of servility, conformity, or blind obedience.[5] In contrast to other critics of content-free conceptions, then, I do not claim that these conceptions are inherently defective.[6] Rather, I claim that, contrary to some proponents of these theories, it is wrong to think that this is all there is to autonomy, or that a content-neutral conception is the appropriate one for well-being as the HPG. The metaphysical and psychological abilities that these content-neutral conceptions identify are only necessary conditions of a richer, substantive conception of autonomy. Indeed, they are also necessary conditions of its contrary: a substantive conception of heteronomy. Just as only reasoning beings can be rational or irrational in their reasoning, so only those who are autonomous in the content-neutral sense can be substantively autonomous or heteronomous.

The plan of this chapter is as follows. In 4.2 I explain my conception of autonomy as a character trait, arguing that it is a deliberative and epistemic virtue, but not a moral virtue. In 4.3 I argue that (i) a person is autonomous just in case, and insofar as, she is intellectually and emotionally disposed to

---

[4] For example, in *The Theory and Practice of Autonomy* (1988), Gerald Dworkin states that someone who endorses the attitudes and preferences of a slave, "the kind of person who acts at the command of others," can still be autonomous (129).

[5] See, for example, Friedman's argument in *Autonomy, Gender, Politics* (2003), chapter 9, that liberal societies should not intervene in minority group practices that fail to respect women's rights if the women have autonomously waived these rights.

[6] These critics include Paul Benson, "Free Agency and Self-Worth" (hereafter "Free Agency") (1994), 650–668; Sigurdur Kristinsson, "The Limits of Neutrality: Toward a Weakly Substantive Account of Autonomy" (2000), 257–286; and Andrea Westlund, "Selflessness and Responsibility for Self: Is Deference Compatible with Autonomy?" (hereafter "Selflessness") (2003), 483–523.

direct herself by her reality-oriented judgments in important areas of her life as a human being and individual, that (ii) she is reality-oriented just in case, and insofar as, she is intellectually and emotionally disposed to track truth or understanding in these important areas, and to act accordingly, and hence that (iii) a person is autonomous just in case, and insofar as, she is intellectually and emotionally disposed to track truth or understanding in important areas of her life as a human being and individual, and to act accordingly. Thus autonomy and reality-orientation are two facets of the same trait, their difference lying only in their focus.

In 4.4 I address some objections to my claim that reality-orientation requires autonomy, and provide a fuller picture of autonomy and reality-orientation, distinguishing them from their simulacra. In 4.5 I respond to the objection that a content-neutral account of autonomy can do everything my substantive account of autonomy can, and in 4.6 to an alleged counterexample to my thesis that well-being as the highest prudential good (HPG) requires autonomy. In 4.7 I argue that insofar as a reality-oriented person succeeds in attaining truth or understanding and, when circumstances permit, acting on it, she is realistic, and insofar as she is realistic, she is morally virtuous. Conversely, insofar as a person is heteronomous and unreality-oriented, she cannot be virtuous, and is likely to fail often in doing the right thing. In 4.8 I consider and reject the view that, to be fully autonomous, we must be able to justify being autonomous. I regard this as an overly-intellectualized conception of autonomy, an expression of philosophical parochialism.

4.2 Autonomy as a Character Trait

4.2.1 A life of well-being as the HPG is a life of one's own, and a life of one's own must be a life in which one is autonomous. For it is only in making our own judgments and (in the absence of external obstacles) acting accordingly that we fully exercise our agency and, thereby, both define and express our identities as individuals. The desire to do so, to "not merely [have] occupied some space for a time, but individuated that space," to have been responsibly involved in the world, is a fundamental drive in most people.[7] Doing so tends to be inherently fulfilling, and is usually the best means to choosing a fulfilling life for ourselves, because we are typically better informed than others about our interests and abilities.

---

[7] Lawrence Haworth, *Autonomy: An Essay in Philosophical Psychology and Ethics* (1986), 185–189. Of course, Haworth's account of autonomy differs from mine.

To live autonomously is to play an active role in shaping our individual selves, instead of slavishly following others, or surrendering direction of our lives to our fantasies, illusions, momentary urges, or inertia. These are all so many ways of surrendering our agency and dissociating ourselves from, rather than directing, the events of our lives. The autonomous person forges a life of her own, and values doing so. By contrast, in letting others or "fate" or his fantasies determine his choices and the shape of his life, the heteronomous person lives a life that, in an important sense, does not belong to him. Even if he evaluates his life as going well for him, the life he evaluates and the perspective he evaluates it from are only minimally *his own*; hence even if he has well-being, he does not have well-being as the highest prudential good.

Like other character traits, autonomy has implications not only for our relationship to the world, but also for our relationship to ourselves and others. Thus, in order to direct our lives by our own judgments well, we need to be able to trust our ability to do so, and this requires a basic self-regard. In turn, self-regard tends to discourage abusive tendencies in others and protect us against abusive behavior. By contrast, the conformist, blindly obedient, or servile person creates unequal power relationships that tend to encourage contempt and abusive behavior in the dominant party.[8] As an excellence of the mind, an epistemic and deliberative virtue, autonomy is required wherever understanding is required. Hence it is required for well-being as the HPG as well as for moral virtue. But autonomy is not sufficient for moral virtue, because it does not guarantee truth or understanding. A moral virtue characteristically or reliably results in the right decision for the right reason, whereas autonomy need not do any of this reliably. Autonomy, the disposition to try and understand things for ourselves—including our own powers of understanding—and act accordingly, is compatible with our reasoning being unsound, or with the matter being beyond our ability to understand. Learning how far to trust our own powers of understanding, how far to rely on others (and which others), and what counts as good evidence, itself requires time, experience—and autonomy. If autonomy were a moral virtue, we would already be in possession of such knowledge.

Of course, an autonomous person cannot be totally clueless about what counts as good evidence, or about his own epistemic abilities, or other

---

[8] For other moral problems with servility, see Hill, "Servility and Self-Respect (1991), 4–18, and Christopher Freiman, "Why Be Immoral?" (2010), 191–205; published online June 2009.

important normative and empirical facts. Indeed, even a heteronomous person can't be totally clueless about them. Someone who is completely cut off from the normative realm, from the distinction between the important and the unimportant, is a psychopath; someone who is completely cut off from the empirical realm, from the distinction between fact and fiction, or someone who cannot make even simple inferences, is insane. Hence even someone who is heteronomous must have some ability to distinguish between the important and the unimportant in his everyday affairs, make valid inferences, take his experience into account, and evaluate the available evidence in making his decisions. What distinguishes the autonomous from the heteronomous individual, insofar as he is autonomous, is his basic attitude towards life.

4.2.2 Autonomy matters. But does it matter equally in every area of life? In the context of a subjectivist theory of well-being, as we have seen, autonomy matters only in those areas that matter to the individual whose well-being is in question. On my conception of well-being, however, this answer will not do, because well-being requires a worthwhile life, and the idea of worth dictates the idea of the important: like other character traits, autonomy must be defined over important areas of our lives. Thus, just as someone who boldly faces up to spiders but not to threats to life or integrity does not count as brave, so someone who chooses his own clothes but borrows others' values does not count as autonomous. Conversely, just as someone who faces up to threats to life or integrity but runs from spiders does not count as a coward, so someone who forges his own goals but leaves the choice of his clothes to his spouse does not count as heteronomous. Both positive (good, admirable, knowledgeable, wise, skillful) and negative (bad, shameful, foolish, unskillful) trait terms implicitly carry a reference to the important, both in the practical and in the theoretical realm. A knowledgeable person in, say, physics, is not someone who knows Who's Who in the world of physics, but someone who knows physics. An independent-minded person in astronomy is not someone who makes stylistic innovations in his writing, but someone who makes theoretical innovations in astronomy. Such normative judgments of importance are inescapable and taken for granted in describing scientists as knowledgeable or independent-minded. But they are equally inescapable in describing people as autonomous in the practical realm.

Of course, what is trivial or unimportant, *simpliciter*, may well be important for particular individuals relative to their commitments or interests. It may also be important for most people in unusual circumstances. For example, sometimes facing up to threats to life or integrity can require facing up to spiders; in such circumstances, a courageous person will be disposed to overcome his phobia of spiders and face up to them. General statements about what is important or unimportant in human life must be understood as *ceteris paribus* statements, not as exceptionless ones.

There is, however, a difference in the way positive and negative traits relate to the important: the former do, while the latter do not, require awareness of the difference between the trivial and the worthwhile, or the less and the more important. This awareness need not amount to knowledge or even a full-fledged belief, but it must be robust enough to motivate aiming at the worthwhile. Thus, a good musician is characteristically motivated by her awareness that being a good musician requires practicing regularly, whereas a lazy musician is either (characteristically) unmotivated by this awareness or actually believes that, for instance, being a good musician is all a matter of luck. A courageous politician is characteristically motivated by the thought that it is more important to speak up against political corruption than to safeguard his position of power, whereas a cowardly politician is either (characteristically) unmotivated by this awareness, or actually believes the contrary.[9,10] Likewise, an autonomous individual is characteristically motivated by her awareness that it is important to make her own decisions in important areas of her life, whereas a heteronomous individual is either (characteristically) unmotivated by this awareness or actually believes that, say, conforming to the group works just fine. Again, the reality-oriented person is motivated by her awareness that, *inter alia*, it is important to understand her own strengths and weaknesses whereas an unreality-oriented person is either (characteristically) unmotivated by this awareness or actually believes that feeling good about herself is more important than understanding herself, ignoring the impact of this policy on her life.

---

[9] The politician who knows what is right but prefers to do the wrong thing acts, as Ronald Milo would put it, from "preferential wickedness," whereas the politician who actually believes that it is more important to safeguard his position of power acts from perverse "wickedness" (*Immorality*, 1984). Aristotle makes a similar distinction in his discussion of vice. In *NE* VII.10 he depicts the vicious man as ignorant of his vice, and therefore of what really matters in life, whereas in IX.4 he depicts him as aware of it but motivated by his vicious desires.

[10] There may well be circumstances under which it would not be cowardly for a politician to safeguard his position of power by not opposing political corruption, for example, when this is necessary for preserving his very ability to keep fighting against corruption. Likewise, there may well be circumstances—and are, as I discuss in Sections 4.4.3 and 4.4.4—under which it would not be heteronomous for a person to rely on others for picking her goals.

As these examples indicate, important areas of human life in general are those broadly identified areas that play a fundamental and pervasive role in human life. Such are relationships of love, work, or play, and intellectual, economic, aesthetic, or physical pursuits. Although the weight of these relationships and pursuits varies from one individual's life to another's depending on each one's abilities, needs, and interests, all of them play some role in the life of everyone who has the ability for them. A community of individuals who lacked these relationships or activities would not be recognizable as a human community.

The next question is: what makes my judgments (evaluations, decisions) autonomous, if informed critical endorsement of them by my own standards, or rational consideration of my ends and means, does not suffice to do so? What is necessary for me to be self-directed? A consideration of what underlies and explains the various ways we can be, or fail to be, self-directed shows that autonomy requires reality-orientation. My strategy for showing this is two-fold. First I canvass common intuitions about heteronomous traits and heteronomous people, and try to show that what is missing from all of them is reality-orientation. Then I do the reverse, canvassing common intuitions about autonomous traits and autonomous people, and trying to show that what they all have in common is reality-orientation.

4.3. Autonomy and Reality-Orientation

4.3.1 Conformity, blind obedience, and servility are among the most salient images of heteronomy in the philosophical and psychological literatures, as well as in the popular culture. A heteronomous individual is servile or slave-like in her attitudes, being disposed, for example, to obey authority just because it's authority, not because she finds it authoritative. She tends to believe and do whatever her society or group or authority figures regard as true, right, or fashionable, either because she lacks confidence in her own judgments, or because she finds it easier to fit in with the crowd, or blindly trust an authority figure, than to think for herself. In all these cases, what she lacks is sufficient concern for understanding what is worth pursuing and how. In common parlance, she "lacks a mind of her own," and no amount of critical reflection on, and endorsement of, her disposition to simply follow others can transform it into an autonomous disposition.

However, simply substituting one's own judgments for those of others does not make one autonomous. An autonomous person is independent-minded and self-possessed. But someone who is disposed to live under the control of his impulses, or his illusions (fantasies, delusions, self-deceptions, or wishful thinking), is the very antithesis of a self-possessed person. To the extent that he is disposed to live in the grip of illusion, he judges and acts without regard for the facts. The same is true of the individual who is given to acting on the desire, inspiration, or "brain-wave" of the moment, without regard for either the likely consequences, or what is worth pursuing. So being disposed to live under the control of illusion or impulse are further ways of being heteronomous.

Another form of heteronomy, sometimes mistaken for autonomy, is exemplified by the "rebel without a cause." The rebel without a cause refuses to conform to others' expectations—to accept social norms, or to obey rules—not because he genuinely judges them to be wrong or harmful, but just because they come from others. The irony is that, at a deep level, he is entirely dependent on others for deciding how to think or who to be, for others constitute his normative frame of reference: he *is* whatever they are *not*. Deep down, then, he is as much in thrall to others as the conformist.

The weak-willed or akratic individual also fails in autonomy because he fails to do what he judges worth doing owing to his unruly appetites or passions.[11] However, he differs in an important respect from other heteronomous individuals: he is autonomous in forming his judgments, but not in carrying them out. Perhaps he is best thought of as "semi-autonomous."

In Feinberg's terminology, the problem in all these cases is that the individual's "I" fails to rule his "me." He is, to adopt Nozick's metaphor, a lightweight, someone who lacks gravitas and, thus, cannot resist outside forces (*Examined Life*, 178). And in all these cases what is missing is the individual's reality-orientation: the disposition to seek truth or understanding about important normative and empirical facts, and (sufficient) motivation to act accordingly. This supports my hypothesis that reality-orientation is essential to autonomy. A look at a character who manages to be heteronomous in all these ways illustrates this hypothesis.

Fyodor Karamazov in Dostoevsky's *The Brothers Karamazov* is the very epitome of such an individual. He is slavish, conformist, a rebel without

---

[11] On the traditional Aristotelian conception, the akratic individual acts against his *correct* judgment of what is worth doing (Aristotle, *NE*, VII.1–10). I adopt this conception in chapter 6, but my point here applies whether or not we conceive of the akratic individual as making a correct judgment. Some contemporary conceptions of akrasia drop this requirement of correctness. See, for example, Donald Davidson, "How Is Weakness of the Will Possible?" (1980), 21–42.

a cause, impulsive, self-deceived, and in the grip of illusions. Dostoevsky depicts Karamazov as a buffoon and a liar whose main preoccupation is to make a certain impression on others. Not only Karamazov's words and actions but even his emotions are a sham, shaped largely by his need to impress others favorably or unfavorably. It is their view of him that is the ultimate molder of his inner and outer life. Thus, when he is put in mind of the fact that people think he is a despicable fool, his usual mode of reflection is to think, "Well, if that's so, I'll act like the fool they think I am and show them that in reality they are stupider and more despicable than I am."[12] Since he cannot gain their respect, he will disgrace himself completely to prove—to them and to himself—that he cares not a whit about their opinion of him. But, of course, his main aim at such times is precisely to get them to form a certain opinion of him—namely, the opinion that he is someone who does not care what they think of him. And so he acts the buffoon, and pretends to feel slighted and offended even when he knows he has not been slighted, sometimes managing to fool himself even more than he fools others. Karamazov is the epitome of someone who is a captive both of others' opinions of him, and of his own rationalizations about his motives and character. Thus, he victimizes himself as much as he victimizes others.

It is instructive to consider how Karamazov's deep-set heteronomy affects his very endorsement of it. The more he reflects on himself, the more deeply he seems to identify with his other-directed, self-deceived attitudes. In other words, his heteronomy infects his very reflection on, and endorsement of, his character.[13] So not only are reflection and endorsement not sufficient for autonomy, they can even reinforce an individual's heteronomy. Karamazov's heteronomy goes hand-in-hand with, and is explainable by, his lack of reality-orientation.

Let us now consider the features commonly attributed to the autonomous person in order to see what underlies them.

4.3.2 An autonomous person has a mind of her own. She characteristically exercises her epistemic powers in forming her judgments about important issues—including the issue of how far she can rely on her own judgment—even if the conclusions she arrives at put her at odds with others, or with her own desires or prior beliefs. In exercising these powers, she exhibits self-reliance, the well-founded confidence that her own powers

---

[12] Fyodor Dostoevsky, *The Brothers Karamazov* (1970), 101.
[13] Cf. Alfred R. Mele in his *Autonomous Agents* (1995), 159.

of perception and thought can deliver truth or understanding—or that, if they don't or can't on some matter, she can acknowledge her limitations and defer to those more likely to be right. Thus, she has a reliable self in charge, a self that she can rely upon to judge well.

The independent person, then, must be distinguished from someone whose unfounded self-confidence frequently derails her attempts at understanding things, or leads her to undertake tasks she is quite incompetent to undertake. To use an example: if I know nothing about car engines except that they either work or fail, then my insistence on repairing my stalled engine myself is not an instance of independence or self-reliance, but merely an instance of my self-delusion—or, else, my pigheadedness. The point of engaging in goal-directed action is not merely to exercise one's agency, but also to achieve the goal of the exercise. The same applies to making intellectual, psychological, or moral judgments: if I do not understand a certain subject matter, or the motivations of the people in a certain situation, or the expected consequences of their actions, then my insistence on forming my own opinion of the subject, the people, or their actions shows not that I am independent-minded but merely that I am opinionated.

To be genuinely independent and self-reliant, then, a person must have a reliable self in charge, and to have a reliable self in charge, she must be reality-oriented. To the extent that she lacks reality-orientation, she either sees herself and the world through the eyes of others, or through the haze of her willful illusions, or else she is impulsive or weak-willed. So either she is an unreliable judge of others and of her own abilities, needs, interests, or circumstances, or her judgments lack the strength or conviction to guide her actions. And thereby she also lacks self-possession and self-direction.

The autonomous person has integrity, the ready disposition to stand up for, and act on, her well-founded judgments. To the extent that she lacks the ability to act on such judgments, she is weak-willed and, thus, lacking in self-possession. But someone who is disposed to stand up for, and act on, her well-founded judgments is reality-oriented. The autonomous person is also disposed to take responsibility for herself, because being committed to guiding her life by exercising her powers of understanding is itself an expression of responsibility—of declaring, in effect, that she will live by her own efforts instead of burdening others. It is also an expression of reality-orientation, as is acknowledging her responsibility when things go awry.

Once again, then, just as a lack of reality-orientation underlies and explains the features commonly attributed to the heteronomous person, the possession of reality-orientation underlies and explains the features commonly attributed to the autonomous person. If I am right about the conceptual connection between autonomy and reality-orientation, it follows that they are two facets of the same trait, their difference lying only in their focus. The focus of reality-orientation is gaining the truth about, or understanding of, important things and responding accordingly, while that of autonomy is living by one's own judgments and decisions. Hence when I talk about either autonomy or reality-orientation, I should be taken as talking about the other as well.

4.3.3 Is there some other feature of the autonomous person that is present in all forms of autonomy, absent from all forms of heteronomy, and explanatorily fundamental? Paul Benson argues that a free agent must have a sense of self-worth, a sense of competence to govern oneself, and that this "involves regarding oneself as being competent to answer for one's conduct in light of normative demands that, from one's point of view, others might appropriately apply to one's actions" ("Free Agency," 660). The addict, the medically gaslighted woman, and the (typical) slave lack this ability to answer for themselves. Similarly, Andrea Westlund argues that taking "responsibility for self" is the hallmark of the autonomous person, and that taking such responsibility requires being "appropriately dialogically responsive to intersubjective demands for justification" ("Selflessness," 502–503). It is this responsiveness to others that is lacking in the self-abnegating "Deferential Wife" (Westlund's version of Thomas Hill's original DF). It is also the feature lacking in the blindly obedient subjects of the Milgram experiment, who are "utterly impervious to the normative force of external critical perspectives" on their decision to obey the experimenter (ibid., 502).

My analysis of autonomy agrees with Benson's and Westlund's analyses that a sense of self-worth or self-regard, a sense of competence to govern oneself, and a sense of responsibility for oneself, are essential to autonomy. But do these qualities entail being, and seeing oneself as being, "competent to answer for one's conduct" in response to others' appropriate normative demands (Benson)? Or being "dialogically responsive to intersubjective demands for justification" (Westlund)? I do not think so. For such responsiveness requires linguistic skills that an autonomous person may lack. The autonomous agent must, indeed, be aware of, and open to, others' perspectives—this follows from the requirement that he be open to truth and understanding, in conjunction with the fact that openness to others' perspectives is important for gaining truth and understanding. But he may lack the skill to justify his actions or policies to others. Being dialogically responsive to others' perspectives may be common in autonomous people, but it is not necessary.

My view might prompt the objection that to be autonomous one must not only be reality-oriented, but also highly informed, empirically and normatively. For reality-orientation does not guarantee success in achieving truth or understanding—indeed, being reality-oriented is compatible with being quite mistaken about important facts—and success, it might be thought, is necessary for being a reliable judge. Suppose, for example, that I have an active and questioning mind that is open to contrary views, but that I live in a culture that is so closed, impoverished, and uncritical as to preclude any expression of, or access to, alternatives to its own deeply mistaken views of human nature. To the extent that I absorb these mistaken views, I am, ipso facto, an unreliable judge of my own and other people's needs and desires. Hence, the objection goes, reality-orientation is not enough for autonomy; autonomy requires realism, that is, both reality-orientation and the relevant empirical and normative knowledge.

This objection would be well-taken if being a reliable judge meant being someone who could be relied upon to get it right every time or even most of the time. But although a reliable judge can be relied upon to get it right more often than an unreliable judge in the same circumstances, all I mean by a reliable judge is someone who can be relied upon to be independent and open to truth and understanding in forming her views and making her decisions, even if her independence and openness lead her into error. No doubt, as noted earlier, such a person must already possess some idea of what, in general, is worth attending to and making up her own mind about, what sorts of things count as good evidence, why and when explanation or justification is called for, and so on. But what makes her autonomous is that she exercises her understanding in arriving at her decisions in important areas of her life. Someone who can maintain such a stance even in a closed and uncritical culture is importantly different from someone who accepts the dominant narrative of her culture by shutting her eyes to contrary evidence or views.

Antigone and Haemon, in Sophocles' play, *Antigone*, are good examples of such reality-oriented and autonomous individuals. When the King of Thebes, Creon (uncle of Antigone and father of Haemon), dishonors Antigone's brother, Polyneices, by ordering that his body remain unburied, to be eaten by birds and dogs, Antigone is the first to defy his orders. She does so not only on the grounds that Creon's order violates Heaven's laws, a myth she has absorbed from her culture, but also on the grounds that the punishment is undeserved and unfitting for a human being. Her autonomy and reality-orientation are shown in her willingness to challenge Creon's authority on the basis of her commonsense conviction, shared by nearly everyone in Thebes, that his order is unjust. When she is caught, she has no hesitation in defending her views and her action. Haemon goes a step further, challenging his father's claim to know better by virtue of his age and rank, and rejecting his commandment to obey him like a dutiful son. "Father," he says, "the gods implant reason in men, the highest of all things that we call our own," and wisdom lies in listening to others' views of the matter and going by their merit, regardless of the others' age. Antigone and Haemon are reality-oriented and autonomous insofar as they seek to be guided by their powers of understanding, even if on some matters the truth eludes them. And they are not only reality-oriented and autonomous but also realistic when the truth does not elude them.

But what about their—or at least, Antigone's—acceptance of the myth that Creon's order violates Heaven's laws? Is that also reality-oriented, though mistaken? To answer this question we need more evidence. If Antigone accepts the myth simply because she has been brought up to accept it, even though she has encountered strong evidence against it, then her acceptance is decidedly not reality-oriented (or autonomous). If, on the other hand, she accepts it because she thinks she has seen evidence of its truth (such as, perhaps, what looks like heavenly punishment for violations of Heaven's laws), and she would be open to evidence against its truth should it present itself (such as, perhaps, what looks like heavenly *rewards* for violations of Heaven's laws), then she is decidedly reality-oriented (and autonomous) in her acceptance of the myth. In between these two polar attitudes lie shades of reality- or unreality-orientation.

Of course, even in our scientifically sophisticated, information-rich culture someone may find himself in a subculture that is permeated by myth. The distinction between reality-orientation on the one hand, and success in achieving truth or understanding on the other, helps us to appreciate the importance of reality-orientation in staying in charge of ourselves, while cautioning us not to dismiss those who hold 'spooky' beliefs as willfully deluded or otherwise irrational. An illustration of both points is provided by Ray Hyman's story of his stint as a palmist.[14] Hyman relates how a desire to supplement his income as a teenager led him to start reading palms. He did not believe in palmistry when he started, but repeated

---

[14] Ray Hyman, "'Cold Reading': How to Convince Strangers That You Know All about Them" (1996), 70–84.

personal validation by his clients over several years led him eventually to start believing in it. It was only when a professional mentalist suggested that he give what palm readers would say was a *mis*reading that he realized that he had been a victim of the "fallacy of personal validation." For to his "surprise and horror... [his] readings were just as successful as ever" (76).

Insofar as Hyman was persuaded that palmistry is valid on the basis of what he reasonably (given his ignorance of the fallacy of personal validation and, let us suppose, of other reasons against palmistry) took to be evidence for this belief, and insofar as he changed his mind again on the basis of further experience and knowledge of this fallacy, he showed himself to be openminded and in charge of himself. Had he based his belief in palmistry on his desire to believe in palmistry, or his disbelief in it on his desire to please the professional mentalist, his attitudes and conclusions would not have been autonomous or reality-oriented. In neither case is it the truth or falsehood of his conclusions, the goodness or badness of his decisions, that decides this issue.

An increase in understanding does, however, bear on reality-orientation in two ways: it enables a person to expand the scope of his reality-orientation and, thus, of his autonomy, and it raises his bar for being reality-oriented. Thus, Hyman's greater understanding of what counts as good evidence, and of the depths of human gullibility, give him reason to believe that untested first-hand experience is not always sufficient evidence for certain beliefs, that one also needs to take the arguments of skeptics into account. His greater understanding thereby enables him to approach other paranormal phenomena with the requisite skepticism. At the same time, his greater knowledge raises the bar for counting as reality-oriented. Thus, had his desire to "believe in something" prevented him from applying his greater understanding to other similar phenomena, such as astrology or tea-leaf reading, he would have shown himself to be less reality-oriented than before.

I have assumed that Hyman was ignorant of the case against palmistry when he started believing in it. But it might be thought that since he was already a practicing magician, he had to be well-aware of the gullibility of human beings. He also knew—or should have known—that palmistry did not fit into the scientific worldview, and that the scientific worldview was better supported than his belief in palmistry. Surely a more reality-oriented person would have given more weight to science than to his clients' personal validation?

But here, as in Antigone's case, we need to ask *why* he didn't give more weight to science than to his own experience. If his reason was a desire to believe in palmistry as a way of becoming a convincing palm-reader, then he was not reality-oriented in his attitude to palmistry. If, however, his reason was openness to the possibility that the scientific worldview as currently understood might have some holes in it—an attitude that cannot be dismissed as 'kooky,' given that the strange claims and theories that emerge from physics are as far beyond the understanding of most of us as the mysteries of the occult—then he was more reality-oriented than someone who closed his eyes to his experience in order not to be shaken from his faith in science. Undoubtedly, however, the most reasonable—the most reality-oriented—attitude would have been to suspend belief until he had an explanation for the apparent clash between his experience and the scientific worldview.

The main lessons of this discussion are that reality-orientation/autonomy can vary in depth as well as scope. The depth of someone's reality-orientation/autonomy is determined by the depth of his motivation to exercise his powers of understanding, and not on the actual truth or goodness of his beliefs or decisions, respectively; its scope is determined by the number of important areas in which he is thus motivated. The truth or goodness of a person's beliefs or decisions puts him in a position to increase the scope of reality-orientation and autonomy, while at the same time raising the bar for being autonomous. To the extent that he is both reality-oriented/autonomous and empirically and normatively informed, he is realistic. And, as I'll argue in chapter 5, to the extent that he is realistic, he is virtuous.

How autonomous must one be to be autonomous? (From now on I will assume that the reader understands that a reference to autonomy is also a reference to reality-orientation and vice versa.) Since autonomy can vary in degree of motivational depth as well as scope, there is no precise formula for how self-directed a person must be to count as being autonomous—other than that she must be self-directed in most important domains of her life, and wholeheartedly so in some of them. Someone who needs to make an effort to be self-directed in some domain is autonomous in that domain, but not wholeheartedly so. Elizabeth Bennett, the heroine of Jane Austen's *Pride and Prejudice*, is highly autonomous and perceptive with respect to the snobbery and shallowness of her class-ridden society, but never questions the assumption that marriage is the only life-choice a woman may make. If we suppose that this assumption is so deep-seated that it not only prevents her from entertaining an alternative, but would prevent her from entertaining it even if someone were to present it to her, we can say that her lack of autonomy in this aspect of her life goes deep.

Nevertheless, not every failure to question an important assumption, or to seek truth or understanding, is a failure of autonomy. Time is limited and some issues are so complex that trying to pursue the truth about them would leave one without enough time to pursue the truth about other issues that are important in one's life. Insofar as someone is autonomous, he is good at judging when he should or shouldn't seek the truth. He is also good at judging when mere acquaintance with a fact is enough, and when he should seek to understand its relationship to other facts—its causes and consequences.

In making these remarks, I have assumed, commonsensically, that understanding requires truth. But some epistemologists argue that not only is truth not necessary for understanding, it can impede understanding, because complex theories, such as those of physics, are better understood by most people in their approximate but simpler form than in their more accurate but more complex form.[15] I am not sure that this applies to practical understanding—understanding of the important facts of one's life and human life in general. But if it does, then for any individual reality-orientation is a disposition to seek only as much truth as is compatible with his ability to understand the issue.

An autonomous person must also care about being autonomous and, thus, about her lapses of autonomy. But how much she cares also does not allow of a precise formula. Some people are more accepting of their failures, both culpable and inculpable, than others; here, as elsewhere, there is a range of acceptable attitudes, and determining the range is a matter of practical wisdom about one's life. Suffice it to say that an autonomous person will care enough about her failures in important matters to revise her estimate of her well-being at least to some extent when she discovers her failures, and that she will revise it more radically if she discovers that her failures were culpable. Thus, Elizabeth regrets the prejudice that clouded her vision of Darcy, and prevented her from seeing his honesty behind his snobbery. Had she seen it, she would have acted differently and fared better. But it is precisely because an autonomous person is reality-oriented that she will keep in mind that she is a human being, not a god, and refuse to take every failure as a permanent dent in her well-being. She is likely to view some of her own failures of autonomy as she views those of others, with a degree of philosophic detachment, accepting that some are

---

[15] See Wayne D. Riggs, "Understanding 'Virtue' and the Virtue of Understanding" (2003), 203–226.

inevitable, as are purely intellectual failures. And if she does, then she will recognize, in Henry Fielding's memorable words, that "the finest composition of human nature, as well as the finest china, may have a flaw in it;...though, nevertheless, the pattern may remain of the highest value."[16] She will cultivate "great discernment...tempered with this overlooking disposition." To do otherwise would be incompatible with a realistic conception of herself and of human excellence and happiness.

4.4. Does Reality-Orientation Really Require Autonomy?

The idea that reality-orientation requires autonomy might be challenged on the grounds that it is possible to acquire truth and understanding by simply accepting the testimony—that is, the say-so—of those more knowledgeable than us, or better positioned than us.[17] This is certainly possible when it comes to truth, but understanding cannot be gained simply by accepting another's testimony. For example, if you trust me, you can believe me when I tell you that I found your joke hurtful, but you can't understand why simply on the basis of my testimony. For that, you must pay attention to my explanation, listen with empathy and without defensiveness, use your imagination to put yourself in my place, and try to link my feelings of hurt with similar feelings you've had in the past when made the target of a joke. Engaging in this process, making an evaluation, and calibrating your response to what you see as the situation—in short, directing yourself by your own rational judgment—is not only reality-oriented, it is also autonomous. Note, moreover, that the process you engage in is shot through with other deliberative virtues: courage, insofar as you face the possibility that you did something shameful; responsibility, insofar as you accept the burden of finding out the truth; and honesty, insofar as you face the facts. And all this remains true even if in the end you conclude, mistakenly, that you did nothing hurtful, and that I'm simply having a bad day.

It might be thought that reality-orientation and autonomy can conflict, hence one cannot entail the other.[18] Suppose someone grows up believing that the best route to truth about what matters in life is not relying on his own judgment, but on the judgment of a wise parent, or a sage such as

---

[16.] Henry Fielding, Book I, chapter 7, *The History of Tom Jones, A Foundling* (1749).
[17.] Karen Jones usefully distinguishes between accepting someone's argument and accepting her testimony in "Second-Hand Moral Knowledge" (1999), 55–78.
[18.] Thanks to Jodi Halpern for raising this objection.

the Dalai Lama or Carl Rogers, someone who is herself or himself both reality-oriented and autonomous. Suppose, further, that to date his experience has never contradicted this belief, whereas the few times he has relied on his own judgment about, say, the trustworthiness of a friend or the suitability of a job, he has landed himself in trouble. Then reality-orientation dictates that he rely on the wise person's judgment rather than his own. In his case, then, reality-orientation requires *not* being autonomous.

This analysis, however, is not quite accurate. The devotee's realization, on the basis of experience and self-examination, that his own discernment in practical matters is impoverished is not only reality-oriented, it is also autonomous. But if he concludes from this that he should continue to depend on the wise person's judgment he is being neither reality-oriented nor autonomous. For in so doing, he is perpetuating the very dependency that has led to his lack of discernment. He wants the right answers handed to him on a platter, but has no interest in understanding what makes them right: why, for example, this person is not trustworthy or that action or judgment is fair or unfair, whom he should befriend, why fairness matters, how it relates (if it does) to kindness or generosity, and so on. For such understanding is necessary for the sensitivity and discrimination we need to convert the rigid rules with which we start on the path to maturity into flexible principles to suit a variety of different situations. Without it he can neither apply what he has learned to new cases nor follow its implications, whether welcome or unwelcome.

The devotee might say that he doesn't want understanding, just detailed guidance to keep him out of trouble. But this proposal ignores the practical and psychological obstacles to getting such guidance. For one thing, even if his sage lives as long as he, he cannot have this sage in tow 24/7. For another, even if he could, there would be a limit to his ability to live on a loaner brain, so to speak. For he must apply the sage's principles to his own life, and to do it in a way that enables him to adopt goals and choose means that fit his abilities, temperament, and circumstances, he must understand these abilities, this temperament, and these circumstances. To be sure, his sage might know things about him that he himself does not, but there are many things only he is in a position to really understand about himself. This is why a truly wise (and, therefore, reality-oriented) sage would want his devotees to take their own situation into account in applying his principles. And to do this successfully, the devotee must learn to live "first-hand"—that is, by his own judgment of the facts. This conclusion stands even if the authority obeyed is not a person but the Church, a holy book, or God.

Like all ventures, living "first-hand" carries risk for anyone who undertakes it, the risk of making a mistake and coming to the wrong conclusion, or of coming to the right conclusion for the wrong reasons. This is one reason why even people with the same abstract philosophy often differ in the values they actually live by. But the risk of making a mistake is even greater if we rely unthinkingly on some admired person or persons, without taking into account the particularities of our own situation, or the possibility that the admired person might be wrong on some crucial points. Wise trust in others—trust that is warranted by the facts—requires that we be reality-oriented in our relationship to others, even those we admire. For this reason, too, we must develop our own powers of understanding and judgment—that is, our autonomy.

Another objection to my claim that reality-orientation requires autonomy might stem from a common picture of the autonomous person as a lone wolf who never relies on others' judgments in any matter of importance. I have already indicated that this picture is false, but it is worth seeing why in more detail. On this picture, autonomy is incompatible with reality-orientation because every sane person, especially a reality-oriented one, is aware that he cannot make an independent judgment on every issue of importance, never accepting anything on trust, especially in a world as technologically, intellectually, culturally, and morally complex as the world of the 21st century. But the problem here is with the lone wolf picture of autonomy, not with the claim that reality-orientation requires autonomy. It is part of lived experience that we need the eyes of others not only to see the external world clearly but even to see ourselves clearly. Insofar as someone is autonomous, he will seek to understand and accept the limits of his powers as the individual he is, and the consequent necessity of relying on others' testimony, example, or judgments. The disposition to do so is but the other side of the disposition to accept the limits of reliance on others and the importance of being independent and living by one's own understanding. As John Benson puts it, "[t]o insist on using one's own eyes instead of the botanist's is as irrational as to insist on using the naked eye instead of a microscope."[19]

---

[19] John Benson, "Who Is the Autonomous Man?" (1983), 5–17, at 5. Benson even defines autonomy as "a mean state of character with regard to reliance on one's own powers in acting, choosing, and forming opinions" (5) or "correctness in the avoidance and acceptance of the testimony and guidance of others" (9) and Roberts and Wood define it as "a wise disposition of balance between hetero-regulation and autoregulation in intellectual practice" (*Intellectual Virtue*, 2007), 257.

The real question is when reliance on others' testimony, example, or judgments is compatible with reality-orientation and autonomy. An obvious answer is, "When we think, for good reason, that the matter is beyond our understanding, or that others are more likely to be right, or that practical demands and time-constraints make such reliance necessary—as is frequently the case." Such reliance is not compatible with reality-orientation or autonomy when we are too lazy to make the effort to think for ourselves, or too neurotically self-doubtful to trust our own judgment, or too desirous of approval to care enough about the truth. All these motivations involve devaluing self-direction.

Awareness of our epistemic limits entails modesty and habitual self-scrutiny.[20] Hence, when our reality-oriented judgments conflict with those of others, we cannot automatically assume that our own are correct. At such times we may need to expand the scope of our deliberation or reasoning, taking new factors into account before making up our minds. Autonomy also precludes rejecting others' views just because they are others' views and we need to prove our independence or cleverness. For such a need to prove ourselves also bespeaks a neurotic self-doubt and desire for approval that puts others in control of our judgments and choices and above our commitment to self-direction. By contrast, deferring to others when we think they are right and we ourselves are not shows self-confidence, as well as honesty and fairness.

But believing or disbelieving someone or something is not the only option. One of the most valuable lessons we can learn from Socrates' conversations with the politicians, poets, and craftsmen of Athens is that it is not necessary to take a position on everything. When our own time or competence is limited, and there is no trustworthy source to reply upon, we can suspend belief. Again, if something seems too good to be true, like internet offers of potions and powders guaranteeing everlasting youth and fitness, we can maintain a healthy skepticism (or, at least, make sure that the offers come with a money-back guarantee).

I claimed in the previous section that relying on others' moral testimony when the matter is beyond our understanding, or when others are more likely to be right, is compatible with autonomy. Some people, however, think that relying on others' moral testimony when there are no practical

---

[20] See Linda T. Zagzebski's lucid discussion of these and other qualities of the admirable epistemic agent in *Virtues of the Mind: An Inquiry into the Nature of Virtue and the Ethical Foundations of Knowledge* (1996), Part 2, chapters 3–5. Zagzebski regards these admirable traits as epistemic and moral virtues.

demands or time-constraints to make such reliance necessary cannot be autonomous, because every moral agent has the ability for moral discernment. Hence, since accepting another's testimony is accepting her judgment simply on her say-so, without understanding her reasons, only laziness or indifference to the moral issue can explain relying on her testimony in the absence of any practical obstacles. However, there is no reason to think that every moral agent has the ability for moral discernment on every issue. Moral discernment requires experience and emotional sensitivity, and an individual may lack the former or the latter or both in certain areas of his life. So if an individual has good reason to believe that the testifier can deliver the truth and he himself cannot, his reliance on the testifier's testimony is no less autonomous than his reliance on a trusted doctor's testimony on some medical matter.[21,22]

There is, nevertheless, a difference in the autonomous person's attitude towards the two cases. Because moral considerations permeate life, and because accepting a moral judgment on testimony does not import understanding, an autonomous person must strive to develop his powers of moral discernment, whereas he might be perfectly content to remain dependent on the testimony of his doctor on medical issues.

A different kind of criticism of my thesis is that if, as I claim, autonomy and reality-orientation are two facets of the same trait, then they are undesirable, because reality-orientation is obviously incompatible with fantasy, daydreams, fiction, and spontaneity, all of which play a valuable role in self-creation and recreation. Sarah Buss is exactly right in noting that "sometimes—we want to be `moved'—even 'carried away'—by the imaginations of others...We want to experience a response we do not 'rationally choose.'"[23] But reality-orientation/autonomy does not preclude the enjoyment of fantasy, daydreams, fiction, or spontaneity. Rather, what it precludes is living at their mercy. Fantasy, daydreams, and impulsive action can provide a valuable sense of freedom from plans, rules, and habits—but only if we have in place plans, rules, and habits that can keep

---

[21.] In *Second-Hand Moral Knowledge* (1999), Jones defends the compatibility of autonomy with the acceptance of moral testimony when the testifier is more likely to be right. But the example she gives suggests that one needn't *believe* that the testifier is more likely to be right. This amounts to holding that autonomy is compatible with blind trust, a position I reject.

[22.] Sometimes sound moral judgment requires empirical knowledge of a specialized kind, such as what counts as consent in the case of Alzheimer's patients, or what the likelihood is of one's aid actually benefiting its recipients. In such cases, we need to rely on the factual testimony of experts in the field.

[23.] Sarah Buss, "Valuing Autonomy and Respecting Persons: Manipulation, Seduction, and the Basis of Moral Considerations" (January 2005), 195–235, at 226.

us free of control by our fantasies, daydreams, and impulses. The ability to surrender to the power of another's imagination without fear of being unable to regain control requires a self-confidence and self-trust that only someone who is well-aware of the distinction between fact and fiction can have.[24]

4.5 Is Substantive Autonomy Really Superior to Content-Neutral Autonomy?

Some critics have argued that my distinction between content-neutral and substantive autonomy is not as clear-cut as I seem to think. One reason is that it is not only on my account that an autonomous person is reality-oriented (disposed to track truth or understanding) but also on the content-neutral account. For reflection on one's preferences and values in light of one's circumstances requires tracking truth and understanding at least about those preferences and values and those circumstances. This is true. But the characterization just given of my account is incomplete; what my account holds is that the autonomous/reality-oriented person is disposed to track truth or understanding about objectively important issues in her life and human life in general. Hence she is disposed to seek truth or understanding not only about her actual preferences and values in light of her circumstances, but also about what is important in human life and, thus, which preferences and values she ought to hold.

Another criticism is that, contrary to my claim, content-neutral autonomy *can* rule out blind obedience, conformity, and servility, whether construed as behaviors or traits.[25] Blind obedience is unreflective obedience, but even content-neutral autonomy requires reflection, so even content-neutral autonomy rules out blind obedience. It also rules out conformity and servility insofar as they are inherently unreflective.

As we saw in chapter 3, however, on the content-neutral account, a person who reflectively and autonomously decides to be a blindly obedient, conformist, or servile person, and behaves accordingly, counts as autonomous in his blind obedience, conformity, and servility. And he counts as autonomous even if his reason for being blindly obedient, conformist, or servile is that it is easier to be thus than to carry the "burden" of being

---

[24.] According to the psychologist Andras Angyal, the ability for self-surrender is as essential to a well-integrated personality as self-determination. Cited in Marie Jahoda, *Current Concepts of Positive Mental Health* (1958), 48.

[25.] This criticism and the next one are by Marilyn Friedman.

a responsible, independent person.[26] So content-neutral autonomy cannot rule out blind obedience, conformity, or servility, either as behaviors or as character-traits.

A third criticism is that, although substantive autonomy is *more likely* to rule out the traits of blind obedience, conformity, and servility, it doesn't *necessarily* rule them out. For example, someone could cultivate these traits as part of his choice of a spiritual life that requires unquestioning obedience to God's will or an earthly religious authority. Or he could cultivate them in order to keep his family safe under a dictatorship. Neither spiritual values, nor the desire to safeguard one's family, are as such contrary to autonomy, so substantive autonomy cannot rule out traits that are cultivated as a means to such values or desires.

It is true that the desire to safeguard one's family is not contrary to autonomy, and that some spiritual values also fall into this category. But values that call for unquestioning obedience to God or an earthly religious authority cannot, for conceptual reasons, be anything but heteronomous. So the only question is whether someone who becomes blindly obedient, servile, or conformist for the sake of his family's safety can be autonomous. That an individual can autonomously decide to renounce his autonomy has already been established in chapter 3 and Section 4.1 above. What he cannot—logically cannot—do is remain autonomous after becoming heteronomous, even if his goal in becoming thus was to preserve an important non-heteronomous value. One acquires traits by engaging in trait-relevant deliberation and behavior, whatever the ultimate goal of acquiring them. Consider this analogy. Having run out of alternatives, an honest man in a famine-struck war zone reluctantly starts stealing to feed his starving family. He uses dishonest means to a not-dishonest goal. Eventually he becomes comfortable with being a thief, and even starts enjoying it; in other words, he acquires a dishonest character. When this happens, he has been transformed into a dishonest man and cannot claim the mantle of honesty just because his goal in becoming dishonest was to preserve an important value not itself dishonest. More generally, whatever someone's *reason* for acquiring a character trait, T, in some domain of his life, once he has acquired it, it follows necessarily that he has T in that domain and

---

[26.] Of course, this is an artificial way of expressing the point. No one acquires character traits simply by deciding to acquire them; by the time we can reflect on them we already have some of the dispositions that constitute them. What we do decide is whether to keep reinforcing them or trying to change ourselves for the better.

does not have non-T. It is irrelevant whether T is acquired only as a means to some other goal or for its own sake.

4.6. Autonomy and Well-Being

A challenge to my thesis that well-being requires autonomy is presented by military training, which, along with combat skills, teaches the habit of unquestioning obedience to authority, and "unit cohesion" through unthinking conformity and loyalty to the group.[27] Even though soldiers are held responsible for obeying illegal orders, their habituation into unquestioning obedience, and the fact that they often must operate under incomplete information, or even ignorance, about the relevant facts—thanks to the fog (and fiction) of war—means that it is hard for them to either be, or see themselves as being, responsible autonomous agents much of the time. According to my theory, then, they cannot have well-being much of the time, even if all the orders they obey are moral. But (the objection goes), this implication of my theory is implausible, since surely many soldiers are happy and, when the cause is just and the war is fought in a just manner, what they do is worthwhile.

This is a complicated challenge that needs careful parsing. The first point to note is that if a soldier really has been thoroughly inculcated into unquestioning obedience to his superiors and conformity to the group, then, even if the orders he receives and obeys are just, their worth accrues not to him but to the order-giver. He is but a tool in the chain of command that culminates in the performance of actions that meet the requirements of justice. Since he acts without understanding, since he would have obeyed the orders even if they had been unjust and harmful in their consequences, he is merely a conduit of worth, not a creator of worth. Consequently, although he can enjoy his activities, find emotional fulfillment in being a member of his unit, and derive a sense of meaning from both, he cannot, qua soldier, have well-being as the highest prudential good.

The second point is that not all soldiers actually learn complete, unquestioning obedience, even when they are at the bottom of the rung. And those who don't are often unhappy enough to leave the military.[28]

---

[27] Jessica Wolfendale, *Torture and the Military Professional* (2007).
[28] Captain Christopher Yalanis, "The Virtue(?) of Obedience: Military Training and Autonomy" (2001). Available online under a slightly different title at http://isme.tamu.edu/JSCOPE01/Yalanis01.html, accessed September 2013.

On my view, if it is true that blind obedience is necessary for the proper functioning of the military, then not only soldiers, but the military system as a whole, is morally bankrupt. But the premise that blind obedience is necessary for its proper functioning is questionable. In his paper, "The Virtue (?) of Obedience," Christopher Yalanis argues that when blind obedience is demanded, it actually creates mistrust of superiors and a high rate of dropouts. It is possible that blind obedience has been rationalized as necessary because those who can like to exercise brute power, even if only because they once had to endure their superiors' exercise of brute power. Further support for the claim that blind obedience is not necessary comes from the Marine Corps, where, reportedly, leadership skills and personal accountability are inculcated at every rank through open discussion and questioning.[29]

4.7. Autonomy, Virtue, and Vice

I argued above that the disposition to be autonomous/reality-oriented is a deliberative and epistemic virtue that requires other deliberative and epistemic virtues such as honesty and courage, modesty and fairness, open-mindedness, and a sense of responsibility (4.4.1). If we understand moral virtue as a disposition to (among other things) do the right thing out of an appreciation of the right reasons, it becomes clear why autonomy/reality-orientation is a necessary component of moral virtue. It also becomes clear why it is not itself a moral virtue: it does not guarantee an appreciation of the right reasons, for such an appreciation requires a measure of constitutive and situational luck. But an autonomous individual far more likely to achieve such understanding and resist his culture's vices than a heteronomous individual in the same circumstances. For example, an autonomous/ reality-oriented person who grows up in a culture that treats racism and chauvinism as virtues is far less likely to acquire these vices than a heteronomous/unreality-oriented person. To the extent that an autonomous/reality-oriented person achieves understanding of the true and the good, and acquires the disposition to deliberate, feel, and act accordingly, he is realistic and morally virtuous.

These claims are illustrated well by the story of Antigone and Haemon. When they take a stand in the face of Creon's tyranny by openly acknowledging and acting in loyalty to their values, in spite of the threat to their

---

[29] David H. Freedman, *Corps Business: The 30 Management Principles of the US Marines* (2001).

lives and well-being, their attitudes and actions evince not only their autonomy/reality-orientation, but also their realism: their correct understanding of the situation and the values involved. Hence their attitudes and actions also evince their moral virtues: their courage and sense of justice, and their integrity and sense of responsibility. Had they opposed Creon not because they correctly thought that his order was unjust, but simply for the sake of defying authority, or simply because they were told by some seer that they ought to oppose him, their motives would have been neither reality-oriented/autonomous, nor virtuous, even though their behavior would have been the same.

Contrast them now with Karamazov. Karamazov's preoccupation with others' opinion of him, his manipulative dealings with them, and his rationalizations evince not only his unreality-orientation/heteronomy and, thus, his epistemic vices, but also his lack of other-regard and self-regard, and the moral vices that go with this lack. Thus, he constantly blames others for his traits and actions, instead of having the courage and honesty to acknowledge his own responsibility for them. This makes him both unfair and dishonest with others, and dishonest with himself about his motives and actions. Although it is possible to be unfair and cowardly without being generally self-deceived or blind, these usually play a large role in vicious traits and actions, and do so in Karamazov's case.

Can an autonomous (and, therefore, reality-oriented) person be vicious? Joseph Raz and Feinberg both claim that autonomy is compatible with an immoral life.[30] "No further analysis," Feinberg declares, "can be expected to rule out as impossible a selfish but autonomous person; a cold, mean, unloving but autonomous person; or a ruthless, or cruel autonomous person" (ibid., 43). If Feinberg is right, we get the odd result that although autonomy is an epistemic virtue, it can be combined with moral vice. So we do need further analysis to see if we can rule this out.

It is certainly possible that an autonomous (and reality-oriented) person might autonomously decide to *act* cruelly or ruthlessly (or coldly, meanly, and unlovingly) when the occasion calls for it; and if there are many such occasions—as, for example, in a violent neighborhood or country crawling with potential and actual enemies, or in a culture in which everyone

---

[30.] Raz, *Freedom* (1986), 380; Feinberg, "Autonomy" (1986). Raz makes this claim about what he calls personal autonomy, which he distinguishes from what he calls moral autonomy. The former, he states, is "a particular ideal of individual well-being," and the latter a claim about the nature of morality. But the distinction is unclear, because he also states that personal autonomy is a "moral ideal which, if valid, is one element in a moral doctrine" (ibid., 370, n. 2).

treats him meanly—he might even acquire cruel and ruthless or mean character traits. But whether these traits are compatible with *continuing* to be autonomous depends on further details of the case. If I am right, someone who has these traits can be autonomous only if he thinks, for good reason, that his situation requires him to be cruel, ruthless, or mean with his enemies, and only if his traits neither make him indifferent to discovering the relevant facts—such as that so-and-so is innocent and deserves to be treated well—nor prevent him from being motivated by his awareness of these facts. If, on the other hand, his cruelty and ruthlessness make him indifferent to finding out if P is innocent, or prevent him from being motivated by P's innocence, it is easy to see that he lacks reality-orientation and, thus, autonomy. He also lacks it if he is too weak-willed to act on his awareness of P's innocence,

In short, Feinberg's claim that the autonomous person can be vicious needs to be qualified. An autonomous (and reality-oriented) person can be cruel or ruthless under some circumstances, but he cannot, *qua* autonomous, be vicious in the sense of being indifferent to important normative considerations, much less opposed to them. In the next section I will argue against the view that autonomy requires the ability for questioning and justifying one's basic attitudes and values, including those of autonomy itself.[31] This view goes beyond that of Westlund and Paul Benson, making autonomy the private reserve of highly articulate and theoretical people.

4.8 Does Autonomy Require the Ability for Justifying Autonomy?

In his discussion of autonomy, Jonathan Lear states that "the value of autonomy has not fully developed in a person's soul if he is not yet motivated to question its value," because "autonomy is a reflexive value; it ultimately calls itself into question."[32] And, presumably, ends by justifying

---

[31] The same requirement is sometimes imposed on the virtuous. According to Annas, "[a]ncient theories require that the virtuous agent be able to articulate and defend her reasons for acting as she does and being the way she is, across the board" (*Morality of Happiness*, 75). In "Prudence and Morality in Ancient and Modern Ethics" (January 1995), 241–257, Annas calls virtue a skill involving "a unified grasp" of "the general principles which define its subject matter," and states that a virtuous person "can explain and, if need be, justify his particular judgments in terms of the general principles" (248). She makes the same point in *Intelligent Virtue* (2011). And in her essay "The Structure of Virtue," Annas argues that possessors of *all* skills, and not only of virtue, have this ability (2003), 15–33.

[32] Jonathan Lear, *Love And Its Place in Nature* (1990), 209.

itself. In "Responsibility for Self" and "What is Human Agency?" Charles Taylor argues similarly that our freedom and responsibility lie in our ability to question our most basic values, and to make "strong," and even "radical," evaluations.[33] Strong evaluations are evaluations of our preferences, actions, and lives overall in the language of "higher or lower...profound or superficial, noble or base" (*Responsibility*, 282), and "radical evaluations" are evaluations of our "fundamental evaluations" (*Agency*, 41–42; *Responsibility,* 297–298). In radical evaluation, Taylor explains, we try to articulate and "bring to definition" our "deepest unstructured sense of what is important"; such evaluation is, thus, "deep" and "total," for it questions even our "fundamental evaluations" (ibid., 41; 298). It is "a reflection about the self, its most fundamental issues," a reflection that arises from the very "nature of our deepest evaluations" (ibid., 42;299). And "it is...the responsibility for radical evaluation implicit in the nature of a strong evaluator, which is essential to our notion of a person" (*Responsibility*, 299).

Since autonomy/reality-orientation is a character trait on my view, and character traits embody a person's fundamental values, it follows that evaluating our own actions or character as autonomous is a fundamental evaluation. Hence, Taylor's view implies that, as persons, we are responsible for engaging in a radical evaluation of our fundamental evaluations. But do we really need to be motivated to call autonomy into question to be fully autonomous, much less to be persons? I do not think so. Someone who lacks this motivation may show every evidence of being autonomous all the same: a commitment to exercising her powers of understanding and judgment, and thus to distinguishing between reality and illusion; the ability to resist both gullibility and total skepticism; and the disposition to be self-confident without being dogmatic. All this requires a perceptive, emotionally engaged, reflective awareness, discerning of self and others, even if she is unable to articulate her perceptions and reasoning and answer the kinds of challenges to autonomy we have encountered above.

Suppose, however, that she does stop to try to call autonomy/reality-orientation into question and to justify being autonomous. She reads postmodernist scholars who purport to show that truth and autonomy are bourgeois Western constructs for keeping the powerful in power. She finds all this quite befuddling, and turns to social psychology for

---

[33.]Charles Taylor, "Responsibility for Self," in *The Identities of Persons*, ed. Amélie O. Rorty (1976), 281–299; "What is Human Agency?" in *Human Agency and Language, Philosophical Papers I*, by Charles Taylor (1985), 15–44. As the in-text references indicate, the two articles are almost identical.

enlightenment. There she reads that mild positive illusions about yourself make you a happier, healthier, and nicer person (see my chapter 5). She also reads that no one is autonomous: we are driven by the desire to fit in with the crowd, or by our unconscious gut intuitions, and the so-called reasons we give for our judgments are typically mere rationalizations.[34] What we call reasoning is usually guided not by a desire for the truth but by a desire to win the case. In other words, much of the time we live like lawyers rather than judges.

She finds that she cannot defend her convictions against these arguments, and mistakenly concludes that they are right. She accepts the view that people who look at life through (unrealistically) rose-colored lenses, or have no trouble following the crowd or willingly conforming to the strictures of their culture or dominant group, tend to be both nicer and happier—to have better lives. So she now has to choose between being autonomous/reality-oriented and having a better life. She decides that the latter is more important and, therefore, that she cannot justify being autonomous. At the same time, however, on a more practical level, being autonomous still seems right to her and she can do no other than continue to live autonomously. Does her life then become less than fully autonomous?

On the one hand, someone who is autonomous because she can be no other is necessarily autonomous. The fact that she cannot justify being autonomous does not render her life less autonomous—it just renders it less theoretical. On the other hand, if her judgment that she ought to eschew autonomy leads to conflict, she is less autonomous than someone who lives autonomously without conflict, wholeheartedly.

What is crucial on my view, then, is wholeheartedness: an integrated intellectual-emotional disposition to live autonomously, whether or not a person can give a justification of autonomy. For one thing, as we have just seen, on the basis of complex but unsound arguments, someone may end up justifying heteronomy. For another, she may not have an incentive for calling her autonomy into question and engaging in a full-fledged articulated reflection on, and justification of, its value. For the course

---

[34] This is a slight exaggeration of Jonathan Haidt's and Fredrik Bjorklund's thesis in "Social Intuitionists Answer Six Questions About Moral Psychology" (hereafter "Social Intuitionists") (2008), 181–217. I agree that we humans confabulate, but not all the time. See also Daniel Jacobson "Does Social Intuitionism Flatter Morality or Challenge It?" (219–232), Darcia Narvaez "The Social Intuitionist Model: Some Counter-Intuitions" (233–240), and Haidt's and Bjorklund's response (241–254) in the same volume. Terry Horgan and Mark Timmons argue against Haidt and Bjorklund in "Morphological Rationalism and the Psychology of Moral Judgment" (2010), 279–295. I discuss the lessons of social and cognitive psychology for virtue in chapter 6.

of her life may provide daily confirmation of its value. Hence she may have good-enough reasons to believe that autonomy/reality-orientation is necessary for a worthwhile life, reasons that are deeply grounded in the web of practical affairs, without being able to hold her own against arguments to the contrary. For example, she may have noticed for years (without being able to say) that people who are not afraid of changing their beliefs, even cherished beliefs, in the face of strong evidence to the contrary, who can openly admit their shortcomings without feeling diminished, who are confident in their own judgments of facts and values, and who lead lives that exemplify their values, seem to enjoy a kind of freedom that people who tend to be defensive, blind, or conformist lack. Her own life may also provide ongoing evidence for the value of remaining autonomous. For she may notice that in those domains of her life in which she is free from the armor of defensiveness, or the constant need to prove herself to others, or the desire to rewrite history to ensure her place on the winning side, she also feels much more at home in the world.

Rejecting Taylor's highly linguistic notion of self-understanding and personhood, Owen Flanagan writes that countless "intrapersonal and extrapersonal feedback mechanisms, by way of feelings of coordination, integration, and integrity, of fit with the social world mediated by the body language of others, and so on," can provide a person with self-understanding.[35] Likewise, they can provide a person with practical justification for becoming and remaining autonomous, even if she cannot verbalize it. Her reading of fiction might support these observations. For example, the fictional characters she identifies with and admires—characters such as Jo March, Elizabeth Bennett, Jane Eyre, and Penny Baxter[36]—are all life-affirming individuals with minds of their own, and an unflinching commitment to seeing things as they are. Baxter knows that life "knocks a man down" again and again, but he still thinks life is a "powerful fine" thing because he has the wisdom to take the knocks "for his share and go on."[37] He seems to understand well the importance of

---

[35] Owen Flanagan, "Identity and Reflection" (1996), 142–70, at 156.

[36] Jo March is the heroine of Louisa May Alcott's *Little Women* and Jane Eyre of Charlotte Bronte's *Jane Eyre*. Ezra "Penny" Baxter is one of the two main characters in Marjorie Kinnan Rawlings's *The Yearling*.

[37] Baxter fits Abraham Maslow's description of the well-functioning person: someone whose "main satisfactions" are relatively independent of his physical and social environment, once his basic needs, such as for love and work, are satisfied. See "Self-Actualizing People: A Study of Psychological Health" (1950), 11–34. In my terms, Baxter is autonomous.

living by his own judgment and facing the facts of his life, even though he evidently lacks the incentive to call his commitments into question or the ability to justify them if challenged. His "knowing practice," in Michael Stocker's words, "embodies, expresses, and really is the knowledge" of the value of autonomy.[38]

Such inarticulable but knowing practices, as both Stocker and Flanagan point out, are common in many areas of human life, from showing someone the way to a house without being able to describe it - to creating questioning, intelligent art without being able to say what the questions are or what the answers - to being a great athlete without being able to say how.[39] Again, the "wisdom" and self-help literatures often embody insights about the value of being reality-oriented and autonomous that are decidedly not the conclusions of theoretically adequate arguments but, rather, of "knowing practice."

The unconscious emotional and cognitive signals constituting the feedback mechanisms that Flanagan talks about seem to help us gain not only self-understanding and understanding of others, but also other sorts of practical, and even theoretical, understanding. Detectives, doctors, and scientists alike rely on hunches or intuitions to distinguish a promising lead from a dead end, to come up with fruitful conjectures, or to find a solution to a problem that eludes their conscious minds. In *Dark Nature*, Lyall Watson talks about the "sixth sense" the naturalist acquires about the workings of nature, a sense that allows him to judge the "health" of a "patch of woodland" or a coral reef from hundreds of yards away, without being able to say how he knows what he knows.[40]

Often, no doubt, these hunches, insights, and intuitions are the result of prior analysis and argument, as Sherlock Holmes never fails to point out to Watson. But this is not always or entirely the case. In both the practical and the theoretical realm, from detective work to medicine to science

---

[38.] Michael Stocker argues for the epistemological priority of emotional practical knowledge in general over "articulated and reflective theory and knowledge" in "How Emotions Reveal Value," R. Crisp, ed. *How Should One Live?* (1996), 173–190, at 186; and with Elizabeth Hegeman, *Valuing Emotions* (1996), 201–202.

[39.] The first two examples are from Stocker, *Valuing Emotions*, 195 and 200–201, the third from Flanagan, "Identity and Reflection," 156–157. Stocker quotes Stuart Hampshire's observation that " 'some kinds of thought, typically human, are remote from rational discourse and are no less interesting'," (*Valuing Emotions*, 200–201). Hampshire's observation is based on his conversations with the artist Giacometti who, according to Hampshire, "had made his art into a series of thoughtful experiments attached to a series of linked inquiries," although he found it hard to "give an explicit account in words of his inquiries, and of their outcomes" (201).

[40.] Lyall Watson, *Dark Nature* (1995), 45–46.

to the choices with which we shape our lives, it seems that insight and intuition are often the result of a sustained implicit training of our senses, emotions, and intellect by experience—akin, perhaps, to the navigational and kinesthetic training of the mind and body as we learn to make our way in the physical environment. Nor is this entirely speculative. The capacity of the unconscious mind is far greater than that of the conscious mind. According to researchers who have tried to quantify our processing abilities, the conscious mind can process only between ten and sixty bits of information per second, whereas the entire mind, including the visual system, can process about 11,200,000 bits of information.[41] These numbers are, of course, highly fallible, but the general point about the vastly superior processing ability of the unconscious mind is not.

In light of these facts, there is no reason to think that those who reliably act autonomously, but cannot explain why they do what they do, much less justify being autonomous, act without any understanding, and thus are not really autonomous. Aristotle, evidently, holds such a view of those who reliably do the right thing, at the right time, from the right desires, but cannot say why they do it, or don't make much sense when they try to say it.[42] His explanation for their success is that they are naturally lucky: they lack understanding of virtue but act from naturally good desires, like naturally good singers who sing without understanding music. He adds that the naturally lucky are better off not deliberating because deliberation can only interfere with their "inspired" way of doing things. He evidently thinks that they don't deliberate because they can't articulate their deliberations; he does not consider the possibility that they do deliberate, but are unable to put their deliberations into words.

No doubt, an articulate understanding of the value of being autonomous/reality-oriented can help some people to apply their understanding to new situations, and might even be necessary for them to do so. But this is not true of everyone. Hence, whether someone should attempt to engage in such understanding depends on whether or not he is good at it. It is rational for someone whose attempts at articulate understanding usually succeed to engage in it, but irrational for someone whose like attempts lead to sophistry or confusion and a subversion of his good common sense. On this point Aristotle is right: those who reliably do the right thing but cannot say why are better off not trying to say why. By the same logic, it

---

[41] Ap Dijksterhuis and Loran E. Nordgren, "A Theory of Unconscious Thought" (2006), 95–109.
[42] *Eudemian Ethics*, trans. J. Solomon (1984), 1247b 18ff. See Annas' discussion of this passage in *Morality of Happiness* (1993), 374–377.

is rational for someone whose intuitions are usually borne out by evidence to rely on them, but irrational for someone whose intuitions are usually contradicted by evidence to do so.

These observations about the ability to understand matters without being able to say how or why are supported by evolutionary theory and experimental research on what psychologists call the "adaptive unconscious" (as opposed to Freud's "dynamic unconscious").[43] This research suggests that our adaptive unconscious does a vast amount of cognitive and emotional work under the radar of our consciousness, from guiding our attention to certain things and away from others, to helping us to interpret them, to helping us set our goals and choose our means. Without the adaptive unconscious, our conscious minds could do little. In light of what we know about the mind from everyday observation, literature, and science, it is safe to say that autonomy need not belong only to a theoretically sophisticated aristocracy.[44]

4.9. Conclusion

I have argued that autonomy, the disposition to live by our own judgments and values in important areas of our lives, is essential for well-being understood as happiness in an objectively worthwhile life, and that it entails, and is entailed by, reality-orientation. Autonomy and reality-orientation are, thus, different facets of the same complex disposition, their difference lying only in their focus. The focus of reality-orientation is gaining the truth about, or understanding of, important things and responding accordingly, that of autonomy living by one's own judgments and decisions in important areas of one's life. To the extent that a person is autonomous/reality-oriented, she cares about being in touch with, and motivated by, the true and the good. If she were to discover that what she had thought were virtues were actually vices, she would downgrade her estimate of her well-being.

[43.] Timothy D. Wilson, *Strangers to Ourselves: Discovering the Adaptive Unconscious* (2002), chapter 1, and Haidt and Bjorklund, ("Social Intutionists") 2008. The adaptive unconscious is an evolutionary adaptation that increases the mind's efficiency in many environments (though not all), whereas Freud's unconscious is largely the repository of repressed material that, according to evolutionary psychologists, usually interferes with the mind's efficiency.

[44.] Here I am paraphrasing Benson's statement that "autonomy ... is not the virtue of a reflective aristocracy" ("Autonomous Man," 1983, 9). Later, however, Benson states that there may be a kind of autonomy that is "exemplified only by the person who is aware of and can articulate his principles," and defend them against contrary principles (ibid., 17). But he doesn't say what this ability contributes to autonomy.

Complete understanding of, or motivation by, the true and the good is impossible, as I argue in chapter 6, but to the extent that she is in touch with, and motivated by, the true and the good, she is realistic and, thus, morally virtuous.

I have rejected the idea that autonomy requires the ability to justify autonomy. This view is far too intellectual, effectively (and counterintuitively) precluding from autonomy all those who cannot engage in such intellectual operations, even those who are, by all other measures, wholeheartedly autonomous. Moreover, the ability for theoretical justification is not necessarily a plus, for in the face of complicated arguments, the attempt at theoretical justification can lead us astray; worse, in moments of weakness it can tempt us into weaving intricate skeins of self-deception to evade unpleasant truths about ourselves and our responsibility for them.

The claim that realism is necessary for a worthwhile life, and thus for well-being as the highest prudential good (HPG), has recently come under attack on empirical grounds. In the next chapter, I will show that these attacks are based on weak evidence and faulty logic, and provide grounds to believe that realism really is good for us.

CHAPTER 5 | Is Realism Really Bad for You? A Realistic Response[1]

The honest or truthful person is "truthful [about himself] both in what he says and in how he lives...simply because that is his...character."

—ARISTOTLE, NE, IV.7.

"[M]en of true wisdom and goodness are contented to take persons and things as they are...The finest composition of human nature, as well as the finest china, may have a flaw in it...though, nevertheless, the pattern may remain of the highest value."

—HENRY FIELDING, Tom Jones

5.1. Introduction

5.1.1 We saw in chapter 2 that philosophers and psychologists have long regarded realism about ourselves and our circumstances as crucial for well-being as the HPG. But this view has also long invited skepticism from some quarters. Recently, this skepticism has found new support in the work of some social psychologists, who claim that far from being *essential* for mental health or happiness, realism is *bad for you*. Certain positive illusions about yourself, they say, are more conducive to health and happiness than their absence. This is a challenge to the very heart of my thesis. I will argue that, properly understood, realism really is good for you. I will start with a brief description of the critics' target.

In her work on mental health, Marie Jahoda notes that most psychologists regard healthy individuals as reality-oriented, as "able to take in matters"

---

[1] An earlier version of this chapter appeared in *The Journal of Philosophy* (February 2008).

they wish were different, "without distorting them to fit these wishes."[2] In a Socratic statement, Gordon Allport declares that "an impartial and objective attitude toward oneself is...a primary virtue, basic to the development of all others....And so...if any trait of personality is intrinsically desirable, it is the disposition...to see oneself in perspective."[3] Abraham Maslow and Carl Rogers also echo the idea that realism is central to mental health and well-being, where realism involves not only characteristically facing up to the facts, but also evaluating them by realistic standards and responding in realistic ways. In the words of Paul B. Baltes, realistic people have "rich factual knowledge about life matters" and "extensive procedural knowledge about ways of dealing with life problems."[4] Such people are also strongly disposed to act accordingly. This conception of realism as including both a certain *attitude*—reality-orientation—and a certain *achievement* (truth or understanding) is the same as the one I laid out in chapter 2. As in my conception, realism in the views of these psychologists does not entail perfection in either of these dimensions. Indeed, it is because realistic people recognize their (inevitable) lack of perfection that they are, as Maslow puts it, self-actualizing, that is, inclined to constantly strive for growth while accepting their own unchangeable weaknesses as individuals and as human beings "without chagrin or complaint."[5] Such people are also happy, because they more fully integrate the "pleasure principle" with the "reality principle," and more fully attain values or virtues such as "serenity, kindness, courage, honesty, love, unselfishness."[6] On this picture, realism is both instrumental to well-being, and partly constitutive of it.

Likewise, in Rogers' view, the healthy or fully functioning individual is open to experience, distorting neither his perceptions of the world to fit his conception of himself, nor his conception of himself to fit his perceptions of the world.[7] He is self- rather than other-directed, avoids façade,

---

[2] Marie Jahoda, "The Meaning of Psychological Health" (1953), 349, and *Current Concepts of Positive Mental Health* (1958), 51.

[3] Gordon W. Allport, *Personality: A Psychological Interpretation* (1937), 422; cited in C. Randall Colvin, Jack Block, David C. Funder, "Overly Positive Self-Evaluations and Personality: Negative Implications for Mental Health"(1995), 1152–1162.

[4] Jacqui Smith and Paul B. Baltes, "Wisdom-Related Knowledge: Age/Cohort Differences in Response to Life-Planning Problems" (May 1990), 494–505.

[5] Maslow, "A Theory of Metamotivation" (1967), 93–127, at 54.

[6] Maslow, *Toward a Psychology of Being* (1998), 171.

[7] "A Therapist's View of the Good Life: the Fully Functioning Person," in *The Carl Rogers Reader*, eds. H. Howard Kirschenbaum and V. L. Henderson (1989), 409–429. Although Rogers talks about the fully functioning person, he also makes it clear that he does not mean the perfectly functioning person, but simply the person who is constantly moving towards better and better functioning (410–411, 416).

pretense, and defensiveness, and is open to inner and outer reality.[8] In other words, the fully functioning individual is autonomous, honest with himself, and honest in the way he presents himself to others. He also has a sense of pride and self-worth that puts a negative value on pleasing others as an ultimate goal (182). On Rogers' view, it is only a fully functioning individual who leads a rich, full, challenging, and exciting life of continual growth, for only such an individual has the courage to launch himself "fully into the stream of life." [9]

Realism, then, has been widely seen as both instrumentally and conceptually necessary for well-being: an important means to happiness, and both a means to, and conceptually necessary for, objective worth. Someone who has well-being is reality-oriented and informed about the important facts of her own life and human life in general, characteristically evaluates and responds to events in the light of these facts, and has a sense of fulfillment that is grounded in them.

This picture of reality-based well-being and mental health is not only internally coherent, it is also intuitively plausible and highly attractive. Directly or indirectly, however, it is this picture of well-being that skeptics challenge when they challenge the importance of realism in our lives. The challenge seems to come both from common sense, and from social and cognitive psychology, with the latter providing support for the former. The challenge is empirical in nature, directed at the claim that realism is an important means to happiness and mental health. But if the challenge is successful, it also undermines, as we shall see, the normative and conceptual claim that realism is partly constitutive of mental health and objective worth and, thus, of well-being as the HPG. This makes it even more important to examine the skeptics' criticisms and see if they are well-founded. I will argue that they are not. In the next section I will address the common-sense challenge, and in Section 5.3 the social scientific challenge.

5.2. Realism Within the Limits of Human Nature Alone

The claim that being realistic (i.e., reality-oriented in one's perceptions, evaluations, and responses, as well as informed about the important empirical and normative facts of one's own life and human life in general) is necessary for well-being seems to fly in the face of an obvious truth, namely,

---

[8.] Rogers, "The Person in Process" (1989), 155–197, at 182.
[9.] Rogers, "A Therapist's View of the Good Life" (1989), 420.

that it is possible to know too much for your own good. The discovery that your kindly grandfather was a gun for hire, or that your loving husband, now deceased, was having an affair with your best friend, seem to be discoveries best not made. Moreover, a reality-oriented person—someone who is disposed to stay in touch with the important facts of her life—is far more likely to make such discoveries than someone who is willing to let sleeping dogs lie. Such a person is also more likely to be aware of her own flaws and the flaws of the human species, an awareness not exactly calculated to create good cheer. This seems to show that being reality-oriented and informed is inimical to happiness, and thus to well-being—that, as *Ecclesiastes* laments, "he that increaseth knowledge increaseth sorrow."

If *Ecclesiastes* is right, then there is a tension at the heart of my conception of well-being as the HPG, since it requires happiness in an objectively worthwhile and, thus, realistic, life. For if knowledge generally increases sorrow, we end up with the strange result that to the extent we are *unrealistic*, our lives are, by hypothesis, lacking in worth, whereas to the extent we are *realistic*, we are likely to feel unhappy. We can try to make our lives *either* objectively worthwhile *or* happy, but we cannot expect to make them both. But *Ecclesiastes* exaggerates. Although knowledge of some facts *can* lead to a sorrow so great that it results in a net decrease of well-being, the sorrow often comes not from knowledge of the truth as such, but from the untimeliness of the discovery. Like surgical procedures, unpleasant truths may need a long prep time. Recognizing this and preparing oneself psychologically for a potentially devastating revelation before proceeding with one's investigations is the better part of realism—of wisdom about one's human and individual limitations. And such wisdom—practical wisdom—after all, is what genuine realism is about, not a mechanical harvesting of all truths, with nary a care for the how, when, or what for.

Nevertheless, it must be granted that there are some truths that are both important and too terrible to face ever. Learning the brutal circumstances of your only child's death might lead to a grief so unbearable that it can only destroy your happiness and, thus, your well-being. And again, the reality-oriented person is more likely to learn such truths than someone who habitually avoids unpleasant facts.

This example, however, is less troublesome than at first it appears to be. What it shows is that being reality-oriented *can* lead to a discovery that diminishes our well-being by increasing our grief and adding nothing of worth to our lives. It does not show that being reality-oriented is *more* likely to diminish our well-being than its contrary: being disposed to self-deception about, or, evasion of, painful or otherwise uncomfortable facts.[10] On the contrary, being characteristically self-deceived is a far more reliable route to grief, since reality is impervious to our wishes, and unwelcome facts do not obligingly retreat from the scene when we choose to ignore them. Moreover, since facts are interconnected, the attempt to evade some facts requires us to evade other facts, which, in turn, requires us to evade yet other facts: "Oh what a tangled web we weave, When first we practice [our selves] to deceive." Thus, whereas the self-deceptive are likely to skin their shins on the rough edges of reality, the reality-oriented, acknowledging that life abounds with pitfalls, prepare themselves to deal with them.

All the same, my reply covertly admits that when the facts are devastating, we might be better off remaining ignorant of them. This seems to contradict my view that well-being as the HPG requires being informed about, and responding appropriately to, important truths about our lives. But appearances are misleading here. What I am claiming is that, when knowledge of a particular fact can only destroy us, whereas ignorance of it has no harmful consequences, then ignorance, even if self-induced, beats knowledge.[11] Some important truths, like some grave dangers or physical pains, are beyond our capacity to bear: far from providing an opportunity to make a courageous or ennobling response, they crush us under their weight.[12] In the example at hand, when you recover enough from your grief to consider yourself somewhat happy again, some of your positive feelings and evaluations will be made possible only by your ignorance of the circumstances of your child's death. Thus, my theory agrees with common sense that some happiness based on ignorance is better than total misery based on knowledge.

Suppose, however, that the brutal death of your child is the result, in part, of your own habitual negligence. Does my theory still hold that ignorance is better than knowledge? The answer to this question depends on

---

[10] Mike W. Martin's definition of purposeful self-deception as an evasion of full acceptance and integration of some fact, or supposed fact—usually painful or difficult—with one's other beliefs, values, and emotions, captures well the main elements of self-deception identified by Sartre, Herbert Fingarette, and others. See Martin, *Self-Deception and Morality* (1986), 14, 15.

[11] Can we really become ignorant of the facts we deceive ourselves about? Or does self-deception entail awareness, however dim, as Sartre insists? This is partly a conceptual issue. Self-deception entails some awareness of the evaded facts, but long practice can turn self-deception into ignorance.

[12] And if some people are constitutionally more fragile than others when it comes to facing certain disturbing truths, like the character of May in Sue Monk Kidd's *The Secret Life of Bees*, then one has to make an exception in their case. It is safe to say that since our epistemic and moral limitations make complete knowledge of important facts well-nigh impossible for us, everyone's happiness (or, for that matter, unhappiness) is, to some extent, based on ignorance and illusion.

the answer to the question why well-being as the HPG requires knowledge of one's character and actions. As I have been arguing, such knowledge is important for improving oneself and avoiding negligent acts in the future, as well as for making a well-grounded evaluation of one's life. In addition, there is something noble about facing the facts and responding appropriately. But if you are already aware of your habitual negligence, have taken it into account in evaluating your life, and are working to improve yourself, then all that knowledge of this particular act can do is make your evaluation of your life more accurate while adding guilt and grief to grief. Hence knowledge of this act is better for you only if nothing else can shake you out of your habitual negligence and prevent future tragedies. If this is the case, *and* you use your newfound self-knowledge to grow in realism, then, and only then, in my view, are you better off knowing about your role in your child's death. But this is no longer counterintuitive. For even as the knowledge increases your unhappiness, it both protects you from further disaster (and, thus, from further unhappiness), and contributes to the objective worth of your life. Thus it contributes to your well-being or, at least, mitigates your lack thereof.

The same sort of analysis applies to the objection from certain metaphysical beliefs. Although our metaphysical beliefs often radically underdetermine how we live our lives, and are thus far less important for realism, this is not always true. The objection is that people who deludedly believe in the existence of an all-powerful, all-knowing, benevolent deity have a source of happiness that atheists or agnostics do not. Religious belief gives people a sense of security, the ability to handle life's problems with grace, and the hope of better things to come in an afterlife or earthly reincarnation. Indeed, this might be most people's main motivation for believing in an all-powerful, all-knowing, benevolent God. But is it true that those who reject comforting delusions are at a comparative disadvantage? Cannot atheists and agnostics derive the same sense of security, the ability to handle life's problems with grace, and the hope of better things to come in this life from their understanding and acceptance of the laws of nature? What can be more comforting than the knowledge that the laws of cause and effect will continue apace, not subject to a powerful and unpredictable Deity's pleasure or displeasure? That whatever the capacities and limits of human nature and the world we live in, they are what they are, and we should and can learn to accept them? That it is possible to adapt to many unfortunate circumstances and find joy in life even after great sorrow? That we have a great capacity to improve our lives, and that when it's all over, our bodies will be one with the earth, nurturing roses and honeysuckle, birds and puppy dogs, and even girls and boys and men and women?

It is consistent with these arguments to acknowledge exceptions for exceptional circumstances. Thus, those who have endured or continue to endure unspeakable horrors—surely hundreds of millions just in the last century—might well need to believe in something beyond this life and this world to wrest some drop of joy and meaning from their existence. It would be both dogmatically wrongheaded and callous to insist that, even so, they would be better off facing the facts and rejecting this source of comfort. Even Boethius, whose circumstances were enviable till he was unjustly imprisoned, needed to believe that God governs the world and will reward the virtuous in order to sustain himself psychologically during his imprisonment.

The lesson of these examples is that although being realistic (informed about the important facts of one's own life and human life in general, and reality-oriented in one's perceptions, evaluations, and responses) is an important means to happiness, and both an important means to, and conceptually necessary for, objective worth, it *can* sometimes come into conflict with happiness. This is one reason why well-being as the HPG, which requires both happiness and objective worth, can be difficult to achieve. Too many objections to the thesis that well-being entails realism either forget that well-being is more than happiness, or assume, mistakenly, that the objective and psychological dimensions of well-being can never conflict.

The scientific challenge to realism, however, has other arguments in its arsenal.

5.3. The Scientific Challenge

5.3.1 In two influential articles, Shelley E. Taylor and Jonathon D. Brown have argued that a vast body of empirical research in social and cognitive psychology suggests that most people harbor certain mild positive illusions about themselves, and that, contrary to the conventional wisdom, these illusions are not only not opposed to mental health and happiness, they tend to promote them.[13] But what do Taylor and Brown mean

---

[13.] Shelley E. Taylor and Jonathon D. Brown, "Illusion and Well-Being: A Social Psychological Perspective on Mental Health" (hereafter "Illusion and Well-Being") (1988), 193–210, and "Positive Illusions and Well-Being Revisited: Separating Fact from Fiction" (hereafter "Positive Illusions") (1994), 21–27.

by happiness? Other than suggesting that it is identical with, or associated with, contentment, they never really tell us. This, as we shall see, is relevant to a proper evaluation of their claim that positive illusions promote happiness. In light of my discussion of happiness in chapters 1–3, I will assume that most respondents in the studies they rely on think of it in terms of a sense of fulfillment, a sense that their life is both meaningful or worthwhile and enjoyable.[14]

Taylor and Brown contend that people with certain "pervasive, enduring, and systematic" but mild, positive illusions about themselves and the world are generally a cheerful bunch, whereas those who are more realistic are generally somewhat depressive ("Illusion and Well-Being," 194). The illusions in question are "unrealistically positive self-evaluations, exaggerated perceptions of control or mastery, and unrealistic optimism" (ibid., 193). Taylor and Brown do not tell us to what extent these illusions are a matter of simple ignorance and to what extent a matter of self-deception or defensiveness.[15] As I shall argue, however, this distinction makes quite a bit of difference to the bearing of Taylor and Brown's argument on the importance of positive illusions in mental health. They also argue that the empirical data show that the somewhat self-deceived or ignorant but cheerful people (call them the Upbeat) do better than the depressed realists (the Downbeat) along all the traditional dimensions of mental health other than realism: "contentment, positive attitudes toward the self, the ability to care for and about others, openness to new ideas and people...the ability to perform creative and productive work, and the ability to grow...and self-actualize, especially in response to stressful events"

---

[14] There are two other problems with Taylor and Brown's understanding of happiness and mental health: (i) They hold that happiness indicates mental health, and unhappiness a lack thereof. But unhappiness is a perfectly appropriate response to misfortune, and large numbers of people in the world, whose lives are an endless struggle for survival, are appropriately (more-or-less) unhappy (ii) Taylor and Brown equate "psychological well-being" with mental health. But since psychological well-being entails happiness whereas mental health does not, well-being cannot be identical with mental health.

[15] Taylor and Brown do distinguish positive illusions from defense mechanisms, but their distinction seems like a distinction without a difference. Positive illusions, they say, "are directly responsive to threatening circumstances, whereas defenses are...inversely responsive to threatening information." Thus, for example, advancing cancer patients typically do not deny or repress information about their deteriorating condition. They are aware that their circumstances have worsened, but within the context of this acknowledgment, they may put a more optimistic spin on their circumstances than conditions warrant" ("Positive Illusions," 25). But a more optimistic spin than is warranted by the facts *insofar as one is aware of them* (an important addition) is possible only if some fact is evaded. The only discernible difference between defense mechanisms and what Taylor and Brown call optimistic spins (positive illusions) is that the former are extreme and the latter mild.

("Positive Illusions," 22). These illusions foster better adjustment as well as "better life functioning."[16]

Although Taylor and Brown do not talk about practical wisdom or virtue, we can infer from these claims that the Upbeat are more likely than the Downbeat to have qualities that are generally thought of as belonging to the practically wise and virtuous: kindness, tolerance, generosity, fairness or justice, a perspective that allows them to take things in stride, and the courage to grow and self-actualize. Hence, in challenging the view that being realistic about oneself is instrumentally important for happiness and mental health, Taylor and Brown are also, by implication, challenging the view that realism is necessary for practical wisdom and virtue.

If Taylor and Brown are right, it follows that wisdom requires the art of tempering self-knowledge with mild self-deception, while taking care not to let it get out of hand. Indeed, Taylor and Brown explicitly recommend nurturing the capacity for self-deception (or, as they prefer to call it, unwarranted "optimistic spins"):

> The individual who responds to negative, ambiguous, or unsupportive feedback with a positive sense of self, a belief in personal efficacy, and an optimistic sense of the future will, we maintain, be happier, more caring, and more productive than the individual who perceives this same information accurately and integrates it into his or her view of the self, the world, and the future. In this sense, *the capacity to develop and maintain positive illusions may be thought of as a valuable human resource to be nurtured and promoted*, rather than an error-prone processing system to be corrected ("Illusion and Well-Being," 205, italics mine).

It should be noted that the phenomena they regard as positive illusions are a mixed bag. It is one thing to respond to "ambiguous, or unsupportive feedback with a positive sense of self, [and] a belief in personal efficacy," and another to respond to "negative" feedback with a positive sense of self. Again, it is one thing to do so on a particular occasion, especially an experimental one, and another to do it characteristically, in one's everyday life. But I will return to this issue later. The thing to attend to now is that, for all the attention their thesis has received, Taylor and Brown's evidence for it is surprisingly weak, and their arguments are riddled with conceptual

---

[16.] Taylor, Collins, Skokan, and Aspinwall, 1989, 115–116, cited in C. Randall Colvin and J. Block, "Do Positive Illusions Foster Mental Health? An Examination of the Taylor and Brown Formulation" (July 1994), 3–20.

and logical problems.[17] Unfortunately, too many people, including philosophers, have tended to accept their thesis as valid without subjecting it to critical scrutiny.[18] Let us start by asking about the evidence and main arguments for their conclusion.

5.3.2 The main source of evidence of widespread positive illusions cited in the 1988 article is experiments with college students, although to broaden the basis of their claims, Taylor and Brown also cite some studies of terminally ill individuals in their 1994 article (see 5.3.6 below). The experiments with students show that most students rate themselves higher on their abilities, achievements, degree of control, and future prospects than they do most of their peers ("Illusion and Well-Being," 195–197). Sixty percent of respondents in surveys of moods also believe that "they are happier than most people" ("Illusion and Well-Being," 198). Taylor and Brown give the following arguments for thinking that the students' positive self-attributions are somewhat illusory: (i) it is logically impossible for most students to be happier or higher in their abilities, achievements,

---

[17] A Google search reports 4,241 citations to date for the 1988 article, and 594 citations for the 1994 article (http://www.google.com/search?hl=en&q=Taylor+Positive+Illusions+and+well-being, accessed July 8, 2011). In addition, Taylor's book, *Positive Illusions: Creative Self-Deception and the Healthy Mind* (1991), and the press reactions to it, have brought the message that illusions are good for you to thousands of people.

[18] For example, in "On Overrating Oneself—and Knowing It" (2005), 115–124, Adam Elga's unquestioned starting point is that it has been shown that people are subject to "persistent and widespread positive illusions (about themselves)" (117). Again, citing Taylor and Brown, Hilary Kornblith states: "While it was once the standard view among psychologists that being emotionally well-adjusted goes hand in hand with an accurate understanding of oneself and the world around one, the evidence against this claim is now quite strong" ("What is it Like to be Me?") (1998) 48–60). When I first completed the article this chapter is based on (*Journal of Philosophy*, February 2008), there was only one critical philosophical article, David A. Jopling's "'Take Away the Life-Lie···': Positive Illusions and Creative Self-Deception" (1996), 525–544. Jopling criticizes the Taylor-Brown thesis on grounds of "ecological validity and phenomenological realism," as well as on the substantive ground that "positive illusions diminish the range of reactive other-regarding attitudes and emotions" (525). Unfortunately, Jopling's substantive criticism is vitiated by his use of a thoroughly self-deceived individual as a counterexample to Taylor and Brown's thesis of the connection between illusions and mental health, in spite of Taylor and Brown's insistence that they are defending only mild illusions.

The best critical article is by the social psychologists, C. Randall Colvin and J. Block, "Do Positive Illusions Foster Mental Health? An Examination of the Taylor and Brown Formulation" (hereafter "Mental Health?") (July 1994), 3–20. They argue that "the logic and empirical evidence used to relate mental health to [positive illusions]···failed to substantiate Taylor and Brown's thesis," and that "more recent studies on positive illusions and mental health also failed to lend support" to this thesis. Since then, the Taylor-Brown thesis has also received a thorough drubbing by Owen Flanagan, *The Really Hard Problem: Meaning in a Material World* (2009), chapter 5. Flanagan's approach is different from mine, but like me, he also questions both the data used by Taylor-Brown and their interpretation of it.

or degree of control than most other students at the same university; (ii) most students rate themselves more positively on their attributes than do observers; and (iii) it is logically impossible for most students to have better life prospects than most other students; moreover, (iv) base rate data cannot justify their optimism about the future ("Illusion and Well-Being," 2; "Positive Illusions," 22).[19]

The first problem with the Taylor-Brown thesis is that it generalizes results achieved from experiments with college students to the American population at large, as though college students are representative of the general population. Given their youth and inexperience, we should expect students to be particularly susceptible to the illusion of control and to exaggerated optimism. Let us grant, however, that most people do regard themselves as being happier and higher on their abilities, achievements, degree of control, and future prospects than they do most others, even most others from a similar socioeconomic background. Does it follow, as Taylor and Brown argue in (i) and (iii) above, that all of them, or even a majority, are laboring under an illusion? It does not. Depending on the figures, it could well be that only a small minority is laboring under an illusion.[20]

Let us suppose that 60% think that they are happier, better, and have a brighter future than 60%. Only 20% of them *have* to be wrong, for it is certainly possible for 40% to outshine the other 60% in all these respects. So only 20% of the population could be laboring under positive illusions. In the absence of a figure for what the respondents have in mind when they compare themselves with "most people," Taylor and Brown cannot conclude from the data that most people are systematically, even if mildly,

---

[19.] Taylor and Brown also state that most people believe that they can control an outcome even in situations of chance. Colvin and Block question this claim by pointing out that in the studies they cite, "the difference between the depressed and nondepressed groups in regard to the illusion of personal control existed only at the outset of the experiment" ("Mental Health?", 8). Colvin and Block surmise, correctly I believe, that the nondepressed subjects' illusion at the outset of the experiment "stems from the application by these generally effective subjects of their typical expectations to an unfamiliar and novel situation." When these subjects learn the nature of the situation, the difference between them and the depressed subjects disappears. Perhaps most damning, Colvin and Block cite research that shows that "[s]light experimental variations can reverse the illusion of control effect such that depressed people overestimate their control of the situation and nondepressed people provide accurate estimates of control" (ibid., 8). Last but not least, even if Taylor and Brown are right that nondepressed people tend to believe they can control situations where they have no control, it would not be germane to their thesis, since such an illusion would be extreme, not mild.

[20.] Colvin and Block also point out that some of the respondents could, in fact, be happier and healthier than most people, but do not draw the conclusion that the vast majority of them could be ("Mental Health?", 14).

deluded about themselves. The same considerations apply to argument (iv), according to which people's optimism about the future is not supported by base rate data. Here again, depending on the figures, it is possible that only a small minority is overly optimistic. Indeed, even if 95% think that they are better and faced with a brighter future than 51% of people, only a minority has to be wrong. For surely 49% could be better and faced with a better future than 51%. That would leave only 46% to be wrong—a large figure, indeed, but not a logically impossible one. At any rate, there is no evidence that 95% of people believe this.

Everyday observation also suggests that most people are neither unrealistically positive about themselves across the board, nor overly optimistic about the future most of the time. Most of us are realistic in some domains of our lives, unrealistically optimistic or pessimistic in some others, and neither consistently realistic nor unrealistic in the rest. Indeed, Taylor and Brown themselves start to importantly qualify their claim that most people live under the influence of positive illusions when they say that "there are ways in which people exhibit self-corrective tendencies over time" because of "the need to monitor reality effectively" ("Positive Illusions," 25). In the rest of the passage, however, they reiterate their view that most people are given to positive illusions most of the time, especially when "they are in an implemental mindset, attempting to put a decision into effect" (ibid., 25–26).

To return to their arguments: (ii) relies on the fact that most people rate themselves more positively on their attributes than do observers ("Illusion," 195–196). But why assume that the observers are more accurate than the subjects?[21] If most people tend to think more highly of themselves than

---

[21.]Colvin and Block also question this assumption, noting that one of the empirical studies cited by Taylor and Brown for the discrepancy between self-ratings and observer ratings used undergraduate observers, and that "the observational basis for the ratings" was brief, leading to an extremely low agreement on the four negative attributes among the observers, and only a .49 on the seventeen desirable attributes ("Mental Health?", 8). Colvin and Block also reveal other problematic features of the study in question, including the fact that although the subject groups consisted of (i) depressed subjects; (ii) "psychiatric control" subjects, that is, non-depressed individuals with other psychiatric problems; and (iii) normal controls, that is, non-depressed individuals without any psychiatric problems, the student observers were told that all the subjects were depressed ("Mental Health?" 8). This negative bias led them to rate, on average, the "members of all three groups as below the midpoint on the dimension labeled as 'social competence'," and, on average, below the ratings of "the members of all three groups" (ibid.). But since depressed people have lower self-esteem, they rated themselves lower than the others, and were thus closer to the ratings of the observers. The lower discrepancy, however, could simply be the result of two equally illusory negatively biased ratings, whereas the greater discrepancy in the case of the "normals" could be the result of greater objectivity on their part and negative illusions on the part of the undergraduate observers. Colvin and Block

of others, it could be not that they are inflating their own merits vis-à-vis the facts, but that they are deflating other people's. Suppose, however, that most people *are* systematically mildly deluded about themselves. On what grounds do Taylor and Brown claim that they are mentally healthy or happy? One reason they cite is simply that most people cannot be mentally unhealthy or unhappy.[22] This conclusion, however, is too quick. There are degrees of mental health and happiness, just as there are degrees of physical health and of virtue. People who are neither depressed nor psychotic (unhealthy) can still be dissatisfied or neurotic to varying degrees (less than fully healthy). The proliferation of therapists, counselors, gurus, and self-help books is evidence enough that dissatisfaction and neurosis are alive and well (a fact that also challenges the claim of widespread positive illusions). So whereas we can agree, for both empirical and conceptual reasons, that most people in a productive, vibrant society such as the United States can't be insane, we have little reason to agree that most people are as healthy or happy (or virtuous) as they can realistically be.

Let us grant, however, that most people *are* as healthy and happy as they can be. On what do Taylor and Brown base their claim that this is so *because* of their illusions? They base it on the putative fact that the more realistic individuals tend to be depressed. But as Colvin and Block have shown, research on the so-called "depressed realists" is contradictory or ambiguous. Indeed, Taylor and Brown themselves acknowledge in their 1994 article that several studies indicate that depressives are negatively biased towards themselves rather than realistic, and that there might *be* no "depressed realists" ("Positive Illusions," 21). This dramatic, but underplayed, admission renders Taylor and Brown's central thesis empty. The thesis, it will be recalled, is comparative: it states that mild positive illusions are *more conducive* to happiness and mental health than realism. So we need a group of unhappy or at least less happy realists to compare with the "normals"—that is, the deluded Upbeat. Taylor and Brown maintain that even if depressed people are not realistic, their original thesis remains intact.[23] But if the Downbeat are unrealistic, *there is no example of depressed realists with whom to compare the Upbeat,* and hence

---

also question the other studies and review articles used by Taylor and Brown to support their thesis.

[22] "Positive Illusions," 22. Taylor and Brown mention only mental health here, but since they think that mental health requires happiness, it is safe to assume that they think their argument applies to happiness as well.

[23] At this point, however, Taylor and Brown reinterpret their original thesis as the relatively innocuous view that "Most healthy adults are positively biased in their self-perceptions" ("Positive Illusion," 1994, 22). But given the fact that there are degrees of health, this is hardly a challenge to the traditional view that we would be healthier without illusions.

no evidence for the thesis that positive illusions about oneself are *more* conducive to happiness and health than realism. The most Taylor and Brown can claim is that those who have *positive* illusions feel better about themselves (unsurprisingly), and are nicer and more creative, than those who have *negative* illusions about themselves. But to say this is hardly a point against realism: it is a point against negative illusions vis-à-vis positive illusions (if you have to drink poison, better sweet poison than bitter.)

For the sake of argument, however, let us assume that future research gives us evidence for the existence of depressed realists. Taylor and Brown's thesis that mildly deluded people are happier and healthier than realistic people still faces problems.

5.3.3 The thesis that positive illusions promote happiness is based largely on self-reports. But how reliable are these self-reports? Like most people, the subjects also likely believe that happiness is, to some extent, an achievement, especially when it is understood (as it often is), not only as contentment but also as enjoyment of life and a sense of meaning. But the subjects who are given to illusions about their other achievements will also be given to illusions about their achievement of happiness. Indeed, we have some of the same reasons for thinking that they inflate their happiness as for thinking that they inflate their abilities and other achievements: *they rate themselves as happier than most people.*[24] Although Taylor and Brown faithfully report this finding, they fail to notice that it undermines their thesis that positive illusions promote happiness rather than simply the *illusion* thereof.[25]

There is also a deeper, conceptual reason why people who harbor positive illusions about themselves must also harbor illusions about their level of happiness. The reason is that the emotions and evaluations that express or constitute their illusions about their abilities, achievements, and future prospects—a sense of self-worth and personal efficacy, and a sense that

---

[24] "Illusions and Well-Being," 198. As I argued in Section 5.3.2, this in itself need not show anything more than that a small minority is deluded about their achievements, etc. My point here is that, whatever the number of deluded people, we have the same grounds for being skeptical about their self-reported happiness as about their other self-reported achievements.

[25] Some readers have objected that there is no difference between self-deceptively believing you're happy and being happy. I disagree. The logical structure of self-deceptive happiness is no different from that of self-deceptive beliefs. If someone believes *p* self-deceptively, it follows that deep down he doesn't *really* believe *p*. Likewise, if someone deceives himself about (the extent of) his happiness, it follows that deep down he is not *really* (that) happy. At best, in the two cases, he sort-of believes *p* and sort-of feels happy, while also believing not-*p* and feeling not-happy, respectively. Or perhaps his feelings and beliefs are unstable, "evanescent," subject to sudden shifts, as self-deceptive feelings and beliefs often are (Sartre, "Self-Deception," in *Existentialism from Dostoevsky to Sartre*, 1975, 299–328).

the future is bright and open to their endeavors—together entail a sense of meaning and enjoyment of life. To the extent that one lacks a sense of meaning or enjoyment, one must either lack a sense of self-worth and personal efficacy, or lack hope for the future. It follows, then, that insofar as happiness consists of these unwarranted evaluations and emotions, the connection between happiness and illusions is a conceptual, and not a causal, one. In other words, people who are deluded about their abilities, achievements, degree of control, and future prospects *must* be deluded about their happiness.[26] Taylor and Brown fail to see this because they fail to see that happiness is not merely a sense of contentment.

In short, the research on which Taylor and Brown base their case does not show that positive illusions promote happiness. To the extent that happiness is an achievement, there are no empirical grounds for thinking that people's positive illusions lead to greater happiness rather than simply to an *illusion* of greater happiness; and to the extent that happiness consists of the positive emotions and evaluations that express or constitute these illusions, the connection between their happiness and their illusions is a conceptual, and not a causal, one.

5.3.4 Taylor and Brown also hold that the Upbeats' positive illusions enable them to be more creative or productive, more able "to grow, develop, and self-actualize," more open to "new ideas and people," and more caring of other people than the Downbeats. But this thesis is subject to the same two counterarguments insofar as the evidence for their greater creativity and so on is based on the Upbeats' self-reports. Taylor and Brown do cite additional research, but this research is only "suggestive evidence" that the ability to be creative, caring, open, and so on is promoted by positive illusions about oneself ("Illusion and Well-Being," 200).

Let us suppose, however, that the credibility of the factual claim is not at issue, and the Upbeats really are all that Taylor and Brown claim them to be. The question now is why we should accept the causal claim that it is *because* of their positive illusions that the Upbeats have these features. Taylor and Brown's argument for this causal claim relies on the prior claim that realistic people are less likely to have these features, because they are more likely to be depressed and lack a sense of self-worth. It is certainly true that if we are down in the dumps about our worth or competence, the motivation to be creative, to be open to growth and change, and to be caring

---

[26.] See also Colvin and Block: "It is not surprising (and perhaps is even tautological or definitional) that individuals high on self-esteem, with a sense of control of their lives, and with optimism about the future are happier than individuals lacking these self-evaluations" ("Mental Health?" 16).

of others, is undercut. In such a state, new ideas and people are likely to be threatening. This is the sort of psychological truism that leads Nietzsche to declare in one of his famous—and famously one-sided–aphorisms that it is not virtue that produces happiness, but happiness that produces virtue (*Twilight*, 58–59). But should we accept the claim that those who are down in the dumps about themselves are down because of their greater realism? So far I have proceeded on the assumption that further research will provide empirical evidence for this view. It is time now to question it.

5.3.5 The view in question is that the Downbeat are more realistic than the Upbeat, and depressed because of their realism. But if the Downbeat really are more realistic about their lives (and do not suffer from a naturally depressive temperament that prevents them from feeling happy, regardless of the facts), then it must be that the truth about their lives really is depressing. Perhaps they have been slothful or weak or pusillanimous, or perhaps they have only been incredibly unfortunate in their circumstances. If this is the case, however, their depression is due not to their realism alone, but also to the sad reality of their lives; after all, if this reality were positive, being realistic about their lives would be uplifting, not depressing. True, if they were extremely deluded about themselves, they could see their sloth, weakness, or pusillanimity as evidence of their good-natured, laid-back, live and let-live attitude towards life and, thus, they could feel good about themselves. But extreme self-delusion, Taylor and Brown agree, is incompatible with the ability to grow and change and other criteria of mental health, criteria that their mildly self-deluded subjects apparently meet. If, however, the circumstances of their lives are positive, and they still come down hard on themselves, then it must be either that they have negative illusions about themselves, or that they see the facts for what they are but have unrealistic expectations of themselves.

The depression and low self-esteem of the Downbeat, then, has to be explained by one or more of the following three factors: they have a naturally depressive temperament; they are realistic, but have nothing to be happy about; or, they have something to be happy about, but lack the realism to see it or to evaluate it by realistic standards. Insofar as they lack this last, they lack the practical wisdom to accept either their own particular limitations or the limitations of human nature or both. In none of these cases is it realism that is at fault; indeed, in the last case greater realism is essential for lifting their depression.

The upshot is that, even if further research were to show a high correlation between realism on the one hand, and depression, low self-esteem, lack of creativity, and so on on the other, Taylor and Brown would not be justified in drawing the conclusion that the depression and low self-esteem were a result of too much realism. Without this premise, however, Taylor and Brown have no grounds for asserting that the greater happiness, creativity, openness to new ideas and people, and so on, of the Upbeat are due to their positive illusions. Indeed, not only do Taylor and Brown lack the empirical basis they need for their claim that positive illusions are more likely to promote happiness and mental health than realism, they have empirical grounds for believing the exact opposite. For there is some evidence that some people are *both* more realistic *and* happier and healthier than Taylor and Brown's "normals."[27] Surprisingly, however, Taylor and Brown have nothing to say about them.

In any case, we can see independently of empirical research why realistic self-perceptions are more conducive to mental health than illusory ones. Growth and change are motivated by a perception of one's shortcomings, or by the aspiration to realize one's full potential by challenging oneself, and openness to new people and ideas is made more likely by a secure sense of self. To the extent that people are given to rosy illusions about their traits, abilities, or achievements, they lack the first motivation for growth and change; to the extent that they have rosy illusions about the degree to which they have fulfilled their potential, they lack the second motivation for change. Moreover, to the extent that these illusions are due to self-deception rather than inculpable ignorance, their psychological investment in their illusions creates barriers against ideas and people who might puncture these illusions. Hence, whatever openness to growth and change people with positive illusions possess must be *in spite of* these illusions, not *because* of them.[28]

It is important to note that there are deep psychological and moral differences between those who are given to self-deception and those who are fundamentally reality-oriented but ignorant of themselves. It is a commonplace that knowledge of the external world is a life-long enterprise requiring experience, attention, and study. But knowledge of the self is no different in this respect. Hence it is not surprising that most of us have large areas of

---

[27] See Colvin and Block ("Mental Health?" 7), who cite studies by W.C. Compton, "Are Positive Illusions Necessary for Self-Esteem: A Research Note" (1992), 1343–1344; and J. Block and H. Thomas, "Is Satisfaction with Self a Measure of Adjustment?" (1955), 254–259.

[28] Colvin, Block, and David C. Funder, "Overly Positive Self-Evaluations and Personality: Negative Implications for Mental Health," provide empirical support for the claim that people with positive illusions about themselves show "poor social skills and psychological maladjustment five years before and five years after the assessment of self-enhancement" (1995), 1152–1162, at 1152.

ignorance about ourselves, that no one is completely self-knowledgeable. And what is true of most adults is even more true of college students. But people whose illusions are chiefly due to lack of experience rather than self-deception can still be fundamentally reality-oriented and, thus, open to new ideas and people, to growth and change. In such people, illusions are always in process of being whittled away. In lumping everyone with positive illusions together, Taylor and Brown fail to appreciate these differences.

Highly realistic people—people who tend to see themselves and others as they are, and who appraise themselves and others by realistic standards—are motivated to grow and change both by an awareness of their shortcomings, and by a desire to challenge themselves. Free of façade and defensiveness, they are unafraid of the truth and, thus, open to the challenge of new ideas and people. Such people are also highly likely to feel fulfilled. If Taylor and Brown were right, however, it would follow that, other things being equal, highly realistic, healthy, and fulfilled people would tend to become healthier (and happier) if they became slightly deluded about themselves. It would also follow that healthy, fulfilled, but somewhat deluded people would tend to become less healthy (and less fulfilled) if they became more accurate in their perceptions as well as more realistic in their expectations and standards. But this amounts to saying that people who have less reason to be open to new ideas and people, and who are thus less likely to grow and change, are more likely to be open to new ideas and people, and thus more likely to grow and change. And his claim is incoherent. Hence it is not only unsupported by any empirical evidence, it is immune to empirical evidence.

5.3.6 One more claim needs to be addressed, namely, that unrealistic optimism among terminally ill patients leads to a greater (unrealistic) sense of control and a reduction in depression, pain, and disability ("Positive Illusions," 24). Taylor and Brown's discussion focuses on a study by Taylor et al. of gay men at risk of AIDS.[29] In this study, men who test positive for the HIV virus apparently show more optimism about not developing AIDS in their responses to the AIDS-specific optimism (ASO) questionnaire than men who test negative. The illusory nature of their optimism is shown by their answers on the ASO, in which some

---

[29] Shelley E. Taylor, Margaret E. Kemeny, Lisa G. Aspinwall, Stephen G. Schneider, Richard Rodriguez, and Mark Herbert, "Optimism, Coping, Psychological Distress, and High-Risk Sexual Behavior Among Men at Risk for Acquired Immunodeficiency Syndrome (AIDS)" (hereafter "Optimism") (1992), 462–473.

of them agree with such propositions as "I feel safe from AIDS because I've developed [or if exposed would develop] an immunity" to AIDS, and "I think my immune system would be (is) more capable of fighting the AIDS virus than that of other gay men" ("Optimism," 469).

Overall, however, both the HIV-positive and the HIV-negative men disagree with the optimistic statements on the six-item ASO questionnaire, with means for the former at 1.94 and for the latter at 1.72 on a scale of 1 to 5 (ibid., 463).[30] So it is misleading to claim that the HIV-positive men's responses show greater optimism rather than simply a little less pessimism. Moreover, even the claim of lesser pessimism is contradicted by the results of various other self-report measures, according to which, as Taylor et al. themselves report, HIV-positive men "see themselves to be at greater risk of developing AIDS," have less of a sense of control over AIDS, and have more worries than the HIV-negative men (ibid., 472). It cannot be true *both* that HIV-positive men are less pessimistic about acquiring AIDS *and* that they "have higher levels of AIDS-related worries and concerns" than HIV-negative men; and it cannot be true *both* that they have "greater feelings of control" *and* that they "see themselves as having less control over AIDS" than HIV-negative men. Perhaps the HIV-positive men's less pessimistic responses to the ASO questionnaire reflect their state of mind when they respond to statements that express optimism, and their more pessimistic responses to statements about AIDS-related worries reflect their state of mind when they respond to statements that express pessimism. But they cannot be both less and more pessimistic overall than the HIV-negative men.

But let us assume that the HIV-positive men are somewhat less pessimistic overall than the HIV-negative men, and ask why this might be so. Taylor et al. offer the plausible explanation that it is because the HIV-positive men have decided to try and prolong their lives by avoiding risky behavior and engaging in various coping techniques ("Optimism," 472). But this, of course, is the reverse of the thesis Taylor et al. (ibid., 460, 470) and Taylor and Brown ("Positive Illusions," 21, 24) set out to defend, namely, that the positive behavior and reduced distress are the *result* of their lesser pessimism. And although it is possible for the lesser pessimism about developing AIDS, on the one hand, and the efforts to prevent it, on the other, to become mutually reinforcing, each cannot be the initial cause of the other.

---

[30] See Colvin and Block, "Mental Health?" 11.

At any rate, those who falsely believe that they are immune to AIDS have no reason to do anything to protect themselves from it. So if they do try to protect themselves from it, it must be because they do not really, truly believe that they are immune—they are merely indulging in a bit of inert magical thinking when answering the ASO questionnaire, thinking that has no effect on their behavior.[31] The other clearly illusory belief, that they can eliminate the virus from their system if they take certain actions, *can* lead them to take those actions and delay or prevent AIDS—but so can the true belief that they might be able to delay or prevent AIDS if they take certain actions, a belief that they also hold.[32] In addition, it is well-known that having a positive attitude has health-promoting benefits of its own. Consequently, if they adopt a positive attitude because they believe that having a positive attitude has health-promoting benefits, then their positive attitude is realistic.[33] So while the false belief and an unrealistically positive attitude *can* produce the desired result, they are not *more conducive* to this result than the true belief and realistic optimism. Moreover, to the extent that people genuinely hold the false belief that they are immune to AIDS or that they can eliminate the virus from their system, they are likely to feel more unhappy when the disease catches up with them. They are also at greater risk of leaving important projects incomplete or undone: financial affairs neglected, frayed relationships unpatched, amends unmade, goodbyes unsaid, and so on. And all this can only add to their unhappiness when they finally do get full-blown AIDS.

Taylor et al. grant the possibility that the "optimists" will feel more unhappy if they develop AIDS. But they also argue that, since

[31] In situations of extreme stress, there is often a tendency to engage in magical thinking ("I'm probably immune to AIDS." "He's not really dead—I'll see him when I wake up in the morning,") even while acting on realistic beliefs.

[32] As shown by the HIV-positive men's low score (1.95) on the Fatalistic Vulnerability scale ("Optimism," 465). This score shows that most HIV-positive men strongly disagree that they will definitely develop AIDS, or that the spread of AIDS is inevitable (ibid., 471). Their disagreement with these statements indicates that they believe (truly) that they can do something about their condition.

[33] It might be thought that whether it is realistic or not depends on the statistics. Suppose they are told that they have only a 5% chance of survival, and that a positive attitude will increase their chance to 10%. Statistically speaking, it is still more realistic for them to believe that they will die. But I am not sure if a positive attitude adopted as a tool to bring about a desired result should be treated like a belief. It is more like a low-risk action taken to avoid a highly aversive result and achieve a highly desirable one, an action that, although unlikely to achieve the desired result, is justified by the expected utility of the result. There are, however, other cases where things work better with false beliefs or the ability to suspend disbelief. These include placebos, being fooled about the identity of a murderer in a whodunit, suspending disbelief during a fantasy film, and so on. None of these, however, involve being unreality-oriented about the important facts of life.

"seropositive optimists as well as pessimists *readily acknowledge their risk and AIDS-related worries and concerns,* it seems unlikely that they will be greatly surprised if they subsequently develop…AIDS" (ibid., 472; italics mine). Moreover, they continue, "inasmuch as optimism has been consistently associated with superior coping…it may be that *the optimists will simply shift their expectations to accommodate the new reality….*" (ibid.)

Given Taylor et al.'s view that the optimists are unrealistic, however, this argument borders on incoherence. If the optimists are as ready to acknowledge the realities of their condition as the pessimists, and better able "to accommodate the new reality" than the pessimists, then they must be more realistic than the pessimists, even if they occasionally espouse some bizarre beliefs. In any case, since very few HIV-positive men espouse bizarre beliefs about their condition, most of those who cope well must do so with the help of realistic optimism. Once again, however, realistic optimists are never even mentioned by Taylor and Brown or Taylor et al.

5.3.7 I have argued that an unrealistically positive attitude *can*, sometimes, be health-promoting, but not more so than a realistically positive attitude. But might there not be many, many situations in which thinking makes it so, and only thinking makes it so, even when the thinking is unrealistic? Self-fulfilling attitudes, whether positive or negative, are a pervasive aspect of human psychology. As the song goes:

> Make believe you're brave
> And the trick will take you far
> You may be as brave
> As you make believe you are."[34]

Might there not be more to the Taylor-Brown thesis than I've acknowledged? I don't think so. Note, first, that both in the case of AIDS optimism and in the case of courage, positive attitudes have the desired result only insofar as they activate or develop a capacity that already exists, or insofar as there is some other causal or non-causal connection (for example, identity) between the positive attitude and the benefit. Thinking can make it so only if one of these is true, and in that case, the thinking is realistic. Thus, if courageous action can be brought about by making believe that one can act courageously on this occasion, it's because it is within one's capacity to do so. The causal mechanism here is akin to the causal mechanism activated

---

[34] From the Richard Rodgers and Oscar Hammerstein song, "I Whistle a Happy Tune," from *The King and I.*

by another's encouraging words, or by stories of courageous behavior or individuals. Making believe that I am a courageous person when I'm not is not an illusion so long as I remain aware that it is only make-believe. Such exercises of imagination are important tools for acting according to the virtue of courage and becoming a courageous person. By contrast, a coward who deceives himself into believing that he is a courageous person, without any intention of acting courageously, cannot, thereby, become a courageous person; acquisition of a virtue requires repeatedly acting in accord with it, in awareness of its importance for one's life, not repeatedly deluding oneself that one already possesses it.

Suppose, however, that I've always acted like a coward in the past. Do I then have any good reason to believe that making believe that I'm courageous will help me to act courageously on this particular occasion?[35] On the one hand, it seems rational to indulge in this make-believe if there is no better way to succeed in acting courageously; but on the other hand, it seems unrealistic and irrational to believe against the odds that there is a high probability that it will lead me to act courageously.

What is realistic or unrealistic, however, depends on the details. Perhaps acting courageously on this occasion is more important to me than in the past, when I failed. Or perhaps in the past I did not make believe that I could act courageously. Or perhaps my imaginative exercises were not accompanied by any intention of acting accordingly, and hence did not lead to anything except for some pleasant reveries featuring a courageous me. If any one of these is true, then the present occasion is relevantly different, and I am justified in believing that "inhabiting" the mind-set of a courageous person can lead me to act courageously now. The alternative—believing that I can't, or most likely can't—is simply false if past occasions have been relevantly different. But even if they haven't been different, my present expectations may be realistic if I've been making progress: every time I try, I'm less afraid and take one more step towards a full-fledged courageous action. For example, the first time I try to act courageously by pretending that I'm courageous I timidly voice my objection to a department proposal I regard as wrong, but quickly lapse into silence when others disagree; the second time I try, I make a fuller case for my view, but then join the majority when the vote is taken. The shame and regret this engenders lead me to resolve to do the right thing the next time. Is it not realistic to believe that the next time

---

[35] Thanks to Hal Thorsrud for pushing me to say more about this issue.

I will vote my conscience? Such incremental improvements with the help of a positive (non-illusory) attitude occur not only in cases of courageous or other virtuous actions, but in many, many other cases: passing a high school exam, cooking a good meal, learning to play the piano, and so on. Of course, there are objective limits to how well or reliably a particular individual can do any of these things, but most of us are capable of achieving a basic competence in most of them if we try hard enough. And this requires realistic optimism. Indeed, as the example of the dancer, Catherine Royce, shows vividly, realistic optimism can help a person in far more dramatic situations.

In a radio essay called "I Always Have a Choice," Royce, a dancer for thirty years, relates that in 2003 she discovered that she had ALS (Lou Gehrig's disease).[36] Facing the facts unflinchingly, she states that over time ALS will "destroy every significant muscle in my body. Ultimately, I will be unable to move, to speak and, finally, to breathe." But "I believe I always have a choice. No matter what I'm doing. No matter what is happening to me. I always have a choice." When she loses the power to type, she has the choice to give up writing—or to learn to use voice recognition software. She does the latter and ends up writing "more now than ever." She also has the choice to live—or to die. "I can choose to see ALS as . . . a death sentence, or I can choose to see it as an invitation—an opportunity to learn who I truly am." She does the latter, discovering "an ability to recognize, give and receive caring in a way far deeper than anything in my life before." Yet she does not pretend that ALS is a blessing in disguise, and she does not have any illusions of control over it. She is optimistic, though fully aware of the terrible course of her disease, and she knows that she always has a choice, though fully aware that her choices are restricted. Her life, until she chooses to die, is both objectively worthwhile and fulfilling, because her realistic optimism not only enables her to cope with her terrible disease, but even use it to enrich her life in new ways.[37]

[36.] Catherine Royce, "I Always Have A Choice." Special Series: "This I Believe." *National Public Radio*, December 4, 2006 (http://www.npr.org/templates/story/story.php?storyId=6560320&sc=e maf).

[37.] Royce chose to die on March 30th, 2009. Richard Knox, "Catherine's Choice: To Die With Dignity." *National Public Radio*. April 13, 2009 (http://www.npr.org/templates/story/story. php?storyId=102923424).

5.4. Conclusion

The claim that realism is an important means to happiness faces challenges both from common sense and from social psychology. I have defended it against both challenges. Common sense is right in holding that some truths can be disastrous for us, robbing us of happiness as well as of the ability to respond in worthwhile ways, and that being reality-oriented is more likely to lead us to such truths. In such cases, some happiness based on illusion is better than utter misery based on truth. But it does not follow from this that being habitually self-deceived or ignorant is more likely to lead to happiness. On the contrary, we have seen good reason to believe that being habitually self-deceived or ignorant about oneself is far more likely to lead to unhappiness.

We have also seen good reason for rejecting Taylor and Brown's claim that most people are given to mild positive illusions about themselves and their future prospects, and that such illusions are more likely than realism to promote happiness. Contrary to the first part of this claim, psychological research gives no reason to believe that most people are given to mild positive illusions about themselves, *simpliciter*. Rather, experience suggests that most people are mixed, harboring (mostly) positive illusions in some areas of their lives, (mostly) negative illusions in some others, and (mostly) realism in yet others. The second part of the claim, that mildly deluded people are happier and healthier, faces even more objections. Even if most people are mildly deluded, to the extent that their delusions are due to self-deception rather than simple ignorance, we cannot, for both empirical and conceptual reasons, use their self-reports to claim a causal connection between their illusions and their happiness. These reasons apply as well to the Upbeats' self-reports of greater mental health. The remaining empirical evidence for a causal connection between positive illusions and health is only "suggestive". Further, there is no good evidence for the existence of "depressed realists," so the thesis that realists are less likely to be happy or healthy than somewhat self-deluded people lacks a referent. But even if depressed realists existed, their depression could be due to a naturally depressive temperament, or to their unrealistic standards for themselves, or to the sad reality of their lives, rather than to realism per se. Indeed, some psychological research provides evidence of realists who are happier and healthier than people with positive illusions. The claim that positive illusions about oneself promote creativity, growth, and so on, even if one is self-deceptively invested in safeguarding those illusions against challenge, defies explanation, whereas the contrary claim is easily explained. Neither empirical research nor philosophical argument supports the idea that illusory optimism about AIDS helps people cope better with their condition than realistic optimism. Make-believe can help to produce positive results when there is some causal or non-causal connection (for example, identity) between the positive attitude and the result, and in such cases, making believe is realistic. The example of Catherine Royce shows how realistic optimism can help a person not only cope with her condition but even enrich her life. Royce is an exemplar of the courageous, life-affirming, well-functioning individual that philosophers and psychologists from Aristotle to Maslow and Rogers have held up as models for us to aspire to. It is hard to see how any illusion about her condition or her future prospects could possibly contribute to her health or happiness.

Realistic optimism about oneself and one's future thus beats unrealistic optimism on both counts: happiness and objective worth. The disposition to be realistic about what matters in human life in general and one's own life in particular, and to adopt realistic standards of evaluation, entails life-enriching traits such as generosity, fairness or justice, a perspective that allows us to take things in stride, open-mindedness, productivity, the courage to grow, fortitude, and overall good functioning. Indeed, it entails all the central (neo-Aristotelian) virtues, since all of them express our recognition, as Aristotle puts it, of the true worth of things (*NE* 1115 b 17–24), and the disposition to act accordingly. This is implicit in the idea that virtue aims at good ends for the right reasons, with the right means, in the right manner, and at the right time.

In the next chapter I explicate and defend a neo-Aristotelian conception of virtue as a psychologically plausible and attractive conception that is well-suited to play an essential role in well-being as the HPG. Actual virtue—virtue as it is instantiated in human beings —is a domain-specific and less-than-perfect trait; this understanding of virtue is necessary for the plausibility of the *eudaimonist* claim that well-being requires virtue. But I reject the claim sometimes made that our characters are not only inconsistent but fragmented, a veritable jumble of good and bad traits, without any rhyme or reason. On this view, too, it is hard to defend the *eudaimonist* thesis.

In chapter 7 I defend the claim that well-being as the HPG entails a virtuous life against a variety of counterarguments; it is only through such successful defenses that the claim can prove its resilience and acquire the thick mantle of plausibility that is its due.

CHAPTER 6 | Virtue

On the whole, tho' I never arrived at the Perfection I had been so
ambitious of obtaining, but fell far short of it, yet as I was, by the
Endeavor, a better and a happier Man than I otherwise should have
been if I had not attempted it.

—BENJAMIN FRANKLIN

No human face is exactly the same in its lines on each side, no leaf
perfect in its lobes, no branch in its symmetry.

—JOHN RUSKIN

6.1. Introduction

Virtue in Aristotle's view is an integrated intellectual-emotional disposition to think, feel, and act "at the right times, about the right things,
towards the right people, for the right end, and in the right way" (*NE*
1106b21–24), and to take pleasure in so doing.[1] In Section 6.2, I argue
that, with some important qualifications, this conception is plausible both
psychologically and normatively. Like much contemporary psychology
as well as ordinary thought, but unlike rival conceptions of virtue, this
conception recognizes that both emotion and intellect play a crucial role
in practical rationality and moral motivation. It also recognizes that virtue requires good ends. Everyday thought is not, of course, consistent on
either of these points, but there are good reasons to accept the stated views
over their contraries. The multifaceted nature of this conception of virtue,
encompassing not only means and ends, but also manner and timing, also

---

[1] All references to Aristotle are to his *Nicomachean Ethics* unless otherwise stated.

constitutes a highly plausible conception of moral excellence, a conception that makes it clear why virtue is worth striving for.

In Section 6.3, I fill out my suggestion in chapter 1 that this conception of virtue and the conception of *eudaimonia* as happiness in an objectively worthwhile life are "made for each other". I discuss and reject a challenge to this claim by Swanton, who argues that although virtue is necessary for *eudaimonia*, it can also be harmful for the agent without the intervention of any bad luck.

I then go on to reject the implicit globalism of Aristotle's conception of virtue, at least insofar as it is thought of as an attribute of real people rather than only an ideal to aspire to (6.4). Globalism holds that, for example, a kind or courageous person is kind or courageous in every sort of situation that calls for kindness or courage—that is, he is globally or cross-situationally consistent in these virtues. But such a person is hard, if not impossible, to come by. So the idea that virtue must be global invites the response that in that case no one is virtuous, and *eudaimonism*, which claims that well-being as the HPG requires a life of virtue, is false, since many people do have well-being. However, if we accept that virtue can be less than global, this objection no longer has a basis. Global virtue is an ideal to aspire to, and a standard of actual virtue, but actual virtue always falls short of the ideal. Indeed, for reasons I give below, it is psychologically impossible for any character trait, other than vice, to be global.

In 6.5 I explicate my conception of virtue (and other traits) as narrowly domain-specific and defend it against objections. Some philosophers who agree that actual virtue falls short of the ideal of global virtue nevertheless insist that *genuine* virtue is global. On this view, if well-being as the HPG requires virtue, it follows that no one has any genuine well-being. This, too, is hard to believe. More importantly, I argue, this conception of genuine virtue contradicts a crucial premise of a *eudaimonist* virtue ethics. I conclude this section by addressing the unity of virtue thesis, and arguing for what I call a "limited" unity.

Another threat to the claim that *eudaimonia* entails virtue comes from the radical thesis that our character traits are not only compartmentalized, they are fragmented, such that we can have a virtue in one narrowly defined type of situation and vice in every other type of situation, or worse, that the same action can be simultaneously expressive of both virtue and vice in the same token situation (Section 6.6).[2] But the idea of fragmented

---

[2.] See John M. Doris, *Lack of Character: Personality and Moral Behavior* (hereafter *Lack of Character*) (2002), chapter 4.

virtue contradicts the inherent generality of moral motivation and practical wisdom, and makes a mystery of virtue acquisition. So does the idea that a single action can express both virtue and vice (and both well-being and ill-being). Indeed, the latter view is incoherent on the neo-Aristotelian conception of virtue (and well-being).

I limit my discussion to the cardinal virtues of justice, honesty, courage, integrity, kindness, and the virtues that are partly constitutive of these virtues: practical wisdom, and regard for self and others as moral agents and patients.

6.2. The Descriptive and Normative Adequacy of Neo-Aristotelian Virtue

6.2.1 What must virtue be like to be the height of moral achievement? What must a virtuous person be like to be a moral exemplar? In this section I provide a sketch of each without making the claim that anyone actually achieves that height in every aspect of her life.

(i) The most obvious requirement for virtue to be the height of moral achievement is that it should make us reliably and appropriately responsive to the morally relevant features of the situations we find ourselves in. Just as a reliable mountain guide is better than an unreliable one, so a trait that makes us reliably responsive to morally relevant features is better than a trait that doesn't. And for this it is not enough simply to have a good heart; one must also have integrated intellectual-emotional dispositions. Someone who has a good heart but not a good head will often act on impulse, without due consideration of the nature of the situation or the consequences of his actions. If he sees a stranger struggling with a large box, he will help him, without asking what the stranger is doing with one leg inside his neighbor's side window at 1 a.m. When friends appeal to him for help, he will give away whatever he has, without thought of how he will pay his rent. Such a person lacks virtue because he lacks practical wisdom.[3]

A virtuous person has an understanding of right ends and right means, and of the costs and consequences of alternative actions, both for himself and for others, and this too is a matter of practical wisdom. It is practical wisdom that turns our "natural virtues" (the positive self- and

---

[3] On practical wisdom, see Aristotle, *NE* 1144b 31–32; John Cooper, *Human Good* (1986), 61ff.; Nancy Sherman, *The Fabric of Character* (1989), 242–243; Annas, *Intelligent Virtue* (2012).

other-regarding propensities that nature has endowed us with), and the emotional dispositions we have acquired in the course of our early moral development to tell the truth, risk danger, help, or empathize, into the moral virtues of honesty, courage, generosity, or kindness. We also need practical wisdom to make our often vague or indeterminate ends determinate, and to analyze the situation we find ourselves in to determine what is appropriate in the circumstances, what feasible, and how best to achieve it. This sort of practical wisdom and, therefore, virtue, comes only with wide experience. (This is just one reason, as we'll see below, why we should not expect anyone to be globally virtuous.)

(ii) Equally, however, someone who has a good head but not a good heart will often fail to notice the morally relevant features of a situation. For example, he might be committed to honesty, but if he lacks sufficient empathy, he might not notice that the recipient of his honesty is in bad shape and cannot handle the painful truth right now, even though it is a truth that must be told at some point. Or he might sincerely want to help, but lack the sympathy and imagination needed for taking another's perspective. Such a person will often fail to strike the right note in certain sorts of situations, and thus end up acting in ways that are, to quote Philippa Foot, "deeply discouraging and debilitating."[4] People like him are less reliable moral agents than those whose emotions are integrated with their (right) intellectual convictions. They seem to lack true feeling for others, or the ability to put themselves in others' shoes. So we need both the right convictions and judgments and well-tempered emotions to be morally excellent. As Aristotle puts it, "Prudence [practical wisdom], this eye of the soul, cannot reach its fully developed state without virtue," the emotional dispositions at the mean (*NE* 1144a 30).[5]

The examples I have just given show that the idea that emotions are essential for moral cognition and motivation is part of everyday thought. But for those who find this idea strange, it may help to observe that it is simply the obverse of the idea that emotions can prevent or disrupt rational thought and action. Just as the emotions of someone who is self-centered, prejudiced, or shortsighted direct his attention away from the morally salient facts and motivate him to do the self-centered, prejudiced, or shortsighted thing, so the emotions of someone who is just, objective, and

---

[4] Philippa Foot, "Virtues and Vices" (1978), 1–18, at 4.
[5] On the importance of emotional training in virtue development see M.F. Burnyeat, "Aristotle on Learning to be Good" (1980), 69–92, and A.W. Price, "Emotions in Plato and Aristotle" (2010), 121–142. Online at DOI: 10.1093/oxfordhb/9780199235018.003.0006, January 2010.

discerning direct his attention to the morally salient facts and motivate him to do the just thing. Emotions involve appraisals of situations or events as, roughly speaking, good or bad, fitting or not fitting, and the appraisals we make depend to a large extent (though not entirely) on our character.[6]

The idea that well-tempered emotions are necessary for characteristically making the right choices is now widely recognized in the philosophical literature and supported by a mass of psychological and neurological data.[7] Indeed, the data support the view that we need emotions to make decisions at all, not only in complex situations, but even in simple ones, where nothing terribly important hangs on our decision.[8] The neurologist Antonio Damasio discusses patients who, after brain surgery or brain damage, emerge with unimpaired IQs but impaired emotional faculties. These patients sometimes become hyperrational, producing endless arguments for and against each of two possible choices, unable to settle on either.[9] One of these patients, Elliot, cannot even decide on an appointment time to see Damasio again, because there are reasons for and against any time Damasio proposes. Elliot also loses the ability to sympathize with anyone, including himself: he is left unmoved by his own tragedy. The problem with people like Elliot, according to Damasio, is that they have

---

[6.] Not entirely, because we are also subject to emotional contagion, that is, to catching other people's emotions and, perhaps, to other sorts of immediate, emotional, reactions to situations. My claim that our appraisals depend to a large extent on our character is consistent with both the cognitive and the noncognitive theories of emotion, an excellent discussion of which appears in Amy Coplan, "Feeling Without Thinking" (2010), 132–151. The cognitive theory holds that emotions are, or necessarily involve, or are subordinate to, judgments or appraisals, and that any feeling or sensation that accompanies them is nonessential. The noncognitive theory of emotion holds that emotions are essentially nonrational, embodied appraisals of stimuli that may or may not be cognitive judgments and that may or may not lead to cognitive monitoring or cognitive reappraisals that either increase or diminish or change the emotion. Coplan argues that only the noncognitive theory is consistent with the claim that rational persuasion is not enough for moral education of our emotions, that different strategies, including stories, are necessary for such an education. But if, as many of us believe, our cognitive states not only affect, but are also affected by, our feelings and sensations, then these strategies are necessary for educating our emotions even if emotions are essentially cognitive judgments.

[7.] See Amélie Rorty, ed., *Explaining Emotions* (1980), and Peter Goldie, ed., *Handbook of Philosophy of Emotion* (2010), for discussions of these and other issues in the philosophy of emotion. Daniel Goleman, *Emotional Intelligence* (1995, 1997), has a lively discussion of the nature of the emotions and their role in our everyday lives.

[8.] More generally still, it seems we need emotions not only for practical reasoning—reasoning about action—but for all reasoning. As Ronald de Sousa argues in *The Rationality of Emotion* (1987), we need emotions to solve the "frame problem", i.e., the problem of knowing what is relevant and what irrelevant in the mass of data on the basis of which we must make inferences, form beliefs, and decide on action (192–196).

[9.] Antonio Damasio, *Descartes' Error: Emotion, Reason and the Human Brain* (1994). Goleman, *Emotional Intelligence*, discusses Damasio's work at 27–29, 52–54.

lost their "somatic markers," the gut feelings that enable normal people to order their priorities and decide what is good for them. Pure reason simply doesn't cut it in our practical lives.[10]

A similar conclusion was reached long ago by the psychiatrist, Hervey Cleckley, on the basis of his experience with psychopaths. Cleckley hypothesized that the psychopath's failure to care about others, or for that matter, himself, is due to an inability to see the significance of things, and that this is due to a stunted emotional capacity.[11] The psychopath can do complex calculations, and even understand, in some abstract fashion, arguments for or against a certain course of action. But none of this seems to *matter* to him, and so he remains unmoved by these rational considerations. As Daniel Goleman puts it, without emotions the intellect is blind (*Emotional Intelligence*, 53).

There is yet another reason why emotions matter to valuing and acting: namely, that some of our central values and disvalues, such as love and hate, or happiness and unhappiness, are themselves emotional states.[12] Hence those who are incapable of love or happiness must find it impossible to understand the nature and importance of these values in human life (think of the difficulty *Star Trek's* Spock has in understanding human love and associated emotions and values such as loyalty). In short, the emotional faculty is crucial not only for understanding and being motivated by certain values, but also for having many central values in the first place. Someone with a normal emotional faculty can, indeed, understand and act on rational considerations even when his emotions refuse to cooperate on a particular occasion. But without it, he can no more understand values than a color-blind person can perceive color.

(iii) A virtuous agent pursues the right ends for the right reasons with the right means, and in the right manner (*NE* II.6). When he loses an argument—or a match, or a race—he not only concedes victory because it is fair to do so, he does so graciously. Someone who recognizes that it is fair to do so, but does it angrily or resentfully—"Fine, fine, you win, but who cares!"—undercuts the very rightness of his concession and leaves a bad

---

[10.] Damasio has since studied twelve patients with frontal lobe damage and found that they, like Elliot, have lost their ability for trustworthy, reliable, responsible behavior, while retaining their IQ, memory, and logical abilities. Damasio's hypothesis is that when a certain part of the frontal lobe is damaged, and can no longer access the emotional memories stored in other parts of the brain, the individual loses the ability to put things in context and make judgments of importance.

[11.] Hervey Cleckley, *The Mask of Sanity*. 1st ed. (1941); 5th ed. (1976).

[12.] See Stocker, "How Emotions Reveal Value" (1996), 173–190, and Stocker with Elizabeth Hegeman, *Valuing Emotions* (1996), 201–202.

taste in his opponent's mouth. Someone who concedes victory graciously, but with a heroic effort, is closer to virtue, but still not quite there; he is *enkratic*. The virtuous person is the one who habitually does the right thing wholeheartedly, and therefore does it in the right manner.

(iv) The virtuous person habitually does the right thing in a more run-of-the-mill sense as well: she does what is apt in the situation. When she wants to give a pleasant surprise to her dog-loving but dog-less friend who lives on the eighth story of a one-room walk-up in New York City, she doesn't present him with a German Shepherd. When her friend's beloved mother dies on his birthday, she doesn't go to visit him with a huge "Happy Birthday" cake. Such acts show a rigidity of character—a tendency to be myopically rule-bound ("wants dog—here's a dog"; "birthday—must have cake")—that amounts to a kind of stupidity. But a virtuous agent has practical intelligence.

On this conception of character traits, then, our traits may be expressed not only in our actions or words, but also in our facial expressions, our gestures, or our bodily posture, and in almost any sort of situation. Henry James makes this very point in his essay, "The Art of Fiction," when he asks: "What is character but the determination of incident? What is incident but the illustration of character?...It is an incident for a woman to stand up with her hand resting on a table and look out at you in a certain way...At the same time it is an expression of character."[13]

It does not follow from this that even in real life character determines *every* incident: after all, both a knave and an honest man can seem sincere; what distinguishes them is that the knave's seeming so is a cultivated knavish trick, whereas the honest man's seeming so is an expression of his honesty. Nor does it follow that even in real life *every* incident of "look[ing] out...in a certain way" expresses character: after all, people can act out of character. Finally, it does not follow that even in real life we can always correctly interpret a person's isolated act without any familiarity with him, for the same nominal act can mean different things coming from different people, or the same person in different contexts. The significance of the passage from James is that it illustrates the myriad ways a person's character is expressed—in her actions, gestures, posture, and manner.

(v) A virtuous disposition must be stable—that is, persist over time. This is part of the very meaning of a character disposition. One can have a motive today but not tomorrow, and likewise a belief or a feeling; but

---

[13] http://public.wsu.edu/~campbelld/amlit/artfiction.html, accessed January 24, 2014.

(barring psychological or neurological trauma) one can no more have an intellectual-emotional-action tendency that's here today and gone tomorrow than one can have a skill at carpentry today but not tomorrow. Stability of a trait, however, does not imply permanence, as Aristotle sometimes suggests.[14] People do change, both for good and for bad. Perhaps the best known case of someone who became "a different person," but only for three years, is that of Oskar Schindler. Although never a believing Nazi, and always concerned about his Jewish workers' safety, Schindler was initially interested chiefly in having a good time and running a profitable business.[15] But when the horror of the evil around him finally struck him with full force, he marshaled all his powers of thought, word, and action to form an ingenious and daring plan to rescue as many Jews as he could, incurring not only great financial losses but also great risks to his life. In those years, his justice, courage, and compassion were deep and stable. After the war he did nothing remarkable, and could not even run a successful business.[16]

(vi) A virtuous or morally excellent act is an act that expresses a habituated intellectual-emotional disposition to make the right choice. For an act that expresses such a disposition is more deeply rooted in the agent than an act whose motivation is not thus rooted, and the depth of an act's motivation is one measure of its excellence. This is true not only of virtuous acts but also of other sorts of acts. For example, the most loving acts are those that express a loving disposition, the finest musical performance is that which expresses the performer's expertise, and so on.

I'll call acts that have the right motive, but do not express virtuous traits, rightly motivated acts in order to distinguish them from virtuous acts. Enkratic or strong-willed acts are examples of rightly motivated acts, as are the uncharacteristically rightly motivated acts of a vicious or akratic person. The fact that people can change for the better implies that it must be possible for someone who, for example, is akratic vis-à-vis food, but newly committed to a diet, to act from the right motive. The same applies

---

[14.] At 1114a11ff Aristotle claims that you can't change a bad character after you have created it. just as you can't get a stone back after you've thrown it, or your health back after you've ruined it. At 1165b 19–21, however, his advice that, if a virtuous friend becomes bad, you should try to rescue his character before giving up on him implies that it is possible to change a bad character.

[15.] See Herbert Steinhouse, "From 'The Real Oskar Schindler'," *Saturday Night*, April 1994 (http://writing.upenn.edu/~afilreis/Holocaust/steinhouse.html, accessed July 2013).

[16.] Analogous phenomena in other spheres of life provide further support for the claim that a virtuous disposition can be stable without being permanent. For instance, a sense of danger can open up reserves of physical strength we didn't know we possessed, a strength that lasts as long as, but only as long as, the danger.

to someone who is intemperate: when he finally acknowledges to himself that the principle of stuffing his face whenever he can is not exactly wise and decides to start eating sensibly, it must be possible for him to restrain himself for the right reasons, even if he finds himself slipping back into his old ways of thinking and acting every now and then. Acts that are outwardly right in that they accord with virtue but are not rightly motivated (such as Kant's shopkeeper who acts honestly only for the sake of a good business reputation) I will simply call acts that are outwardly right, or acts that only accord with virtue.

I stated earlier that, because virtue is an excellence of character, it must aim at good ends, but that common sense seems divided on this view. This view, however, is controversial enough to merit more discussion.

6.2.2 Soon after the terrorist attacks on the World Trade Center in September 2001, Bill Maher, a TV talk show host, declared that at least the terrorists had courage. This led to some of his viewers feeling outrage at his seeming praise of the terrorists, and some feeling admiration for his seeming honesty. Both sides had a point. Calling someone courageous is often meant as praise for his goals and action, or his character—hence the outrage at Maher's remark. But it is also often meant to praise a non-moral aspect of someone's action or character—hence the praise for Maher's remark. This kind of ambiguity is common in much everyday discourse about the virtues: people say that generosity is a virtue, but also that so-and-so is generous to a fault; that honesty is a virtue, but also that so-and-so is cruelly honest, and so on. The virtues are treated as psychological propensities to act in certain ways, regardless of the agent's goals, motives, or context. But this pre-philosophical conception of the virtues has some highly counterintuitive implications. It implies, for example, that the cleverness and self-confident fearlessness of a gang leader who preys on innocent people is no different, morally, from the cleverness and self-confident fearlessness of an individual who goes to their defense, or that the psychological perspicacity of Iago is just as admirable as the psychological perspicacity of Solomon. The common view of the virtues thus leads to conclusions at which common sense balks.[17]

To avoid this result, one must accept the view that, since virtuous traits and virtuous acts are morally excellent, they must be aimed at good ends.[18]

---

[17] See my "The Limited Unity of Virtue" (hereafter "LUV") (1996), 306–329. For other problems with the common view, see Gary Watson, "Virtues in Excess" (July 1984), 57–74.

[18] Foot suggests a different solution. Instead of saying that a virtue cannot be used for bad ends, she says that when it is so used, it fails to act like a virtue, just as when poison fails to kill or injure, it

On this view, the terrorists might have been fearless and confident, but not courageous. The "cruelly honest" person is blunt and tactlessly truthful, but not honest, because her (perhaps unconscious) motive and goal is a desire to hurt others for no good reason. Iago is insightful about certain kinds of motives, but not practically wise. A wise Iago's insight and cleverness would have been prompted, supported, guided, and informed by thoughts and desires different from the cruel Iago's.

Nevertheless, the common view of the virtues does capture the important intuition that there is something inherently desirable about psychological propensities like confidence and fearlessness, or cleverness and insight, just as there is something undesirable about their contraries: chronic self-doubt and fearfulness, stupidity and blindness. But the desirability of propensities like confidence and fearlessness, or cleverness and insight, can be explained by the fact that they are necessary for—indeed, central components of—the virtues of courage and practical and theoretical wisdom. They are psychological excellences that become virtues when informed by practical wisdom and aimed at good ends. By contrast, self-doubt and timorousness, stupidity and blindness, have nothing going for them—they are psychological defects. We can all be grateful for the stupidity of our enemies if this prevents them from harming us. But we cannot *admire* them for their stupidity.

6.2.3 The discussion to this point has, hopefully, shown some of the ways in which virtue and *eudaimonia* are well-suited to each other. Their fit is both structural and substantive. Structurally, just as a *eudaimonic* life is the highest prudential good, so a virtuous life is the highest moral good. Substantively, both happiness and virtue involve emotional, deliberative, and evaluative dispositions: dispositions that, in normal circumstances, are to a significant extent up to us—only to a significant extent, however, because both also require some constitutive (genetic) and circumstantial luck for their development and maintenance.[19] Furthermore, the integration of emotional dispositions with intellectual (especially deliberative) dispositions, which is required by virtue, makes virtue highly conducive to happiness, since a common source of unhappiness is conflict between our emotions and our evaluations. Indeed, since the

---

fails to act like poison ("Virtues and Vices," 15–16). Hence, in the wicked, courage, temperance, and so on *typically* fail to operate as virtues because of their "systematic connection with defective action rather than good action" (17).

[19] Williams discusses circumstantial luck in his *Moral Luck* (1981), chapter 2, reprinted in *Moral Luck*, ed. Daniel Statman (1993), 35–57. Nagel discusses constitutive luck in his *Mortal Questions* (1979), chapter 3, reprinted in Statman, ibid., 57–73.

virtuous agent necessarily takes pleasure or joy in acting virtuously, virtuous activity is inherently productive of some happiness. It also promotes happiness insofar as the achievement of worthwhile goals is a source of happiness, and virtuous activity enables the virtuous agent to achieve them. This is obvious in the case of virtues like honesty, courage, responsibility, and integrity in their self-regarding aspects; but it is arguably also true of these virtues in their other-regarding aspects, as well as of purely other-regarding virtues such as justice, generosity, and kindness. The neo-Aristotelian moral exemplar is very far from the self-abnegating poor woman "who sacrifices even the pittance she has for some impersonal cause."[20]

These claims are compatible with the recognition that virtue can be turned into a weapon against the virtuous by the vicious, or that, in certain circumstances, a virtuous act can destroy the agent's happiness. But it is not compatible with the claim that virtue and virtuous activity all by themselves—that is, without the intervention of bad people or bad luck—can be the cause of their possessors' unhappiness, much less their ill-being. This, however, is precisely what Swanton argues in *Pluralistic View* (2003). I address her argument in the next section.

6.3 Unhappy Saints

6.3.1 Swanton tries to make her case with the help of three examples of (putatively) virtuous characters who are clearly unhappy, arguing that their unhappiness is due to their virtue and not to bad luck. I raise questions both about the virtue of her characters, and (granting for the sake of argument that they are virtuous), about her claim that their unhappiness is due only to their virtues.

The first example is of an aid worker who devotes herself to the relief of suffering in the jungle, repeatedly contracting malaria and dysentery (*Pluralistic View*, 82). She is always exhausted, neglects her health, takes no joy in her work, and finally dies of a viral infection. This example of lethal virtue is, however, surprising for someone like Swanton, given her view that "self-love is part of the profile of all virtue, and certain kinds of damaging self-sacrifice are thereby precluded" (ibid., 81). For what is obviously present in the choices made by this saint of the jungle is her damaging self-sacrifice—and what is obviously absent from them is her

---

[20] John Cottingham, "Partiality and the Virtues" (1996), 63.

self-love. The mere fact that the aid worker is living according to her personal ideals does not mean that she is acting with self-love, for personal ideals can be ideals of damaging self-sacrifice. At any rate, if this worker's self-neglect and joyless persistence in the face of her personal woes are not examples of such self-sacrifice, it is hard to see what could be. Hence, as far as I can see, not only is this saintly woman not virtuous on my neo-Aristotelian conception of virtue, she is not virtuous even on Swanton's own conception of virtue.

Swanton next offers the example of a manic-depressive artist who "struggles to realize her creative goals, constantly feels she has failed, and commits suicide having achieved no recognition" (82). Twisting the knife in her artist's side one last time, Swanton adds that this artist does not achieve any posthumous recognition either. The artist's devotion to her art is commendable because she does have something important to say—yet, according to Swanton, it is the cause of her suffering. Swanton rejects the idea that it is bad luck and not her virtue that leaves her unhappy, because lack of recognition is the usual fate of the artist. A "more reliable bet for flourishing would have been for her to have deflected or curbed the artistic passion which make her such a driven personality" (83).

But can a chronically self-doubtful person be seen as virtuous in the very realm in which she is self-doubtful? Chronic self-doubt in the face of real talent bespeaks a lack of self-knowledge, and being driven to suicide because one has fared no better than other artists bespeaks a lack of perspective and courage. The underlying problem, of course, is the artist's manic-depressive illness, which, although not a character flaw, is incompatible with virtue, since to the extent that the artist is in its grip, she lacks autonomy, reality-orientation, and practical understanding.[21]

The third example features a prescient environmentalist who is passionately devoted to the cause of environmental preservation and warns people of the environmental disaster to come, but who is not taken seriously by anyone in spite of his "interpersonal skill" (83). The stress this causes leads to a heart attack and he dies in despair, although he has some posthumous success, when people start heeding his warnings.

Here again one might wonder how virtuous Swanton's environmentalist really is. A virtuous person, one might think, would be made of

---

[21.] Swanton doesn't say why her artist doesn't seek medical help, but let's say that she has and it hasn't worked, or that it does work, but only at the cost of depriving her of her artistic passion. Either way, this is a case of bad luck, because in most cases the right drug at the right dose actually helps bipolar people become both happier and more productive (see chapter 2, n. 23).

sterner stuff, would be a little more self-sufficient and not quite so dependent on success. One might also wonder how this environmentalist arrived at his conclusion of impending environmental disaster without the cooperation and agreement of other scientists, and why absolutely no one takes him seriously if he is so skilled at communication. At any rate, if he had been a stronger person, his failures would not have stressed him to the point of a heart attack, and his success would not have been posthumous.

Swanton might argue that, on her "threshold" conception of virtue, the aid-worker, the artist, and the environmentalist are virtuous and self-loving, in spite of the self-neglect of the aid-worker, the manic-depressive illness of the artist, and the lack of self-sufficiency of the environmentalist. This, however, is a very different conception of virtue from the one I am defending in this book, and so even if Swanton succeeds in showing that her virtues can lead to ill-being by their very nature, she will not have shown that neo-Aristotelian virtues can do so. For the sake of argument, however, let us abstract from these characters' negative traits and attitudes, and grant that the aid-worker is virtuous insofar as she perseveres in a worthy, beneficent cause; the artist is virtuous insofar as she struggles to give expression to her important vision; and the environmentalist is virtuous insofar as he is passionate about his cause and tries to spread the truth about the impending disaster.

6.3.2 Is Swanton right to claim that it is the aid-worker's virtue that causes her suffering? Given the aid-worker's neglect of her health and the unpleasant circumstances in which she has chosen to exercise her beneficence, I see no reason to accept Swanton's verdict. There *are* people who find working in malaria-infested jungles challenging and fulfilling, just as there are people who find walking a tight rope over Niagara Falls, or risking frostbite and broken limbs scaling Mount Everest, challenging and fulfilling. But Swanton's aid-worker is decidedly not one of them. As Henry David Thoreau declares in *Walden*, "You must have a genius for charity [in infested jungles] as well as for anything else." In choosing such work, this aid-worker has either sadly neglected to find out what is suited to her nature or failed to act on her self-knowledge. *Eudaimonia* requires attention both to what is worth doing for a human being, and what, among the many worthwhile pursuits open to us, is both suited to our talents and personally fulfilling or, at least, not damaging. It is the aid-worker's ill-chosen work and self-neglect that are responsible for her suffering, not perseverance in a beneficent endeavor as such. Indeed, such perseverance is necessary for *eudaimonia*, because without it (though not necessarily in relief of suffering, or under grueling conditions), our lives would lack the meaning and richness that are essential to *eudaimonia*.

I also see no reason to accept Swanton's claim that the artist's suffering is due to her struggle to express her creative vision. How can dedication to a project you rightly believe is worthwhile be a cause of suffering? Would the artist suffer if she gained recognition, did not have chronic self-doubt, and did not have manic-depressive illness? It is hard to see why she would.

The example of the prescient environmentalist also does not show that his suffering is due to his virtue. Since he's a good communicator, isn't it just bad luck that no one believes him? After all, the usual problem is that people are only too willing to believe predictions of disaster, whether it be the Doomsdays beloved of pastors, or the mass starvations beloved of Malthusians.[22]

There is a common problem underlying Swanton's arguments in all three cases: they do not establish that it is in the very nature of beneficence, perseverance in a worthwhile creative struggle, and passionate devotion to the truth, in a world like ours, to lead to suffering. Merely showing that they lead to suffering when they are conjoined with self-neglect, manic-depressive illness, lack of mettle, lack of success, and unfavorable circumstances shows only that they are not *sufficient* for *eudaimonia*, a claim that is, indeed, true of all the virtues. But had Swanton succeeded in showing that the virtues in question have an inherent tendency to make their possessors suffer, then well-being would require that we avoid acquiring them, and the *eudaimonist* thesis that well-being as the HPG requires virtue would be dead-on-arrival, at least with respect to these virtues.

In the next section I address the issue of the scope of virtue and whether human nature makes virtue well-nigh impossible.

---

[22] Erin Prophet's book *Prophet's Daughter* (2008) is but the latest tale of a cult whose members spent years of their lives and a vast fortune to build an underground shelter to save themselves from a nuclear holocaust. Paul Ehrlich and Lester Brown have been making dire predictions of mass starvation from a population bomb, and other horrors, for decades, even though every decade refutes them by producing more food than people. In spite of being proved wrong every time, they continue to garner praise and awards for their dire prophecies. In *Future Babble* (2011), Dan Gardner reviews the innumerable mistakes made by experts over the decades, and discusses psychologist Philip Tetlock's explanation of experts' unshaken confidence in themselves in terms of various kinds of biases, and of their audiences' unshaken confidence in them in terms of their desire for certainty.

6.4 Global Virtue?

6.4.1 Most philosophers now agree that actual virtue is not global, so it might seem that arguing against this claim is like beating a dead horse.[23] However, at least some philosophers still hold out hope for globalism, while some others, as mentioned in 6.1, take the position that, since no one is globally virtuous, no one is genuinely virtuous, from which it follows that no one is genuinely *eudaimon*.[24] Globalism also continues to have a deep hold on the human psyche. It is common to hear people dismissing an individual as a good-for-nothing because he abandoned his family, or praising him as a real mensch because he was a great boss and colleague.[25] This way of talking betrays the same implicit commitment to the idea that virtue must be all-or-nothing, a commitment that threatens *eudaimonism*. Another brief discussion of the issue should, then, be useful, especially to readers who have not been following this debate. In earlier work I have argued on both philosophical and experimental grounds that human beings cannot (psychologically cannot) be globally virtuous, but nevertheless most people do have some genuine virtue.[26] I still hold this general view,

---

[23] The anti-globalist camp includes Robert Adams, *A Theory of Virtue: Excellence in Being for the Good* (hereafter *Excellence*) (2006); Jesse Prinz, "The Normativity Challenge: Cultural Psychology Provides the Real Threat to Virtue Ethics" (2009); and Daniel Russell, *Practical Intelligence and the Virtues* (hereafter *Practical Intelligence*) (2009).

[24] Nancy E. Snow, *Virtue as Social Intelligence: An Empirically Grounded Theory* (2009), still holds out hope for global virtue. Becker, *Stoicism* (1999) and Annas, *Intelligent Virtue* (2012), argue that genuine virtue must be global and unified, while acknowledging that no one is genuinely virtuous. Paul Bloomfield, whose view I discuss in 6.5.4, argues that we can have respect for ourselves as ends *iff* we have respect for everyone else as ends.

[25] This is not to say that people are consistently globalist. Even as they dismiss some people as worthless on the basis of one misdeed, they accept the flaws of people they are close to as minor spots on a character otherwise excellent. Some people think that Asians don't make globalist judgments, citing as support some studies done in the province of Orissa in India which show that its inhabitants give highly contextualized descriptions of close acquaintances more often than Americans do. For example, instead of saying, "She's generous," they'll say, "She brings cakes to my family on festival days." Doris takes this to show that Indians are less prone to global attributions than Americans (*Lack of Character*, 105–106). But the behavioral description could simply be a way of evading the question of whether the individual in question is generous (in case she isn't), or a way of explaining why they think the individual is generous. That Indians are as globalist in their conceptions of character as Westerners can be readily seen in Indian matrimonial ads calling for "beautiful girl of good character for decent boy from good family," or in Bollywood movies featuring virtuous heroes pitted against vicious villains. These give a far more accurate picture of Indians' conception of character than the studies that Doris cites.

[26] In "LUV" (1996) I argue for this position on the basis of the demanding nature of Aristotelian virtue and the commonly observable limitations of human nature, and in "The Milgram Experiments, Learned Helplessness, and Character Traits" (2009) on the basis of the experimental literature.

but my position has changed in certain respects, and revisiting it here will allow me to revise some of my earlier arguments.

6.4.2 The thesis that the virtues are global is a tacit assumption of Aristotle's argument for the unity of the virtues, not something he argues for. Indeed, it might seem at first blush that he *cannot* believe that the virtues are global, given his view that each virtue has its own sphere of application: physical danger for courage, material wealth for generosity, and so on. But this view is entirely compatible with the globalist thesis that someone who is courageous or generous must be courageous or generous whenever courage or generosity are called for. At any rate, I will ignore Aristotle's rather artificial conception of spheres of application in favor of the more commonsensical view that, for example, courage is relevant in all situations of danger, whether physical, social, or some other; generosity is relevant to the giving of one's possessions for another's benefit, whether these possessions are material, temporal, or psychological; and so on. And I will argue that the requirements of global virtue are beyond our psychological capacity to meet.

Aristotle depicts a person of practical wisdom (and virtue) as someone who has a true conception of what is good or bad for a human being (1140b 4–6), not in "some restricted area" such as health or strength, but "in general" (1140a 28), and of the best means to good ends (1144a 8–10). Thus, a practically wise person understands when to help and how, when to tell the truth or keep silent, how to raise children, and so on. This understanding of good ends and means is not a mere abstract understanding of what is required, the sort that an insightful philosopher or dramatist might have, but an understanding that informs a wise person's perceptions of, and responses to, particular situations (1142a 12–16).[27] It is an understanding that shows itself in the nitty-gritty of everyday life: in first perceiving and correctly interpreting a situation and then appropriately responding to it in word, gesture, and action. Only such an understanding constitutes practical wisdom, and only with the appropriately habituated emotions and desires—that is, with virtue—can one have such an understanding (1152a 8–1152a 9). In other words, practical wisdom entails virtue, for it is virtue that makes our overall goals correct (1144a 8–10, 1145a 5). "Vice perverts us and produces false views about the origins of actions"

[27.] At 1143a7–15 Aristotle distinguishes between comprehension, which is an ability to *judge* well of practical matters, and practical wisdom, which is concerned with both *judging* well and *acting* well. So an ethical or dramatic work can show comprehension, but not practical wisdom (although, again, the activity of choosing to write it and writing it can).

(1144a 34–1144a 36) (i.e., about the ends worth striving for), the way disease spoils the taste and makes sweet things appear bitter (cf. 1113a 27–1113a29). A vicious person may be *clever* in achieving his ends, but not *practically wise*, because either his ends or his means are bad (1144a 24–1144a28).[28] Conversely, a virtuous person is practically wise. A fully good or virtuous person is disposed to respond appropriately to situations in thought, feeling, and action. She knows which ends are worth striving for, how to prioritize them, and how best to achieve them. And this, in part, is the work of practical wisdom.

But why does Aristotle hold that practical wisdom must be global or, in his words, "a single state" (1145a 2)? The mere fact that practical wisdom is "concerned with action about what is good or bad for a human being" (1140b 5–6) does not entail that it must be global. For surely it is possible for someone to understand what is good or bad for a human being and (especially) herself in, say, her professional life, but not in her family life, or vis-à-vis religious authorities but not scientific authorities. Presumably, Aristotle thinks that practical wisdom is holistic or indivisible because he thinks that the human good itself is causally interconnected, and ignorance or misunderstanding of one aspect of it can skew our overall understanding of, and pursuit of, the good.[29] In contemporary terms, one false value can affect our understanding and pursuit of all our values. Conversely, one true value requires an understanding of other values in all areas of one's life, and of the connection between them. Thus, in order to be courageous, one must understand what is worth fighting for, and in order to understand that, one must understand what one risks by fighting, and the relative importance of what one risks (Annas, *Happiness*, 76). For example, risking one's life to right a minor wrong gives neither one's own life and well-being, nor the life and well-being of those one cares about, the importance they deserve. The virtue of courage thus requires an understanding

---

[28.] This suggests that the only alternative to virtue is vice, or that practical wisdom is incompatible only with vice. But since Aristotle also believes that practical wisdom involves a sensitivity to particulars and a readiness to act rightly, it has to be incompatible with akrasia as well. Akrasia involves comprehension (see n. 23 above), but not practical wisdom. The case of enkrateia is less clear. Enkrateia embodies some sensitivity to particulars and the ability to act rightly, but not with the readiness of the virtuous individual. Perhaps Aristotle would agree that the enkratic person is close to possessing practical wisdom. I will return to this point in 6.5.1 below.

[29.] Terence Irwin, "Disunity in the Aristotelian Virtues" (hereafter "Disunity") (1988). Aristotle is not, however, consistent on this point, for he states that "large-scale" virtues like magnificence require special knowledge and habituation: generosity plus lots of wealth is not sufficient for becoming magnificent. Elsewhere, too, he presents the virtuous as not necessarily virtuous across the board. See n. 48 below.

of what is worth fighting for in the context of one's life as a whole, and such understanding requires practical wisdom. It also requires the other virtues, such as the virtues involved in parental love and parental obligations. Hence, since practical wisdom is global, and practical wisdom and virtue entail each other, one virtue entails all (unity of virtue thesis). (From now on when I talk about virtue I should be understood as talking about practical wisdom as well and conversely.)

6.4.3 On this view, however, it seems that the concept of virtue can only be the concept of an ideal that actual virtuous agents will always fall short of. The obstacles we must overcome to become habituated into, and then maintain, global virtue are many: the vastness and complexity of what we need to understand to be virtuous, the limited resources of time and energy with which to do it, the uneven nature of our cognitive and emotional endowment, our inconsistent moral education, and the early fears or emotional traumas that can affect us, sometimes even without our knowledge, for the rest of our lives. When we consider the demanding requirements for being globally virtuous in conjunction with the undeniable limitations of human nature, it is easy to see why we should not expect globally virtuous people to cross our paths. Let us look at Aristotle's and Hume's portraits of such a person, portraits that most of us would agree are of a virtuous person, and then consider the epistemic and emotional obstacles to global virtue and practical wisdom. (I will leave out from the portrait some of the features of Aristotle's virtuous person that don't fit in very well with the rest of what Aristotle has to say (and that strike us as ridiculous), in order to keep the focus on the issue at hand.)

The "good person is correct," says Aristotle, about the "three objects of choice," namely, the "fine, expedient, and pleasant," and the "three objects of avoidance," the "shameful, harmful, and painful" (1104b 31–35). The good person knows what does or does not matter in human life, and what sorts of things matter more. Hence he is just, temperate, courageous, and generous. He is also open, not devious, and although he despises the truly despicable, he doesn't sit in judgment on people for trivial faults (1125a 6–9). He is objective in his judgments of both friends and foes, acquaintances and strangers; thus he is neither ingratiating nor quarrelsome (1126b 11–20). He doesn't gossip or nurse grievances but is, instead, mild-tempered and "ready to pardon" (1126a 1). He seeks "to share pleasure and avoid causing pain" (1127a 2–5) and helps "eagerly" (1124b 18). He knows himself well, and is truthful "both in what he says and in how he lives," because he is neither boastful nor self-deprecating (1127b 2–4). He is honest in all these ways because he loves honesty. He also doesn't let others, except friends, "determine his life," because that "would be slavish" (1125a 1–2). And even in great misfortune, "what is fine shines through" (1100b 27–31). In short, the ideally virtuous person is a happy person whose life illustrates a sure grasp of the true worth of things (1115b 17–24), and a sure grasp of how to use them, for "the best user of something is the person who has the virtue concerned with it" (1120a 5ff.).

Hume's portrait of Cleanthes, whom he regards as "a model of perfect virtue," is strikingly similar, even though his theory of virtue is rather different from Aristotle's. Cleanthes is fair to everyone, kind, witty, friendly, highly accomplished, and knowledgeable without being vain, and above all, serene and even cheerful in the face of great trials and misfortunes.[30]

Given the absence of heroics, these portraits make it seem easy to be ideally virtuous. But the appearance conceals the difficulties we must encounter in trying to become like these persons. To achieve the sure grasp of things of the ideally virtuous person, we must possess not only true "universals" or principles, but also experience of particulars and true empirical generalizations. The most important such empirical generalizations concern human nature and one's own nature as individuals, generalizations that often require theoretical knowledge. Hence understanding human nature and one's own nature—one's character, personality, subconscious desires, emotional blocks, unconscious needs and aspirations—is no less a work in progress than understanding the world outside us. And for some people it is harder, through no fault of their own, than for others.

One factor contributing to this difficulty is a person's genetic endowment. Some people have a reduced capacity to identify emotions, their own and others', hence a reduced capacity to understand themselves and others. The same is true of people who naturally have less empathy than others.[31] Some people with normal empathy are deficient in their ability to grasp the theoretical knowledge necessary for virtue. The "learned helplessness" experiments by Martin Seligman and Steven Maier strongly suggest that some people (as well as dogs and rats) have a greater capacity for helplessness and a smaller capacity for resilience in the face of failure than other people.[32] To be exact, this number is 65%—the same as the

---

[30] David Hume, *An Enquiry Concerning the Principles of Morals*, ed. Eric Steinberg (1751/1983), Section IX, Part 1, 173–74.

[31] An extreme incapacity to identify emotions is a subclinical condition called alexithymia. A general impairment in empathy, in understanding of social cues, and in communication skills and (usually) intellectual ability, is typical of autism. See http://www.autismspeaks.org and http://www.ninds.nih.gov/disorders/autism/detail_autism.htm#243513082, accessed September 2013.

[32] See Seligman, *Authentic Happiness* (2002), 23. Seligman also claims that one out of eight subjects is helpless to begin with (both people and animals? Seligman does not make this clear).

number of those who continue to shock the "learners" to the very end in three variations of the Milgram experiments, a startling coincidence that I discuss in "Milgram Experiments."[33]

In addition to these genetic obstacles to the epistemic and motivational requirements of virtue, early experiences can reinforce certain bad tendencies, and lead to blocks in our cognitive and emotional repertoire that prevent us from even seeing some of our problems as problems, much less correcting them. These problems are magnified by a confusing and inconsistent moral education. Children are taught, for example, to stand up for what is right—but also to be 'realistic' and willing to bend their principles when necessary for getting along with others; to have moral integrity—but also to be 'team players' and 'not make trouble'; to have self-confidence— but also to never presume to know more than others.

6.4.4 Our natural and learned tendencies can also make us highly susceptible to situations in all the wrong ways, often without our awareness. A clear picture of the depths and divisions of the human mind, both innate and acquired—its mechanisms of defense, repression, and confabulation, and its capacities for learning and unlearning—is a late arrival in human history.[34] For instance, although we've always known that situations can affect us powerfully—parents commonly admonish their children to keep good company, Odysseus asked to be tied to the mast to prevent him from following the Sirens, and so on—it is only in recent decades that, thanks to the brilliant work of some social psychologists, we have become aware of how easily unobtrusive situational factors can tap our propensities to obedience, conformity, irresponsibility, cruelty, or indifference to others' welfare.[35] In short, we have only recently become aware of how fragile our commitments and character can be in the "right circumstances"—and of how little we are aware of their fragility. Yet knowledge of our fragility is surely crucial to our ability to be virtuous.

The point here is not that without knowledge of the situationist experiments we simply cannot learn about our fragility. We can learn a lot

---

The original experiment is described in Seligman and Maier, "Failure to Escape Traumatic Shock" (1967).

[33] These three experiments are 2, 5, and 8. In all of these, the experimenter is in the same room as the subject, and the learner is in a different room. Unfortunately, in "Milgram Experiments" (2009), I wrongly stated that the experimenter is in a different room.

[34] Haidt, *Happiness Hypothesis* (2006), gives an overview of the new discoveries about the mind in the first chapter, "The Divided Self."

[35] More precisely, it is only in recent decades that *some of us* have become aware of this fact; most of the human population is still unaware of it and will remain unaware of it for centuries. Equally distressingly, even many people who know about these experiments tend to pooh-pooh the results.

from good literature about the limitations of human nature—if we take the trouble to apply its lessons to ourselves and others. We can also learn a great deal from historical and contemporary events. We have real-life analogs of the Milgram experiment in the so-called Strip Search Prank Call Scam, in dictatorships, and most of all, in the tendency of people (including the media) to side with the government against whistleblowers who expose government abuses committed in the name of security. We also have many real-life analogs of Zimbardo's Stanford Prison Experiment (SPE) in real prisons (and schools and colleges) around the world; real-life analogs of the Asch experiments in many social settings; and so on.[36] But nothing brings home the everyday roots of evil acts like these experiments, for here we see people "like ourselves" obeying the authority figure for no other reason than that it is the authority figure. Hence in circumstances that test our propensities to obedience, conformity, cruelty, or submissiveness, we can profit greatly from knowledge of these experiments: to be forewarned is to be forearmed.

In one way or another, all these experiments show that the underlying flaw in the subjects who do the wrong thing is a lack of autonomy/reality-orientation. The obedient majority in Milgram obeyed the authority figure against their own values and judgment of the situation, the subjects in the Asch experiment went against the evidence of their own senses in order to conform to the majority opinion, and the "guards" and "prisoners" in the SPE lost sight of the fact that they were subjects in an experiment as the former started behaving like real guards and the latter like real prisoners. Indeed, even Zimbardo, who played the role of prison superintendent, and the others on his research team, got sucked into what he later called "the full-blown madness of this place," finding it hard to keep their grip on the fact that it was just an academic experiment with real students, not a prison with real convicts.[37] "Only a few people," Zimbardo confessed,

---

[36] See my discussion in "Milgram Experiments" (2009). The Strip Search Prank Call Scam is described, with links to external sources, in http://en.wikipedia.org/wiki/David_R._Stewart, accessed May 6, 2013. There were over seventy incidents from about 1994 to 2004 in thirty US states before the culprit, David Stewart, was arrested. The single best discussion of the Obedience experiments is by Stanley Milgram himself in *Obedience to Authority* (1974). For the Zimbardo experiment see Philip G. Zimbardo, *The Lucifer Effect: Understanding how Good People Turn Evil* (2007), and for the Asch experiments, Solomon Asch in "Opinions and Social Pressure," *Scientific American* (1955), 193: 31–35.

[37] This fact by itself suffices to meet Nancy Snow's objection in *Virtue as Social Intelligence: An Empirically Grounded Theory* (2009), that the manipulation of the subjects undercuts any real-life implications of the experiment (109–111). In addition, even when the experimenters intervened on behalf of the prisoners, the guards did not change their behavior. For other such objections and my replies to them, see "Milgram Experiments" (2009). Milgram also addresses these and other issues

"were able to resist the situational temptations to yield to power and dominance while maintaining some semblance of morality and decency; obviously I was not among that noble class" (69–71).[38]

Cognitive psychology has identified yet other obstacles to virtue and practical wisdom: situational and innate factors that interfere with both theoretical reasoning and practical deliberation and motivation. Thanks to our tribal evolutionary past, we are subject to a whole host of biases, including implicit racism, which may have helped us to survive at one time but now do little except bode conflict. Again, our minds are constructed to use heuristics to make quick calculations that serve us well in many situations but that also lead to certain sorts of statistical errors, errors that even those trained in statistics often can't help making. Thus the very architecture of our minds both enables and hinders sound reasoning. Our decisions and actions are often subject to the "framing effect," which leads us to opt for an action or policy when its outcome is positively framed and reject it when it is negatively framed, even though the outcomes are identical.

These biases and propensities are hard to control because we are typically unaware of them. Nevertheless, it is an exaggeration to say that "most of a person's everyday life is determined not by their conscious intentions and deliberate choices but by mental processes that are put into motion by features of the environment and that operate outside of conscious awareness and guidance."[39] For our goals and the means we take to them determine our environment to a large extent. Further, as we learn about our unconscious racist, authoritarian, or conformist impulses, or our susceptibility to statistical errors or the framing effect, we can gradually extend our control over them by monitoring ourselves in situations that are likely to trigger them and being more open to others' reactions to us.[40] In Freudian terms, we can

---

regarding the use of laboratory experiments for drawing lessons about the general population in *Obedience*, 170–178.

[38] Zimbardo, 175, 180; and Zimbardo, Christina Maslach, Craig Haney, "Reflections on the Stanford Prison Experiment: Genesis, Transformations, Consequences" (2000), 193–237. Zimbardo credits Christina Maslach, a recent PhD, from Stanford who saw the experiment with fresh eyes for the first time on the fifth night, for prevailing on him to terminate it on the sixth day instead of letting it run its course for the projected two weeks (214–220).

[39] J.A. Bargh and T.L. Chartrand, "The Unbearable Automaticity of Being" (1999), 462.

[40] For these and other suggestions, see Snow, chapter 2 (2009), Kamtekar, "Updating Practical Wisdom" (2012), and Maria W. Merritt, John Doris, and Gilbert Harman, "Character" (2010). Snow is the most optimistic about our abilities to overcome these problems, Merritt et al the least optimistic. I address the cognitive challenges in "Reasoning about Wrong Reasons, No Reasons, and Reasons of Virtue" (2014).

try to put ego where id was. But we must acknowledge the fact that our success will be incomplete. Once again, then, we must reject the possibility of global virtue.

To conclude: although everyday experience, history, and experimental social and cognitive psychology are consistent with the *logical* possibility that a small minority of people are globally virtuous, we have good reason to believe that global virtue is *psychologically* impossible. Attention to the epistemic requirements of virtue alone make this conclusion inescapable. I have discussed the obstacles in the path of self-knowledge and knowledge of others. The obstacles in the path of knowledge of the external world are just as serious. The upshot is that we all hold many morally significant mistaken generalizations about many matters of psychology, economics, and society. Thus, many people still believe that without the American government's war on drugs, we would be overrun by gangs and addicts.[41] So they continue to support a war that has led to violent gangs, undermined the rule of law, militarized American society, killed countless innocent people, and incarcerated and destroyed the lives of thousands of young people merely for getting high in a manner frowned upon by those in power. Support for these policies does not amount to vice, since it does not come from immoral principles or vicious dispositions, but it does amount to a lack of virtue (a lack that, interestingly, Aristotle's fourfold taxonomy of character traits cannot accommodate).

Global virtue is an attractive and coherent ideal to try and approximate, but an individual can no more expect to reach it than she can expect to reach global theoretical wisdom. On this issue, Christian and Kantian ethics, with their emphasis on our flawed nature, are far more realistic, however unacceptable their explanation or analysis of our flaws.[42] All the virtues of all human beings put together may add up to one "global" human being's global virtues, but no one human being has been or can be globally virtuous. To think otherwise is either to seriously misunderstand the nature of Aristotelian virtue—or our own human nature.

---

[41] This and other myths are exposed by Ryan Grim in "Five Myths About Drugs in America" (August 9, 2009).

[42] On the Christian view, Adams points out, human virtue is frail and dependent on our social circumstances (and divine grace) (*Excellence, op. cit.*), 157.

6.5. Domain-Specific Traits and Domain-Specific Unity of Virtue

6.5.1 Virtue, I argued in "LUV," is domain-specific, a domain being an area of practical concern that *can be compartmentalized,* that is, isolated from influence by other domains (psychological criterion), and that is *important enough to justify the ascription of virtue* (normative criterion).[43] In "LUV" I thought of domains as neatly demarcated areas of concern, such as social danger or physical danger. I am now persuaded that an individual's virtue is unlikely to fall into such neatly demarcated domains. For example, an individual is more likely to be courageous in the face of some kinds of social danger and some kinds of physical danger than in the face of social danger *tout court,* or physical danger *tout court.*[44] There are, of course, other kinds of danger as well, such as danger from injury or ill health, and it is only too possible for someone who is courageous on the battlefield to be cowardly in the face of illness. The pattern of our character is not like a political map, with clearly demarcated boundaries, but like a physical map, with its complicated contours made by the rivers and crisscrossing streams.

An individual's lack of courage in the face of some kinds of danger might be due to a lack of practical understanding or to a lack of motivation or to the wrong motivation. For example, if Hypatia understands what is worth fighting for and how when her little brother is being bullied by his classmates, but not when he is being mocked by his instructor, then her practical understanding of the two kinds of social danger is compartmentalized. Or if she understands what is worth fighting for and how in both kinds of situation but tends to be afraid—or else reckless—in her response in the latter kind of situation, then her emotional dispositions in the two kinds of situation are compartmentalized, such that she is courageous in the former and akratic or foolhardy in the latter. Our individual and social histories, our particular biological endowments, our personalities, the quality of our reflection, and our moral education all play a role in how we compartmentalize domains. Hence different people have different domains of virtue. But our shared evolutionary history, and the fact that we first learn virtue within the family, also leads us to have some domains in common. Thus, most of us are more likely to be

---

[43] "LUV" (1996), 306–329.
[44] Adams, *Excellence* (2006), and John Doris. *Lack of Character* (2002).

virtuous towards members of our in-groups (whatever the criteria for the in-groups) than towards members of out-groups, even when the demands of virtue are identical in the two cases.[45]

As this discussion shows, a domain consists of several or many types of situations. So when I say that so-and-so is very courageous or pretty courageous, I mean that she is courageous in most or many kinds of dangerous situations, respectively. It is important to note, however, that even in domains in which someone is very virtuous, there is no reason to think that she will always act virtuously in *every* token situation, actual or counterfactual, that falls under that domain. Nor is this required for virtue. Virtue requires only that she *characteristically* act virtuously. There is also no reason to think that even when she does act virtuously, she will display the full "profile" of the virtues in every instance.[46] A person's virtue can go all the way from excellent, as when her deliberations, emotions, and actions are right in every respect but short of the very best, to superlative, to exceptional. Virtue is like an A grade, which can go from A- to A+, or like an uneven plateau, rather than a mountain peak. As a result, virtue is what Swanton calls a "threshold" concept (*Pluralistic View*), or what Russell calls a "satis" concept (*Practical Intelligence*).[47] Both agree that to be virtuous enough is to be virtuous *tout court*. The same, I would add, is true of the other character traits. Hence, the boundary between the lowest level of virtue and the highest level of *enkrateia*, or strength of will, is unclear.[48]

6.5.2 The fact that domains of virtue—and, as I argue in Section 6.7 below, of akrasia and *enkrateia*—are highly individualized has important

---

[45] I add the qualifier "even when the demands of justice are identical in the two cases" because, as I argue in "Friendship, Justice, and Supererogation" (1985), I do not believe that they are always identical.

[46] The lovely phrase, "profile of the virtues," is from Swanton, who uses it to refer to the "constellation of modes of moral responsiveness or acknowledgement which comprise the virtuous disposition," modes such as "love, respect, creativity, and promotion (*Pluralistic View* (2003), 2).

[47] Others who recognize that actual virtue comes in degrees include Hursthouse, *On Virtue Ethics*, Introduction and chapter 7; Joel J. Kupperman, "The Indispensability of Character" (2001), 239–51; and Adams, *Excellence* (2006). This view departs from Aristotle's conception of virtue, at least as expressed in some of his remarks and as usually interpreted. Shane Drefcinski, however, argues that Aristotle presents two pictures of virtue, ideal and realistic, and that on the latter, he acknowledges both that virtue comes in degrees and that the virtuous can sometimes do vicious things ("Aristotle's Fallible Phronimos" (1996), 139–154). See also Howard Curzer, "How Good People Do Bad Things: Aristotle on the Misdeeds of the Virtuous" (2005), 233–256. I discuss Aristotle's realistic view in connection with situationist challenges to virtue ethics in "Reasoning about Wrong Reasons, No Reasons, and Reasons of Virtue" (2014).

[48] If both virtue and *enkrateia* come in degrees, how do they differ from each other? I would say that virtue is, at worst, hesitant, but never reluctant, whereas *enkrateia* is, at best, somewhat reluctant. But with vague concepts like these, there will always be borderline cases that belong clearly to neither category. Thanks to Heather Battaly for raising this issue.

implications, both positive and negative, for moral psychology and the possibility of *eudaimonia*. If (as is only too plausible) many of the obedient subjects in the Milgram experiments obeyed the ostensibly immoral orders of the experimenter because of a disposition to place excessive trust in scientific authorities and too little in themselves, the domain-specific theory cautions us not to conclude that they would also have obeyed immoral orders from, say, the police. On the contrary, they might have a great deal of integrity, courage, and justice with respect to many kinds of authority. It is true, as opponents of the idea of compartmentalized virtue point out, that virtue in one domain can be undermined by akrasia or vice in another domain if the two domains intersect frequently.[49] But it does not follow from this that compartmentalized virtue is not really virtue: permanence is not a necessary property of the real. If someone's virtue is undermined in domain D1, it follows that she is no longer virtuous in that domain. But it is just as possible that the (frequent) intersection of domain D1 with domain D2 will bring her akrasia or cowardice in the latter domain home to her, and give her the wherewithal to overcome them.[50] How likely she is to succeed in overcoming her faults depends largely on how deeply she cares about becoming more virtuous. Since a virtue is an intellectual-emotional disposition to characteristically do the right thing for the right reasons in the right spirit, acquired and maintained through practice, anyone who is virtuous in some domains must have some degree of "care for the soul". So whenever she finds her lack of virtue in a domain she has hitherto neglected undermining her virtue in another, she has an incentive to improve herself. In short, even compartmentalized virtue can be quite enduring, although the greater the scope and depth of a person's virtue, the more enduring it will be.

6.5.3 It might be thought that even if *human* virtue is domain-specific, such virtue is only so-called virtue, because genuine virtue requires practical wisdom and practical wisdom must be global. This view, however, contradicts the crucial *eudaimonist* premise that a defensible conception of virtue and of well-being must take into account the nature of human beings and the nature of the world they live in. If this nature makes global

---

[49] In allowing that virtue in a domain can coexist with vice in another, I am rejecting my own earlier view in "LUV".

[50] At 1150b 35, Aristotle states that "the vicious person does not recognize that he is vicious, whereas the incontinent person recognizes that he is incontinent." But Aristotle does not always depict vice as involving such ignorance; at IX.4 he depicts the vicious person as conflicted, self-hating, and self-destructive. Such people are, as Ronald D. Milo puts it in *Immorality* (1984), "preferentially wicked."

virtue unattainable, then genuine virtue cannot be global. The defenders of global virtue also fail to explain why only practical wisdom and virtue are required to be global in order to count as genuine; after all, they don't require medical or theoretical or craft wisdom to be global in order to count as genuine. For example, globalists wouldn't deny that someone can be an excellent ophthalmologist without being an excellent oncologist, notwithstanding the fact that our bodies are an "organic whole," and the doctor's lack of medical expertise in oncology can, in principle, undercut her medical expertise in ophthalmology. Nor do they deny that someone can be a great physicist without being a great chemist (or the other way around), notwithstanding the fact that his lack of knowledge in one field can, in principle, mislead him in the other. In other words, they seem willing to recognize that domain-specific excellence in medicine or science is still genuine excellence. Hence there is no good conceptual reason for insisting that practical wisdom/virtue must be either global or non-existent; like wisdom and excellence in other areas of human life, they vary in scope and are never global.

6.5.4 Another variant on the argument that virtue must be global (and that well-being requires such virtue) comes from outside of virtue ethics. In a recent article, Paul Bloomfield argues that recognition respect is a matter of justice, and recognition respect for self entails recognition respect for others, and conversely.[51] Justice in this sense consists of recognizing that we all have worth as ends in ourselves, and reliably acting on this recognition. Such recognition arguably underlies all other virtues, so someone who lacks recognition respect for anyone at all can have no virtue. Bloomfield also argues that such global justice is necessary for well-being, so someone who lacks it can have no well-being. These are extremely strong claims, implying as they do that only perfectly just people can have any self-respect or any well-being. Fortunately or unfortunately, I do not think they are true.

Why does Bloomfield believe that recognition respect for others and oneself stand in a relationship of mutual entailment? Because he holds that just people see their relationship to other people accurately, and this requires them to have "self-correcting reflexive attitudes" which help to make their self-assessments responsive to who they actually are (ibid., 48). Someone who is characteristically either arrogant or servile is unjust to himself as well as others, because he fails to see his relationship to other

---

[51] "Justice as a Self-Regarding Virtue" (January 2011), 46–64.

people accurately. He also violates the formal principle of justice, which tells us that like cases must be treated alike (50). Hence, the failure to treat like cases alike involves at once a psychological misrepresentation (judging x to be –x), a logical inconsistency (judging x to be x at one time and –x at another), and a normative mistake (51–52). The principle of treating like cases alike "is therefore not only a moral principle, but a principle of thought or epistemology" (52).

There is much here that is important and obviously in line with my own view about the connection between realism and virtue. I agree that the arrogant individual who characteristically places himself above all others, and the self-abnegating individual who characteristically places himself below all others, both fail to have genuine self-respect because they do not assess themselves accurately. What I question is Bloomfield's view that one cannot see *anyone* accurately without seeing *everyone* accurately, hence that one must see *everyone* as an end in order to have self-respect. As he puts it:

> Since making accurate judgments about one's self requires that one treats like cases alike, one must also make accurate judgments about everyone relevantly similar to oneself (56).

> And if we are concerned with recognition self-respect, then we will have to see ourselves as equals to everyone else who deserves recognition respect, since we will fail to have self-knowledge if we judge ourselves to be better, or worse, than everyone else (59).

It is true that we fail to have self-knowledge and, thus, genuine self-respect, if we misjudge everyone else. We cannot know ourselves as human if we do not recognize anyone else as human because conceptual understanding is general. For the same reason, we cannot see ourselves as ends if we don't see anyone else as ends. The arrogant individual might see himself as superior to everyone because he has power and status, while the self-abnegating individual might see himself as inferior to everyone because he lacks power and status. But neither understands anyone's inherent worth as a human being. However, none of this entails that we fail to have genuine self-respect unless we "make accurate judgments about *everyone* relevantly similar to oneself" and "see ourselves as equals to *everyone else* who deserves recognition respect" (emphasis mine). This would be like saying that someone who, seeing a skyscraper for the first time, doesn't recognize it as a dwelling place for hundreds of people, has *no* idea of a dwelling, even though he can recognize huts, shacks, and single-story buildings as dwellings. Or that a red-green colorblind person who can't recognize the redness of red roses or the green of grass has *no* idea of redness or greenness, even though he can recognize the redness of rubies and the green of emeralds. In short, it is to deny that moral development, like conceptual development, occurs over time and is not an all-or-nothing affair.

Bloomfield does qualify his view later in the essay by acknowledging that the harm done to one's self-respect by one small act of injustice, such as an act of rudeness, is much less than the harm done to it by one large act, or by many small acts (60). But this concession still allows that many large injustices done over a lifetime are incompatible with *any* self-respect. And this entails that the vast number of human beings over history, perhaps the majority, have no self-respect, since they have characteristically disrespected large numbers of people they regarded as inherently inferior to them, fit only for serving as their tools or, at best, their servants. But there is no reason to think that, for example, slave masters did not or could not see other free people, especially other slave owners, as fully human, and accord recognition respect to them and to themselves.

Bloomfield's argument also goes wrong when he states that, in treating any others as though they are either below or above me, I treat myself and them as if we are better or worse *than we are* (56). This conclusion does not follow because, as the slavery case shows, a mistaken comparative judgment about some people is perfectly compatible with an accurate absolute judgment about other people, including oneself.[52]

To conclude: just as we are not justified in attributing a global virtue to a person simply on the basis of her consistently virtuous dispositions across several domains, so we are not justified in withholding the attribution of domain-specific virtue simply on the basis of an inconsistency across domains. Doing so would be justified only if it had been shown that we cannot characteristically do the right thing for the right reason at the right time with the right emotions and in the right way in some important areas of life and not others. But this has not been shown. That the virtues can be parceled out across different domains is an idea that is both commonsensical and commonly forgotten. It is of no small interest, then, to

---

[52.] Bloomfield's argument that "when I arrogantly place myself above others, ipso facto, I place them below me," and that this is a failure of justice because it is a failure to treat like cases alike, also raises other questions (56). Since the justice at issue concerns recognition respect, placing others below me presumably means failing to see them as ends in themselves. But does this entail failing to see myself as an end in myself? If it does, then how can I have an inflated view of myself? If it doesn't, then how can it be impossible for me to have self-respect?

note that even Aristotle succumbs to its force when he remarks, inconsistently with his general position, that a coward in war can be generous with money (1115a20–22).[53]

6.5.5 If global virtue is psychologically impossible, then it is trivially true that a global unity of virtue is psychologically impossible. It does not, however, follow that domain-specific unity is impossible. Indeed, the complexity of human life and the multifaceted nature of normative situations suggest that no major virtue can stand on its own and that every cardinal virtue entails a cluster of virtues. Let us return to Hypatia and her courage in defending her little brother when he is bullied by his classmates. To be characteristically courageous in this sphere, Hypatia must have a particularized understanding of the situation and certain emotional and action dispositions. Like other virtues, courage requires the ability to recognize when it is called for; hence it requires the ability to discern when her brother is being treated unkindly or otherwise bullied. In order to do this, Hypatia must be able to distinguish between ridicule and good-natured teasing, intimidation and rightful assertion of authority, inappropriate pressure and rational persuasion, and so on. To make these distinctions with the ease and fluency that are needed for courage, Hypatia must have the virtues of social intercourse (friendliness and wit), mild-temperedness, i.e., the disposition to be angry only for good cause (instead of never angry or indiscriminately angry), fairness (in judging the actions of the alleged bullies), and kindness (towards her brother). If she was merely enkratic in some of these respects rather than virtuous, then given that *enkrateia* (like the other traits) comes in degrees, she would either fail to make these distinctions at all or not make them as readily or act on them as willingly.[54] For there is no finite list of rules or cues or signs that can tell a person when someone's behavior counts as ridicule, intimidation, or inappropriate pressure; for this she would need, in addition to the right commitments, the right emotional sensitivities that are part of the supporting virtues (see 6.2 above). So courage in some domains requires the other relevant virtues in those domains—relevant. because some virtues might not be needed in some domains. Hypatia must also, of course, have the practical wisdom to judge when intervention is likely to be both safe and successful, lest she

---

[53] If virtue is global, then someone who is generous with money must be generous with it even in war. But if he's a coward in war, then, by the unity of virtue, he can't have any virtue in war.
[54] Here I disagree with Russell's argument that a virtue can get all the support it needs from moral decency, which differs from virtue in lacking the "level of stability and firmness of character, as well as practical intelligence" of virtue (*Practical Intelligence*, 357).

end up as yet another victim of the bullies. Generalizing from this: one virtue in a domain entails the other relevant virtues in that domain. I call this the limited unity of the virtues. It is important to note that Hypatia can be courageous in the type of situation just discussed without being particularly kind in her treatment of her little brother after the danger has passed. For example, she might be too awkward to offer him the sort of spontaneous, tactful solace a kinder person—someone whose kindness is deeper or broader—would offer. Since such kindness is not, strictly speaking, necessary for dealing appropriately with the threat her brother faces, its absence does not show that Hypatia isn't really kind or courageous in saving the victim from ridicule.

Because virtue is not global, and life offers plenty of evidence that most people are virtuous in some domains of their lives, it follows that most people satisfy a necessary condition of well-being as the HPG in some domains of their lives. There is, however, another threat to the thesis that virtue is a necessary condition of well-being as the HPG that needs to be addressed: namely, the claim that character is fragmented and virtues are local, or situation-specific. This is the position John Doris takes in *Lack of Character.*

6.6. Local Virtue?

6.6.1 Doris states that character is "an evaluatively disintegrated association of situation-specific local traits" (64, 166). This thesis actually consists of two distinct ideas.

(a) The idea that character is evaluatively disintegrated is simply the denial of the idea that there is a global unity (or reciprocity) of traits. It is important to note, however, that the unity thesis has never been asserted of all traits, only of virtue. And of course, as has already been pointed out, if the virtues are not global, they cannot be globally united. But this is compatible, as explained above, with domain-specific unity.

(b) The second claim in Doris' thesis is that character is merely an "association" of local or situation-specific traits, such as dime-finding-dropped-paper-compassion or sailing-in-rough-weather-with-one's-friends-courage (115).

Doris does not provide a definition of "local traits," but his examples suggest that, in contrast to domain-specific virtues, which must range over several or many kinds of situations within their sphere of concern, local traits are confined to just one type of situation. Thus, not only are there no brave people, *tout court*, there are only people who are brave in the face of storms when sailing with friends and nowhere else, or soldiers who are brave under rifle fire but not under artillery fire—or, presumably, any other kind of danger, such as from storms, heights, or wild animals (*Lack of Character*, 62). If our virtues really are so fragmented, then well-being as the HPG must also be fragmented. But are we really so fragmented? Given that virtue and well-being are dispositions that require practical under-standing of different sorts of situations and motivations that are integrated with such understanding, is it even possible for virtue or well-being to be so fragmented?

Adams points out that the situationist literature does not support the idea that people's virtues are confined to just one narrowly specified type of situation. There is no reason to suppose that someone who has cour-age in one narrowly specified type of situation can't or is unlikely to have courage in many other (narrowly specified) situations. Hence it is quite possible for her to have courage in the majority of types of situations that call for courage (*Excellence*, 181–182).

But even if the empirical literature did support the claim that some-one can deal with danger or behave compassionately in just one narrow situation-type and no other, there is no reason to think that the behav-iors are expressions of the *virtues* of compassion or courage. Virtues, as we've seen, are intellectual-emotional dispositions to act in certain ways for certain reasons, and reasons range over different types of situations. A narrowly circumscribed understanding, such as the understanding of how to treat friends (but not non-friends) when sailing in rough weather (but not walking or running in rough weather) can no more be regarded as practical wisdom than an understanding of colds (but not coughs) can be regarded as medical wisdom. Understanding—whether practical, theoretical, or both, such as medical—is general, because it involves a grasp of principles and an ability to apply them to a range of situations, including novel situations. Someone with practical wisdom must have some understanding of the nature of a good human life and the point of being virtuous, just as someone with medical wisdom must have some understanding of the nature of a healthy human body and the point of medicine. A similar point applies to motivation: just as being motivated to treat patients for colds but nothing else is not enough to make some-one a doctor, so being motivated to do the right thing in one kind of situation and no other is not enough to make someone virtuous in even that kind of situation. Someone whose motivation is thus circumscribed cannot be said to care much about virtue or a good human life. Local or situation-specific "virtues" must, therefore, be ruled out on conceptual grounds.

The view that virtues are local also makes a puzzle of virtue acquisition. We learn virtue in complex situations, situations that have many different features and dimensions. We learn to balance different considerations against each other, to prioritize our goals, to weigh the costs and benefits of using these means over those for achieving our ends, and to distinguish the central from the peripheral, the urgent from the non-urgent, the short-term from the long-term, and so on. It is through such thought and action that we acquire the ability to discern the mean. It would be impossible to learn to do this in just one kind of situation—or two or three—isolated from other kinds of situations. Experience of many kinds of situations is essential to acquiring virtue, and when it is acquired, it is acquired for many kinds of situations, including at least some novel ones. The nature of virtue acquisition thus provides another reason to reject the idea of local virtues.

6.6.2 Even more radical than the fragmentation thesis is Doris' claim that some people have inconsistent traits in the same token situation: character is a veritable hodgepodge. He approvingly repeats Primo Levi's claim that the same person can be both brutal and compassionate "'in the same moment,'" and Robert J. Lifton's statement that Dr. Mengele could be very "'kind to the children,'" bringing them sugar, thinking "'of small details in their daily lives...And then, next to that...the crematoria smoke, and these children, tomorrow or in a half hour, he is going to send them there'" (*Lack of Character*, 58).

For reasons we have already seen, however, inconsistent actions in a particular situation give us no ground for inferring inconsistent traits. Since practical wisdom and virtuous motivation are general, a person's traits can be inferred only from his actions, his reasons for his actions (which themselves must be inferred), his emotional responses, and other features in a variety of situations. If we keep this in mind, there is no good reason to think that Mengele's "kindly" actions expressed either the virtue, or even merely the motive, of kindness. Rather, when we keep Mengele's other actions and his commitments and goals in mind, the most likely explanation for his "kindly" actions were his sadism and love of power. Perhaps Mengele enjoyed the fact that the very same children whose trust he was gaining and who were becoming fond of him, calling him "Uncle Pepi," were going to be his helpless prey the next day. For he surely didn't forget that he was going to massacre tomorrow the children he was pampering today: amusing toys to be disposed of when he tired of them. What greater power could a man have than the power to dispose of helpless, trusting human beings at will, like some god? Alternatively, perhaps he had a need to be seen as decent by *someone, anyone*, and the children's love and trust satisfied that need.

The thesis that virtues are neither global nor local but, rather, domain-specific, is compatible with the recognition that global virtue is a worthy ideal to try to approximate. If our practical understanding or motivations were fragmented all the way down, as the idea of local traits entails, or if we had inconsistent traits in the same situation, we would have no general understanding of a good life, and so we could not even endeavor to approximate global virtue. Neither could we endeavor to approximate global well-being. But we have seen both psychological and conceptual reasons to reject the fragmentation and inconsistency theses. The fact that not only virtues, but also (as I argue below) vices and akratic traits, come in clusters, shows that our character exhibits a certain coherence and integration, both for good and for bad.

6.6.3 It might be objected that my argument against Doris' fragmentation thesis hoists me with my own petard: if virtue cannot be fragmented, how can it be compartmentalized? My reply is that my arguments against fragmentation are based on the nature of practical understanding and virtuous motivation, as well as on the nature of virtue acquisition. None of these arguments tells against the sort of compartmentalization I have argued for. Nor do my arguments against global virtue, ranging from the demanding requirements of virtue and the limitations of human nature, to the absence of any good evidence for globally virtuous people, show that virtue must be fragmented. It follows, then, that it is possible to have well-being as the HPG in some domains of our lives and not others.

6.7. Akrasia, *Enkrateia*, and Vice

Some of the same arguments that show that global virtue is psychologically impossible also show that global *akrasia* (weakness of will) and *enkrateia* (strength of will) are psychologically impossible.[55] Global *akrasia* and *enkrateia* entail a consistent cross-situational understanding of goodness accompanied by a struggle to be good in the face of wayward appetites or emotions. But we have seen the obstacles in the path of global understanding.[56] Moreover, it is hard to imagine someone who cares about

---

[55] My argument in this section is taken almost entirely from my "Milgram Experiments" (2009).
[56] Aristotle himself restricts continence and incontinence to the appetites we share with the beasts—food, drink, and sex—and the emotion of anger, but there is no good reason to accept

being good being consistently *enkratic* or consistently *akratic*. The life of a consistently *akratic* man would be full of struggle and regrets, that of a consistently *enkratic* man full of struggle and frustrated appetites or emotions. Their unhappiness would provide both with a strong incentive to either give up the struggle and become vicious, or succeed in integrating their wayward appetites or emotions with their convictions and become virtuous in some domains. Perhaps this is why Aristotle states that, unlike vice, *akrasia* is "curable" and not "continuous" (1150b 33 ff.). The same, of course, is true of *enkrateia*.

By contrast with the other traits, everyday experience as well as social psychology show that global vice is all too possible.[57] Someone who is coldly indifferent to others' weal or woe is devoid of all goodness, as is someone who is afflicted by a deep and universal misanthropy. And cold indifference or universal misanthropy are both doubly incompatible with well-being: they are incompatible with worth, and they are incompatible with happiness. Coldly indifferent or misanthropic people may be subject to occasional impulses of fellow feeling, but impulses are neither dispositions, nor a form of practical understanding. Vicious people may have charm—as Stalin evidently did in some situations; they may be gentle with furry little animals—as Hitler evidently was; and they may eat healthy—as Pol Pot perhaps did. But in the context of their overall vicious goals and nasty dispositions, none of these dispositions makes a dent in their vice. There are also individuals who, while less than universal in their indifference or misanthropy, have such warped values that they must be seen as thoroughly vicious. Such seem to be the Mengeles and Himmlers of the world.

It is sometimes asserted that someone who is sincerely committed to evil principles can't be all bad, because he is, after all, acting on his conscience. But acting on one's conscience is, at best, only formally right, and it is not even formally right when that conscience has been corrupted by one's own choices in the face of better alternatives.[58] Nevertheless, the role of moral luck in what we become cannot be denied, and sometimes even

---

this restriction: it makes perfect sense to see the sphere of incontinence and continence as being coextensive with that of the virtues and vices.

[57] On the evidence from social psychology, see my discussion of some of the obedient subjects in the Milgram experiments in Section 6.7 of "Milgram Experiments" (2009).

[58] See Alan Donagan, *The Theory of Morality* (1979), 134–139, on the distinction between formal and material rightness. Donagan argues that Huck Finn is both formally and materially right in his decision to help Jim escape, because although doing so is contrary to his conscience, it is true to "his deepest consciousness."

global vice is due entirely to luck. As we have seen, virtuous habituation requires a great deal of knowledge of human psychology and human institutions, and habituation into appropriate emotional dispositions. But such knowledge and such dispositions depend to a large extent on the resources available to us—and the resources may be impoverished. This dependence opens up vast possibilities for inculpable ignorance and inculpable vice. On the most abstract level, an individual may be brought up on false metaphysical and moral theories and habituated into perverse emotional dispositions. For example, a young Taliban boy, forced to memorize the Koran without understanding it, kept ignorant of other viewpoints on the world, taught to be intolerant of all disagreement with his religious dogmas, and made to view with suspicion or hatred the pleasures of sex, music, and play, has little chance of understanding himself or others. Indeed, he has little chance of ever understanding the value of life on this earth. His vice is complete through no fault of his own. A son of the Pharaohs brought up to believe that he and his family have a divine origin, and are meant to rule the ignorant and base masses, can hardly be expected to see through the sham, especially as everyone around him, including those base masses, reinforces this belief through their words and actions. He is less unfortunate than the Taliban boy, because he is at least taught to appreciate and enjoy many goods of the mind and the body. But both he and the young Taliban boy are condemned to lives of injustice toward the many, in ignorance not only of their victims' natures and aspirations, but also their own, unless some fortuitous alteration in their environments offers them a way out of their mental traps.

6.8. Conclusion

I have argued that the neo-Aristotelian conception of the virtues as integrated intellectual-emotional dispositions (or, in the language of empirical psychology, cohesive cognitive-affective dispositions) to deliberate, feel, and act appropriately is both descriptively and normatively adequate. The demanding epistemic and emotional requirements of virtue, on the one hand, and the cognitive and motivational architecture of our minds, on the other, make global virtue psychologically impossible, whereas the nature of practical wisdom and virtuous motivation, as well as the nature of virtue acquisition, make fragmented virtue both conceptually and psychologically impossible. Virtue is always domain-specific and comes in degrees, as indeed do continence and incontinence. Only vice seems capable of being global. Because virtue comes in degrees, the boundary between virtue and continence is not always clear-cut. But no virtue can stand alone: because a virtue is a disposition to respond appropriately to the normative features of our world, and every situation is normatively complex, it follows that every domain-specific virtue entails other relevant domain-specific virtues.

These facts caution care in our evaluations and expectations of ourselves and others. For example, it would be hasty to conclude on the basis of some virtue in an individual that she is flawless. It would also be hasty to conclude on the basis of a vice that she is a moral loser and can have no well-being as the HPG. But this does not mean that we are barred from making any generalizations or predictions. Since the virtues come in clusters, we are justified in our common practice of using evidence of one virtue to predict others and, should the prediction turn out to be false, in either narrowing the scope of our initial judgment, or rejecting it altogether.

A realistic attitude toward ourselves and others embodies an understanding of these facts about virtue and the human powers and limitations that explain them, an understanding that tempers disappointment and allows optimism. A realistic attitude thus allows us to live with ourselves even as we aspire to improve ourselves, and to appreciate others' virtues without being blind to their faults. A realistic attitude thereby aids happiness in a worthwhile life.

In the next chapter I address four challenges to Aristotelian *eudaimonism*. One claims that thoroughly bad people can have all the prudential goods that a virtuous person can have, and so virtue is not necessary for *eudaimonia*. The second claims that Aristotelian *eudaimonism* is internally unstable. The third claims that the view that virtue, rather than happiness, is primary in *eudaimonia* is implausible. And the fourth claims that even if *eudaimonia* requires a worthwhile life, a worthwhile life does not require virtue, and so *eudaimonia* does not require virtue. I also argue against the newly-revived Stoic thesis that virtue is both necessary and sufficient for *eudaimonia*.

PART THREE | Well-Being and Virtue

CHAPTER 7 | Happy Villains and Stoic Sages,
External Goods and the
Primacy of Virtue

"Imaginary evil is romantic and varied; real evil is gloomy,
monotonous, barren, boring. Imaginary good is boring; real good is
always new, marvelous, intoxicating."

—SIMONE WEIL

7.1 Introduction

In chapters 2 and 3, I argued that the idea of well-being as the highest prudential good (HPG) is internally coherent and plausible, and that to meet
the constraints of the HPG, well-being must be conceived of as happiness in
a worthwhile life. I also addressed the main subjectivist arguments against
objectivist theories of well-being. These arguments turn on the nature of
well-being which, subjectivists hold, does not admit of objective standards
of worth. Without these standards, however, subjectivist conceptions fail
to pass the test of descriptive and normative adequacy. In order to pass the
test, the more sophisticated subjectivist theories illicitly smuggle in standards of authenticity or good functioning, standards that cannot be justified
in terms of their own premises. But since these theories interpret authenticity or good functioning in a way that is consistent with almost any way of
life chosen by an individual, they still fail to meet the test of descriptive or
normative adequacy and the conditions of well-being as the HPG.

In this chapter I begin by addressing Bernard Williams' and Brad
Hooker's arguments against the claim that virtue is constitutively or
non-instrumentally necessary for *eudaimonia*, arguments that, so far as

I know, have never been seriously challenged (Sections 7.2 and 7.3). I then address arguments that purport to show that Aristotelian *eudaimonism* fails in its own terms (Sections 7.4 and 7.6). The basis for these objections is the complex structure of Aristotelian *eudaimonism*: happiness or sense of fulfillment in a virtuous life with an adequate supply of external (including bodily) goods. External goods are necessary not only as material for virtuous activity, which is the primary element in *eudaimonia*, but also as sources of happiness in their own right. (What this means I explain below.) Since I endorse this conception of *eudaimonia*, the objections apply to my neo-Aristotelian view as well. One objection to this view is that it is "unstable" because it pulls us in two opposite directions.[1] I address this objection in Section 7.4. In Section 7.5, I critically discuss Terence Irwin's claim that the primacy of virtue entails that the virtuous agent is more *eudaimon* than anyone else, regardless of the circumstances.[2] I argue that this does not follow from the primacy of virtue thesis and is, indeed, incompatible with the Aristotelian view that external goods are essential for *eudaimonia* in their own right. Then I turn to Haybron's objection that the primacy of virtue thesis is intuitively implausible, because it entails that more virtuous but less happiness-making activities contribute more to well-being than less virtuous but more happiness-making activities (Section 7.6). In Section 7.7 I argue against the newly revived Stoic thesis that virtue is both necessary and sufficient for *eudaimonia*.[3] The Stoic theory is simpler and theoretically more satisfying in certain respects, but this advantage comes at the cost of a drastic, and utterly implausible, revision of the idea of *eudaimonia*. I end this chapter by discussing the objection that well-being does not entail any other-regarding moral goodness, because a person can lead a life that is happy and overall objectively worthwhile without it (Section 7.8). If this claim turns out to be true, then all *eudaimonist* theories must be declared false.

I hope to show that Aristotelian *eudaimonism* and, thus, my view, can survive these challenges, and so we do not need to replace it either with a weaker thesis, or with the stronger, Socratic-Stoic thesis. I will start with Williams' influential critique in his *Ethics* (1985) of the claim that *eudaimonia* requires virtue, and show that he misses his target twice over, because

---

[1] Annas, *Happiness* (1993).
[2] "The Virtues: Theory and Common Sense in Greek Philosophy" (hereafter "Theory and Common Sense") (1996).
[3] Annas, *Happiness* (1993), chapter 18; Becker, *Stoicism* (1999).

neither his conception of well-being nor his conception of virtue is the conception used by any *eudaimonist* thesis.

7.2 The "Dangerously Flourishing" Villain

7.2.1 Williams argues that "an adequate psychology of character" will recognize many types of people whose happiness or unhappiness is either inversely related to their ethical state, or is independent of it (*Ethics*, 45). There is the villain, "rarer perhaps than Callicles supposed, but real, who is horrible enough and not miserable at all but, by any ethological standard of the bright eye and the gleaming coat, dangerously flourishing" (ibid., 46). Williams acknowledges that flourishing villains seem more plausible when separated from us in time—they "seem sleeker and finer at a distance. Some Renaissance grandee fills such a role with more style than...tawdry" fascists or gangsters (46). Nevertheless, Williams believes that psychologically healthy and not miserable villains are possible. His description of his villain suggests someone who survives and succeeds in his pursuits ("bright eye and gleaming coat") by exercising dominion over his circumstances and the people around him ("dangerously flourishing by any ethological standard").

This, however, still leaves an important question unanswered: even if the villain is not miserable, does he have a sense of self-worth and does he feel secure in his power? Now assuredly, the answers to these questions are in the negative for most tyrants and gangsters, who are typically insecure about their public image, anxious about possible enemies, and either filled with hostility and resentment or affectively flat.[4] Let us grant, however, that Williams' villain does have a sense of self-worth, feels secure in his power, and enjoys his life. He gets a kick from people's pretended admiration for him or, perhaps, simply from their suffering. Perhaps he feels justified in oppressing people because he regards himself as superior to them in intelligence, practical skills, physical prowess, or character. Or perhaps he doesn't care about being justified: enough, for him, that he controls them,

---

[4] See, for example, Steven Cox, *Blood and Power: Organized Crime in Twentieth Century America* (1989), and Nathan McCall's autobiographical *Makes Me Wanna Holler: A Young Black Man in America* (1994). McCall recalls his penchant for holding a grudge, for hatred and vengeance (ibid., 106) not only toward the oppressive whites, but also toward other blacks, the chief victims of his predatory activities (86). See also Joseph Pistone, *The Way of the Wiseguy* (2004) and the movie, *Donnie Brasco*, for an undercover FBI agent's firsthand account of the friendless and miserable lives of the wiseguys.

and feels confident that he can always outwit them. This sense of power, he thinks, is what anyone with any spirit would desire for his own enjoyment. Being vicious, he either "does not recognize that he is vicious" (*NE* 1150b 35), for "vice perverts [him]...and produces false views about the principles of actions" (1144a 35–6)—or he recognizes his own viciousness and is undisturbed by, and maybe even proud of, it.[5] If this is the psychological condition of the vicious man, then we must grant that he feels happy.

But there are two problems with a happiness that comes chiefly from power over others—a power that requires his victims to be relatively weak, fearful, cowardly, or stupid. One is that even though the tyrant or gangster feels secure in his power, his power rests on shaky foundations, since people are prone to hate their oppressors and plot against them. As Hobbes pointed out, those who are weak individually may still be strong collectively. The more serious problem is that, even if they fail to overthrow him, his sense of worth and positive assessment of his life are based on a fiction, the fiction that his superiority entitles him to oppress them or that oppressing them is the thing to do for anyone with any spirit. He either fails to see, or fails to care and act upon, the fact that each of his victims is as much a center of experience, as much a source of valid claims, as he himself. He makes of the other "a ghost, as the imprudent man makes of his future self a ghost."[6] His blindness, or his lack of motivation, may be due to long habituation in self-deception and cruelty, or to an inborn deficiency in his capacity for empathy. If he is blind to others' status as ends in themselves, then he is also blind to his own status as an end, since to understand oneself as an end, a person, requires seeing oneself, to paraphrase Nagel, not only as an 'I,' but also as one person among (at least some) others.[7] But even if his problem is not that he is completely blind to his own and others' status as ends, but that he is insufficiently motivated to treat others as ends, he is, like the severely retarded man, impeded in the functioning of a central human capacity, and fails the reality test of well-being. Hence he cannot have *eudaimonia*.

---

[5] Aristotle's portrait of vicious men in *NE* VI.12 and VII.8 suggests that they are free of conflict, since all three parts of their souls—reason, emotions, and appetites—are in harmony. He does not recognize the possibility, described above, that vicious men may recognize their vice and simply not care. In IX.4, however, he states that vicious men are self-destructive out of self-hatred and shun their own company, and that out of "cowardice or laziness" they "shrink from doing what they think best for themselves" (1166b 10–14).

[6] Royce, *The Religious Aspect of Philosophy* (1885/1976), 159.

[7] Nagel, *The Possibility of Altruism* (1970).

Williams' next argument, if sound, poses a stronger challenge to my thesis.

7.2.2 Williams imagines people who are miserable *because* they "try hard to be generous and to accommodate others' interests" (*Ethics*, 45). The implication is that not only is other-regarding virtue unnecessary for *eudaimonia*, the attempt to be other-regarding can actually be inherently misery-making for some people. One possible explanation for this, Williams continues, is that they are "victims of a suppressed self-assertion that might once have been acknowledged but now cannot be, still less overcome or redirected" (ibid., 45–46).

Presumably, Williams means that these miserable people would be better off if they could stop trying to be other-regarding and accept their "suppressed self-assertion" instead. But if so, then Williams' explanation of their misery as due to their "ethical state" (their attempts to be other-regarding) is only a partial explanation. The full explanation is that they are trying to be other-regarding without being properly self-regarding ("victims of a suppressed self-assertion"). They are fundamentally out of touch with their own needs and interests and so, like the "flourishing villain," they fail the reality test for well-being. By the same token, their failure is also an ethical one, since on the *eudaimonist* view, a proper concern for one's own well-being is a central part of one's "ethical state".

Williams' underdescribed example raises another question: do these miserable individuals try to accommodate others' interests because they believe that they owe this to others, or simply because they want others to think well of them? If they do it because they think they ought to, then even though their actions frustrate their desires and cause some feelings of unhappiness, their actions must be at the same time a source of pride and self-worth. At any rate, the failure to do these actions would lead them to think less of themselves and also cause unhappiness. So it is inaccurate to say that they are miserable from their ethical states. Rather, they are miserable because they have not yet succeeded in integrating their emotions and desires with their judgments. If, however, they try to accommodate others' interests only for the sake of being well thought of by others, then, even though their actions might have some good effects, their motives are not virtuous and their actions are intrinsically unrewarding to them. And so, once again, it is inaccurate to say that their unhappiness is caused by their ethical states.

Williams then imagines another putative counterexample to the Aristotelian thesis to show that *eudaimonia* and moral goodness can be inversely related, depending on the individual's psychology. He imagines someone who is "horrible and rather miserable," but who is "successful and has some pleasures, and if he were less horrible he would not be successful, and would be no less anxious, because he would be frustrated..." (46). But what is he successful at, and what is meant by being "less horrible"? The suggestion is that what he is successful at is itself something unsavory, since being less horrible would stand in the way of his success. And Williams' point seems to be that if he were better ethically he would be worse off prudentially. But would he? Less pleasure and lack of success (in horrible projects) is not identical with less happiness. Even happiness requires a sense of worth, and *eudaimonia* requires, in addition, objective worth. Moreover, if the horrible individual's horribleness consists of envy, jealousy, greed, spite, or malice, then it is inherently unpleasant, so whatever pleasure he gains from success in his endeavors has to be weighed against the unpleasantness of his character.

Consequently, if he were to become better ethically, his life would have one less source of unpleasantness, and greater objective worth. Again, whatever sense of worth he might derive from his existential success would be replaced by a sense of worth from his success in improving his character. He may end up no closer to *eudaimonia* if his moral improvement is miniscule and his lack of success significant. But this is perfectly consistent with the thesis that virtue is necessary for *eudaimonia* as the highest good, since the individual in question lacks virtue.

There are too many questions about Williams' examples to allow us to come to any firm conclusions, but the general point is clear. A successful argument against the claim that virtue is necessary for *eudaimonia* must keep in mind that *eudaimonia* requires both objective worth and a sense of fulfillment. If *eudaimonia* is equated simply with pleasant feelings or enjoyment, and objective worth with actions that benefit others, with no thought of self, it should not be surprising to find that the two may be inversely related.

In the next section I address Brad Hooker's challenge to *eudaimonism*.[8] His challenge is important because it shows that the common view about the relationship of moral and epistemic virtues to what are widely taken to be important prudential goods is mistaken.

---

[8] See Hooker, "Is Moral Virtue a Benefit to the Agent?" hereafter "Moral Virtue" (1996), 141–155.

7.3. Upright vs. Unscrupulous

7.3.1 Hooker assumes that the objective list theory of well-being is the only alternative to subjective theories, and accepts the usual view of objective list theorists: that pleasure, knowledge of important things, achievements of various sorts, friendship, autonomy, "and perhaps the appreciation of beauty," are constitutive or non-instrumental "fundamental categories of prudential value" (*Moral Virtue*, 149). He then asks whether moral virtue can be defended as a fundamental and constitutive or non-instrumental prudential good on this theory. At this point, two clarifications are in order. First, the virtues that Hooker is concerned with are other-regarding virtues, such as justice, generosity, and so on, but I will also consider epistemic virtues. Second, as is clear by now, *eudaimonism* is not an objective list theory, but Hooker's question can be directed at any theory of well-being that takes virtue or moral goodness to be partly constitutive of the agent's good.

Hooker proposes a novel thought experiment as the best way of answering his question. He invites us to imagine that Upright and Unscrupulous have equal and maximal amounts of the acknowledged fundamental prudential goods in their lives (ibid., 152). Their only difference is that Upright's life contains the pleasures of morality and moral achievements, whereas Unscrupulous's life contains the pleasures of immorality and non-moral achievements. Unscrupulous, as the name suggests, is very, very bad, not just morally mediocre. Hooker indicates that gangsters and pirates qualify as the sorts of people he has in mind, and doubtless would agree that anyone who lives a life of violent predation qualifies. The question now is: do we feel sorry for Unscrupulous for lacking virtue, as we would if he lacked friendship, knowledge of important things, pleasure, or autonomy?[9]

Hooker argues that many people who have not already made up their minds that moral goodness is a fundamental prudential good would not feel sorry for Unscrupulous for lacking it (149–150). The question is: "Why?" After a consideration of various alternatives, he concludes that

---

[9.] Hooker first imagines that Upright and Unscrupulous both lead "sad and wretched lives," although Upright is morally virtuous and Unscrupulous is immoral, and asks if we feel *sorrier* for Unscrupulous than for Upright (149). If moral virtue is a fundamental prudential good, Hooker argues, then we *should* feel sorrier for Unscrupulous, since he is not only sad and wretched, but also immoral. So if we don't feel sorrier for him, it must mean that we don't really believe that moral virtue is a fundamental category of prudential value on par with the others on the list. My answer to this is basically the same as my answer to the case I discuss above.

the best explanation for the lack of sympathy is that many of us do not think that Unscrupulous's immorality is bad for him. In other words, we do not believe that morality is a fundamental prudential good. Rather, at best we believe that it is "a subcategory of achievement" whose absence may be outweighed by forms of achievement open only to the immoral (155).

7.3.2 I grant that we would not feel sorry for Unscrupulous if he had all the prudential goods that Upright has. But this is a big "if." Hooker's arguments rest on the widely-shared but dubious assumption that someone completely lacking in morality can have fundamental prudential goods.[10] There are many reasons why this is dubious. One reason, already discussed, is that horrible people usually have horrible dispositions and motives such as hatred, jealousy, envy, malice, rage, and so on. The psychological state of most horrible people is, therefore, inherently unpleasant, indeed, unhappy. Still, this is not the case with all such people. Badness can be due to indifference to people outside one's own community or in-group. And whatever the explanation for nasty motives or indifference, so long as they are not directed at *everyone*, there is room in a nasty individual's life for *some* prudential goods, such as friendship. But this, I will argue, means that there is room in his life for virtue, no matter how narrow in scope. Hooker acknowledges that people capable of friendship must have "some concern" for another, even though this is not enough "to qualify [a]…life as a moral one" (152, n. 21). I agree with Hooker on the latter point, but I think that "some concern" might not quite capture the virtue implicit in a genuine, close friendship. But I will start by asking how likely it is for people who are overall just plain bad to have genuine friendships or the other fundamental prudential goods.

The first point to note is that genuine friendships, friendships in which there is an active concern for each other's good, are extremely rare among unscrupulous people. Even among the family-oriented Mafia, rarely do fathers encourage their sons to use their education to seek a safer, more rewarding, and more worthwhile life for themselves. Their affective ties, then, not only do not typically enhance their sons' highest prudential good, they limit it. Moreover, the very possibility of forming genuine friendships is highly limited, because not only is there inter-gang warfare, there is also infighting that leads to the splintering of gangs into sub-groups that survive by fighting each other.[11] In some gangs, there is not much difference between a friend and an enemy because there is not much honor or justice even among the gang members. As Lefty, a character in the film, *Donnie*

[10.] Sumner makes the same assumption in "Is Virtue Its Own Reward?" (1998).

[11.] http://en.wikipedia.org/wiki/Crips; http://en.wikipedia.org/wiki/Bloods, accessed July 2013.

Brasco, tells Brasco: "When they send for you, you go in alive, you come out dead, and it's your best friend that does it."[12] And any attempt to leave incurs the real risk of being "whacked" by their erstwhile comrades.

Do gangsters fare any better on autonomy? The disposition to think and choose independently in important areas of one's life is not a quality that is highly valued among gangsters. As Lefty says, "Who the fuck am I? Who am I? I'm a, a spoke on a wheel. And so was he, and so are you." Everyone must obey the boss unquestioningly.[13] The boss himself becomes a boss only by obeying blindly, and never knows how long he will be boss before he is "whacked" by a "friend" wanting to take his place.[14]

Nevertheless, genuine, close friendship is certainly possible among gangsters, including street gangsters. Leon Bing's book, *Do or Die*, describes how older kids in the Crips or the Bloods, often those who've been paralyzed or otherwise badly injured, sometimes develop genuine love for younger draftees into the gang, and teach them how to read and write—and escape gang life. To love someone genuinely is to love him as an end, to care for him for his own sake, and not only as a means to other ends. Such love entails wishing him well, and this in turn entails understanding and responding appropriately to his needs, desires, and abilities as a human being and as the individual he is. In turn, this requires, as these gangsters recognize, wanting their friends to get out of the gang—for life in a gang is nasty, brutish, and short. Hence these gangsters must have a fairly robust, but narrowly confined, set of virtues—kindness, generosity, courage, justice, and loyalty—towards those they teach and help to escape.

Perhaps it is improbable to hold that anyone can have these traits in such a narrow area of life without having any moral decency in any other area of life. For understanding a friend requires understanding human beings in general, not to mention friendship in general, and understanding is likely

---

[12] The film is based on the true story of an FBI agent who infiltrated the Bonanno crime family in New York, posing as a jewel thief expert called Donnie Brasco.

[13] See, for example, Virgil W. Peterson, *The Mob: 200 Years of Organized Crime in New York* (1983) on the use of torture and murder to punish double-crossers, and the fear of violence to maintain "rigid discipline" (426). See also the minutes of the Oyster Bay Conference of organized-crime-control specialists, describing the structure of various organized crime groups: "They are totalitarian in nature — The leader of the organization has absolute authority over the life and death of the organization's members" (cited in Dwight C. Smith, Jr., *The Mafia Mystique* [1975]), 247.

[14] The 5th commandment of the Cosa Nostra states: "Always being available for Cosa Nostra is a duty—even if your wife's about to give birth." Of course, a secret agent might have the same duty. But if he fails, he is fired, not finished. And he treats only some institutions and some members of some foreign governments as his (government's) enemies, whereas gangsters treat any and all institutions and members of civil society anywhere as actual or potential enemies.

to bring some concern for other people's good. If this is the case, then genuine friendship with another gang member requires decency towards at least some people outside the gang, and a gangster who doesn't have any such decency cannot have a genuine friendship. Either way, the gangster must be virtuous towards his friends to have the prudential good of close friendship.[15]

Hooker suggests that Unscrupulous can have morally neutral achievements to make up for his lack of moral achievements, but does not give any examples. Perhaps he has in mind skills that are a justifiable object of admiration to others, and a source of pride for the person who has them. Consider, for example, the dry wit and clever repartee of some of James Bond's adversaries, the ingenious planning of the evil warlord, the daredevilry of the ruthless double agent who leaps across buildings trying to escape from law and justice, the ambidextrous expertise of the six-shooter who tries to slay the hero—all these can evoke our delighted admiration, even as the ends they serve evoke our abhorrence. But the significance of these achievements pales by comparison to those open to Upright as a trustworthy member of a cooperative community held together by justice and mutual trust. Upright can have all the qualities and do all the things that Unscrupulous can have or do—have a rapier wit, be a daredevil or an ambidextrous six-shooter, make ingenious plans—and much more besides. It is not an accident that street gangsters or the Mafia or, for that matter, tyrants are not known for being good entrepreneurs, inventors, writers, artists, or intellectuals (although some tyrants have a predilection for being seen as such).[16]

There are, however, deeper reasons why they do not boast more or more important achievements, namely, that as in the case of friendship, some moral decency is part of the very structure of most worthwhile achievements. This is why (most?) Mafia enterprises fail to be achievements even when they do something useful, such as providing goods and services arbitrarily outlawed by the state, such as alcohol under Prohibition, gambling, and so on. For they do it with the help of violence to drive out competition and raise prices. Their stock in trade is extortion, violent seizure of people's businesses, killing would-be competitors in order to establish a monopoly on trades, preying on small farmers and shopkeepers, or

---

[15.] I discuss the virtues inherent in friendship in "Friendship, Justice, and Supererogation" (April 1985), 123–131. However, I did not there entertain the possibility that even murderous gangsters might be capable of genuine friendships.

[16.] Hitler fancied himself a great painter, Mao some sort of great intellectual, and Saddam Hussein a great poet and novelist.

sucking the wealth out of a country or community by driving out would-be entrepreneurs and investors.[17] What drives them to do this is nothing more exalted than money-and power-lust. Their achievements in business are, thus, no more genuine than the achievement of an athlete who "wins" a competition by cheating or breaking his rival's legs—and no more admirable. What prevents their activities from being genuine achievements is precisely their injustice and dishonesty. Just and honest behavior in exchange and in competition are partly constitutive of achievement in business, as they are in sports.[18] Only trade without force or fraud counts as voluntary trade, and only money made honestly counts as earned.

I say "just and honest behavior" rather than the *virtues* of justice and honesty, or even a principled commitment to justice and honesty, for good reason. A person who reliably acts in a just and honest manner only because he thinks that justice and honesty are good policy can have the prudential good of achievement. He would do better, however, if he were to develop a principled commitment to justice and honesty, and even better if he were to develop the virtues of justice and honesty, both because his behavior would then be even more reliable, and because acting on principle, and even more so from virtue, brings an emotional reward that acting merely on a useful policy does not.

Again, gangsters and tyrants are not usually known for their intellectual achievements in science, philosophy, etc.—and for the same sorts of reasons. Intellectual inquiry requires an adherence to the canons of rationality and a desire to pursue the truth. And this, in turn, requires honesty with oneself, openmindedness to others' views, respect for certain epistemic norms and for one's intellectual peers or superiors, and the courage to surmount obstacles to one's search and accept one's mistakes. In short, intellectual achievement requires intellectual inquiry, and such inquiry is partly constituted by certain epistemic and moral virtues.

---

[17] This has happened in Sicily. See "Best of Sicily: A Guide to Sicilian Travel and all things Sicilian" at http://www.bestofsicily.com/mafia.htm. But there has been some encouraging news recently, thanks largely to the initiative of the anti-Mafia movement, "Libera Terra." See http://www.globalpost.com/dispatch/italy/091027/libera-terra-food, accessed January 27, 2014.

[18] This is a good place to point out that predatory activity is not limited to outlaws. Every time a politician threatens to shake down a business unless that business supports his campaign, or every time a business or other special interest group lobbies politicians for special favors, that politician, business, or special interest group engages in predation. A political-economic system in which this is common is rife with prisoners' dilemmas: a business does better by lobbying for special favors whether or not its competitors do, and since other businesses reason and act the same way, they all do worse than they would if such lobbying were prohibited.

Still, it must be admitted that there are some great achievements that do not require any other-regarding moral goodness. Suppose that Unscrupulous has a great inborn talent for singing, which he develops because he enjoys singing and the adulation of the crowds, but that he has only contempt for, or indifference towards, the crowds, and those who care for him or try to help him. Since he is Unscrupulous, he also hates other singers who seem any good, and tries to harm them. But he does have knowledge of some important things related to his success as a singer, such as who is the best voice coach. He also has autonomy in the sense of the freedom to decide what to sing when, whom to harm, and so on. In order to keep this sense of autonomy distinct from my own, namely, the intellectual and emotional disposition to live by one's reality-oriented judgments in important areas of life, I will call it autonomy*. So now he has five of the items from Hooker's list of fundamental prudential goods: great achievement, some enjoyment, knowledge of some of his own interests, autonomy*, and some appreciation of beauty.

Is he a counterexample to my claim that an individual without any other-regarding goodness cannot have any well-being as the HPG? Not quite. Note, first, that knowledge of important things without the appropriate motivation (and Hooker makes it clear on pp. 146–147 that motivation to act on one's knowledge is not one of the goods on his list) is not of much use to its possessor. For example, knowledge of his own interests becomes a prudential good to its possessor only when it is appropriated and used in a fitting manner. It is not a benefit to him if he fails again and again to be motivated to further his interests through akrasia or apathy or vanity.[19] Thus, Unscrupulous' knowledge of who is the best voice coach is useless if his vanity leads him to hire coaches who will flatter him instead of pushing him to improve. So to "knowledge of some of his own interests as a singer" let us add "with the appropriate motivations" and call it knowledge*. Again, autonomy* in the sense of freedom to decide what to sing when is useless if the singer's decisions are made on a whim, or out of jealousy of other singers, and lack all concern with which program or which venue would serve his interests as a singer. So to "decides autonomously*" let us add "in the light of some concern with his interests as a singer". Now Unscrupulous's knowledge* and autonomy* are of some prudential value to him as a singer. But since his only sources of fulfillment are his singing,

---

[19.] And theoretical knowledge of important things is of little benefit to the knower if he takes no joy in the process of acquiring it, builds nothing on it, and doesn't enjoy contemplating it.

the adulation of the crowds, the effort he puts into developing his talent, and perhaps the pleasures of cruelty, and all of these are undercut by his jealousy, rage, and contempt, his life is too bleak to be happy, giving him little to celebrate.

Let us therefore add that this unscrupulous singer has one close, genuine friendship. Now his life gives him a little more to celebrate. But now it also contains some other-regarding virtue. For as we have already seen, close, genuine friendships entail some other-regarding virtue towards friends, and perhaps also some concern for other people. Even so, however, Unscrupulous leads a highly reduced life, barring himself from many sorts of achievements and many sorts of fulfilling relationships, and filling it with unpleasant emotions like jealousy and hatred. And this is because his knowledge* of important things and his autonomy* are minimal. If they were great enough for leading a full life, he would be realistic and, thus, virtuous. If, in addition, he was also happy, his life would be *eudaimon*.

7.3.3 If I am right so far, then we must reject Hooker's very question, the question whether other-regarding virtue—more generally, other-regard—is a fundamental prudential good like pleasure, friendship, achievement, adequate knowledge*, adequate autonomy*, etc. For this question assumes that other-regard is something over and above—or alongside—all these goods. But as I have argued, moral and epistemic virtues or goodness do not occupy their own special rarefied realm. Rather, they are part of the very structure of genuine, close friendships, and of some important achievements. Without them, these goods fail to be. Hence we must reject Hooker's assumption that Unscrupulous can have exactly the same quantity of prudential goods in his life as Upright. If this were true, Unscrupulous would not be Unscrupulous—he would be Upright.

Unscrupulous' problem can be summed up as follows: he either fails to understand the role of worthwhile activities in well-being, or he fails to be motivated by his understanding. In his callousness towards others, he either fails to understand that others are as much sources of valid claims as he himself, or he fails to be motivated by his understanding. In the exception he makes of himself and the few he may care about, he fails to see or to care about the fact that he and his friends are only, in Nagel's words, "one person among others". Hence, Unscrupulous fails in realism in a large swath of his existence. In other words, his lack of moral goodness implies a lack of realism and, thus, of well-being. If most of us still don't feel sorry for him, it is because we don't feel sorry for people who are willing to harm us and cause us misery. This lack of sympathy is deepened if he doesn't even suffer pain for his actions. Yet when we focus on his blindness to his own needs and motives rather than on his victims' suffering, we see that he is a sorry specimen of a man. And then we can feel pity for him.

It might be thought that it is fairly easy to show that there is nothing to be said for being thoroughly unscrupulous, for being the kind of person who pillages and assaults as a way of life, or who, like my Unscrupulous singer, treats others as mere means to his (legitimate) ends. But what about those whose vice is more mundane, involving no violence? Or those whose vice is largely self-regarding? If they make up for their vice by their gains in happiness, are they really making such a bad deal? On my theory, of course, to the extent that they are vicious, they lack well-being, since well-being on my theory is happiness in a worthwhile life and, by hypothesis, their lives are moderately unworthwhile. But it might be thought that if moderate immorality can be crowned with success and happiness, then it poses a challenge to my conception of well-being.

An example of moderate vice is provided by Rosamond, a secondary character in George Eliot's *Middlemarch*, whose "[e]very nerve and muscle…was adjusted to the consciousness that she was being looked at," and who "even acted her own character, and so well, that she did not know it to be precisely her own."[20] Her guiding interest in life is to occupy a high social rank, her mind presenting a "blank unreflecting surface" to her husband's passion for his scientific work (Loc. 10170–10171). "He once called her his basil plant…[because] basil was a plant which had flourished wonderfully on a murdered man's brains" (Loc. 14310–14316). Yet she is so closed to his feelings, his perspective, that she is free of all guilt for continually frustrating his wishes by her stratagems, and insisting that he give up his dreams in order to provide her with the rank and wealth she "deserves". Indeed, she sees herself as a martyr for tolerating his occasional frustrated outbursts. She has no understanding of either him or herself. He dies prematurely at fifty, whereupon she marries an older wealthy man who indulges her whims. She is pleased to tell everyone that she has finally been "rewarded," ostensibly for her patience with her first husband (Loc. 14305–14310). She sees herself as finally happy, and it is true that she is not unhappy. But if happiness is a sense of fulfillment in a meaningful life, if it is a psychic affirmation of one's life, then what she has is

---

[20.] George Eliot, *Middlemarch*, Illustrated Kindle edition, 2011. Kindle Loc. 2237–2239.

not happiness. Her constant preoccupation with social rank, with being praised above other women, with being the cynosure of all eyes, almost certainly comes with constant anxiety about every new woman who enters her social circle, and about her own looks as she ages, especially as she has nothing deeper or "more her own" to absorb her attention and serve as a source of fulfillment. So while her shallowness protects her from unhappiness, it also prevents her from achieving happiness. And although she is not evil, and even exhibits a spark of goodness towards Dorothea, the novel's heroine, her life is far from being a worthwhile life.

The following example of moderate vice for the sake of happiness might provide a stronger challenge to my thesis. Suppose that honesty or courage with his social group would make Lonesome the odd one out, maybe even lead to ostracism. All the empirical evidence we have on exclusion and ostracism points to its painfulness. And so, in order to reduce social dissonance and fit in better with the crowd, Lonesome suppresses the doubts and questions he has about the going ideology and surrenders his independent judgment. To secure his position in the group, and make himself immune to doubt, Lonesome reads only the publications or listens only to the programs that spout views that those who count in his universe agree with. If he reads contrary views, or listens to contrary viewpoints, it is only for the sake of finding their weak spots and refuting them. Now he is "happily" one with the group in its echo chamber.

This kind of attempt to silence the self for the sake of fitting in with the group sometimes creates an internal disharmony that can be just as pernicious—or more pernicious—than being rejected by one's group. Gays who have finally come out after years spent repressing their feelings and deceiving themselves about their sexual orientation report their unhappiness and/or their self-alienation in those years, and regret the fact that they lost years of possible sexual and romantic happiness with a partner. Someone who surrenders his independent judgment for the sake of fitting in with the crowd suffers a similar loss. He doesn't look for people who might share his values, people with whom he can have the sort of open conversation and discussion that is part of a friendship of equals. Moreover, by avoiding dialogue and argument, he never finds out to what extent his own values and beliefs, or those of his group, are justified.

Of course, with time Lonesome might internalize his new system of beliefs and values, so that he is almost completely free of conflict. His evasion of uncomfortable facts then becomes second nature to him and is constantly reinforced by those around him. He can achieve a most desirable harmony with his colleagues and, to his delight, even acquire a loyal fan base on Facebook that daily showers him with plaudits for his right-thinking posts. He might even become the moral leader of his group, pronouncing judgments that others feel compelled to agree with. And so, at last, he might be happy.

If this picture is accurate, then, in surrendering his integrity— his reality-orientation and autonomy—in order to avoid loneliness, Lonesome seems to have gained much in exchange for a small sacrifice of integrity. Note, however, that even if we assume that the system of values and beliefs he has adopted contains as much truth as, and no more falsehood than, his previous system of values and beliefs, the fact remains that he has acquired it and maintains it through a willful blindness to contrary values and beliefs. Moreover, should the composition and ideology of his group change, even his leadership position in the group might not protect him from rejection by the other members of his group. So even if Lonesome is happy, his happiness is both insecure and dearly bought. In some highly communal, closed societies, it may have been necessary for Lonesome to sacrifice some integrity for the sake of happiness, for in such societies, it is harder to find people who don't toe the communal line. But in the kind of society that he (and the readers of this book) inhabit, it is possible, even if hard, to find congenial companions and happiness without sacrificing one's integrity. And whatever the nature of one's society, such a sacrifice always entails the sacrifice of some happiness as well, since integrity itself is a source of happiness, and its surrender a source of unhappiness. To conclude this section: neither mundane nor moderate vice challenge my conception of well-being as the HPG. Although Rosamund is too shallow (as well as too fortunate in her circumstances) to be unhappy, she is also too shallow to be happy. Her determined superficiality and narcissism mean that there is little in her life that can serve as a source of deep fulfillment. Her preoccupation with others' views of her means that whatever pleasure she takes in life is almost entirely dependent on others. Lonesome does have some happiness, but his sacrifice of integrity and independence is doubly pointless: it brings with it a sacrifice of a far more secure source of happiness than acceptance by his group, and it is unnecessary even for such acceptance, since with time and effort he could have found a more congenial group. To the extent that Rosamund and Lonesome lack reality-orientation and autonomy, they not only lack a worthwhile life, but also the happiness such a life affords.

In the next two sections I will address objections that are internal to Aristotelian and neo-Aristotelian *eudaimonia*.

7.4. Is the Necessity Thesis Unstable?

In common with Socrates, Plato, and the Stoics, Aristotle holds that *eudaimonia* requires us to regulate our desires, goals, and actions by virtue in order to have both internal harmony and harmony with other virtuous agents' goals and actions. Of all the goods, virtue alone can never be misused.[21] Virtuous activity (or virtue, for short) thus contributes to our happiness and makes our lives worthwhile. Unlike Socrates and the Stoics, however, Aristotle holds that an adequate supply of external goods and a degree of success in our endeavors are also necessary for *eudaimonia*, not only as material for virtuous activity, but also in themselves.[22]

> [H]appiness [*eudaimonia*] evidently also needs external goods to be added...since we cannot, or cannot easily, do fine actions if we lack the resources...Further...we do not altogether have the character of happiness [*eudaimonia*] if we look utterly repulsive or are ill-born, solitary, or childless; and we have it even less, presumably, if our children or friends are totally bad, or were good but have died (1099a 30–1099b 6).[23]

We may not agree with Aristotle's judgment that all the external goods he lists, such as, for example, children, are essential for *eudaimonia*, but his general point that external goods are essential sources of *eudaimonia* in their own right is only part of common sense. But what exactly does this mean in the context of a theory that states that virtuous activity is the controlling element of *eudaimonia*? Surely external goods are sources of *eudaimonia* only insofar as we use them or respond to them according to virtue. So what additional contribution do they make to our *eudaimonia*,

---

[21] Irwin, "Theory and Common Sense" (1996).

[22] In *Human Good* (1986) Cooper interprets Aristotle as saying that external goods are necessary for *eudaimonia* only *qua* material for virtuous activity. On this interpretation Aristotelian *eudaimonia* is essentially the same as Stoic *eudaimonism*. Regardless of interpretive issues, however, I think that the correct view is that certain external goods are needed for happiness in their own right.

[23] Aristotle's remark about the importance of not being "utterly repulsive" is supported by the true story of the Elephant Man, Joseph Merrick, who led a terrible life until he was rescued by a doctor and became something of a celebrity in London high society (see the Wikipedia article, http://en.wikipedia.org/wiki/Joseph_Merrick, based on Ashley Montagu's *The Elephant Man: A Study in Human Dignity* (1971/2001), and other sources).

over and above the contribution made by our virtuous response to them or virtuous use of them?

My view is that external goods like reputation, wealth, health, decent friends, and a presentable appearance fulfill certain deep needs that cannot be fulfilled without them, no matter how virtuous our lives. We can be virtuous even if we lack these external goods by, for example, bearing our misfortune, or endeavoring to improve our circumstances, with courage and hope. But it is only if we both possess these goods and respond to them, or use them, according to virtue, that we can enjoyably exercise many of our powers and capacities and satisfy our basic human needs for society, security, and pleasure. With them, the virtuous person can live more fully and enjoyably than without them. This interpretation is supported by Aristotle's claim below that the lack of such goods involves pain and impedes "many activities":

> Many major strokes of good fortune will make it [a virtuous person's life] more blessed [*eudaimon*]: for in themselves they naturally add adornment to it, and his use of them proves to be fine and excellent. Conversely, if he suffers many major misfortunes, they oppress and spoil his blessedness, since they involve pain and impede many activities. And yet, even here what is fine shines through…And since it is activities that control life…no blessed person could ever become miserable, since he will never do hateful and base actions…but neither will he be blessed if he falls into misfortunes as bad as Priam's (NE 1100b 25–11101a 8).

Annas, however, argues that Aristotle's view is unstable because the claim that external goods are essential to *eudaimonia* in their own right, and not merely as material for virtue, does not sit easily with the claim that virtue is supreme, the controlling element in *eudaimonia*. Since I agree that external goods are essential to *eudaimonia* in their own right, Annas' objections apply to my view as well. Annas identifies three problems with this view.

(1) The first is that it does not offer any obvious way of determining the minimum amount of external goods essential for *eudaimonia* (*Happiness*, 381).

I would suggest that the minimum level of external goods necessary for *eudaimonia* is the level that allows a person to live a life that is both happy and worthwhile. Someone who spends most of his time in a joyless struggle to make ends meet, or cope with his physical disabilities, with little time or energy left for doing something positive with his life, does not have the minimum level. It would be a mistake, however, to think that poverty or physical disabilities in themselves are enough to rob a person of *eudaimonia*: a lot depends on his other circumstances and his native energy, talent, and personality. In some cases, as I discuss below, severe deprivation might actually lead to an enhancement of a person's life. In other cases, it might prevent him from being *eudaimon* without reducing him to misery. Ramón Sampedro, who became a quadriplegic after a diving accident at the age of twenty-five, and fought a thirty-year campaign for the right to die, is a case in point.[24] His plight called forth his heroism, and his heroism, good nature, and charismatic personality made him the object of love and admiration by many. His life was neither entirely unhappy, nor worthless; he wished to die because he found it humiliating to be totally dependent on, and a burden for, his family, especially the sister-in-law who was his chief caregiver.

(2) Annas' second objection to making external goods essential to *eudaimonia* is the reverse of the first: we cannot place an upper limit on external goods. For example, if "good health is required to make me happy, surely excellent health will make me even happier?" And so on for the other external goods, because the more of them I have, the greater is "the range and scope of my virtuous activity" (ibid., 381). Yet this runs into the claim that *eudaimonia* is that to which nothing can be added to make it better.

This is a real problem if we understand a *eudaimonic* life as a peak on a mountain, or an A+ on a grade sheet. But it is not a problem if we understand it, as we do virtue, as something that allows of degrees, both diachronically and synchronically: an uneven plateau with dips and rises, something that can go all the way from A- to A+, depending on its scope and depth.

I would also question Annas' substantive suggestion that on the Aristotelian view the more external goods I have, the greater is my *eudaimonia*. This might seem uncontroversial, at least of perfectly virtuous

---

[24.] The movie, *The Sea Inside* (December 2004), tells the story of Sampedro's struggle. See also the article on the making of the movie by Gregory Jordan, "Into the Life of a Man Fighting for the Right to Die," *New York Times*, December 15, 2004, http://www.nytimes.com/2004/12/15/movies/15samp.html, accessed July 2013; and these reports on his death and the issue of euthanasia in Spain: http://www.nytimes.com/1998/03/09/world/a-suicide-tape-on-tv-inflames-the-issue-in-spain.html, March 9, 1998 and http://web.archive.org/web/20110628230407/http://www.time.com/time/magazine/1998/int/980126/file.live_and_let_die.sh11.html, accessed July 2013. Before dying with the help of friends in 1998, Sampedro invented things that made his caretaking easier for his caretakers, and published a book of essays and a book of poetry.

agents, since such agents will use external goods in the most worthwhile and fulfilling manner. But even perfectly virtuous agents' time, energy, and interests are limited. So above a certain level, more external goods are a waste or a burden to them. At any rate, since there are no perfectly virtuous agents in my view, the truth value of the claim that the more external goods someone has, the greater is his *eudaimonia*, must be assessed for imperfectly virtuous agents. And the following examples show that, for such people, more external goods may increase their *eudaimonia*, leave it unaltered, or decrease it.

The last possibility is illustrated by the phenomenon of playboys who drift through life dissipating the huge fortunes left them by their parents, but who, without this fortune, would most probably have behaved like most other people and done something worthwhile with their lives. The second possibility, that more external goods might leave my *eudaimonia* unaltered, is illustrated when I neither use them to expand the scope of my worthwhile activities, nor, after an initial boost in happiness, manage to stay happier than before. The latter is a common phenomenon, explained by the well-known fact that we tend to adapt to our circumstances, both good and bad. For example, lottery winners typically return to their original levels of happiness after a period of intense happiness, and people who become quadriplegic typically return close to their original levels of happiness or unhappiness after a period of intense unhappiness (Haidt, *Happiness Hypothesis*, 84–85). The first possibility, that more external goods might increase my *eudaimonia*, is illustrated when I either use them to expand the scope of my worthwhile activities, or experience a permanent boost in my happiness, or both.

These facts show that the right level of external goods for an individual is the level compatible with her ability—time, energy, interests—to use these goods virtuously and happily. Possessing more than she can enjoy or put to worthwhile use, now or in the future, is a waste and a burden, and undertaking more, or more difficult, projects than she can do both enjoyably and virtuously detracts from her *eudaimonia* rather than adding to it. Like the minimum amount, then, the maximum amount of external goods needed for *eudaimonia* is also relative to a person's capacity for virtuous employment and enjoyment of them. This is true even of health. If excellent health would enable me to do more worthwhile things enjoyably, then excellent health would increase my *eudaimonia*. But sometimes it is bad health or physical disabilities that induce a person to make the best of his time and abilities, to learn to use them to achieve important goals, and to enjoy doing so. Writing about the effects of motor neurone disease on his life, Stephen Hawking reports that before he was diagnosed with it, he had been "very bored with life. There had not seemed to be anything worth doing."[25] After he was diagnosed, and told that he might not live long, he found to his own surprise that he was "enjoying life in the present more than before." He "began to make progress with...[his] research," and "got engaged to...Jane Wilde...," an event that, he says, "changed my life" and "gave me something to live for."

(3) The third problem Annas identifies with the thesis that external goods are required for *eudaimonia* has to do with the loss of external goods. If their loss makes you less *eudaimon*, Annas argues, "there should surely come a point where losing enough external goods makes you not happy [*eudaimon*] at all" (382). Yet as we have seen, Aristotle holds that "the blessed person could never become miserable," no matter how great his misfortune, because "he will never do hateful and base actions." Annas argues that Aristotle is trying to "hold two theses that sort ill together" (383).[26]

I am not sure why Annas thinks that these theses are in tension. They would be in tension if misery were the only alternative to *eudaimonia*. But as the examples of Sampedro, Boethius, and Admiral Stockdale (chapter 2) illustrate, there are many stages between *eudaimonia* and sheer misery. Although virtue is not enough to make a virtuous person *eudaimon* in the face of great misfortunes, it is enough to prevent him from becoming miserable. The fact that he can accept his fate with dignity and continue to act with integrity and justice, feeling the loss but not so much that he collapses in agony, is enough to protect him from sheer unhappiness. Boethius is particularly interesting in this regard. After initially giving in to despair, he recovers his equanimity and his agency by reminding himself (or having his imaginary Lady Philosophy remind him) of the fortunate life he has led till now, and of the power he still has to overcome his despair, and ends up writing the still-treasured *Consolations of Philosophy*. His betrayal by those he trusts and his subsequent imprisonment surely rob him of *eudaimonia*. But it is only if he loses that minimum level of external goods

---

[25] "Prof. Stephen Hawking's Disability Advice" (http://annalsofneurosciences.org/journal/index.php/annal/article/viewArticle/48/951, 2009, accessed January 2014). Recall, also, the story of Catherine Royce in chapter 6.
[26] In *Intelligent Virtue*, 167–168, she makes the stronger and somewhat different criticism that there is "a latent incoherence in thinking of happiness [*eudaimonia*] as made up both of living virtuously and of items such as money and status, which belong with life's circumstances rather than the living of it." However, as I've argued (following Aristotle), money and status can expand the range of our activities in worthwhile and enjoyable ways.

necessary for acting virtuously and maintaining his equanimity that he will be miserable. In his case, the goods he needs are, in addition to food, water, and shelter, pen and paper and the opportunity to write.

So far, then, the idea that virtue is the controlling element in *eudaimonia* seems to be compatible with the Aristotelian claim that we also need some external goods for happiness, and thus for *eudaimonia*. No amount of external goods can make us *eudaimon* if we lack virtue altogether, but with virtue, we can be *eudaimon* with very little. Both virtue and external goods are sources of happiness, but only the virtuous use of external goods gives us happiness in a worthwhile life, and only virtue can protect us from misery when we are deprived of nearly all external goods. Terence Irwin, however, interprets the supremacy of virtue thesis in a way that seems to threaten this compatibility, even though he believes that, according to Aristotle, we need external goods for happiness.

7.5. Must the Virtuous Person be the Most *Eudaimon* in all Circumstances?

7.5.1 Irwin argues that because virtue is "superordinate" or supreme for Aristotle and other *eudaimonist* philosophers, it follows that virtue more than anything else must increase a person's *eudaimonia*, and that "the virtuous person is in all circumstances happier [more *eudaimon*] than anyone else."[27]

If virtue and the other traits are global, then it is easy to see why this must be the case. Akratic people typically do the wrong thing and are filled with regret. In addition, their lives are not very pleasant, being full of conflict between their emotions or appetites on the one hand, and their rational wishes on the other. Enkratic (strong-willed) people also lack harmony between their emotions or appetites on the one hand, and their rational wishes on the other, although in those who are close to being virtuous, the disharmony is muted. Further, because they do the right thing for the right reasons, they are rewarded by a sense of pride in their rectitude. But their lives would be more worthwhile, and their emotional reward in such a life greater, if they were virtuous. Wicked people are the worst off, because they lead worthless lives, and many are also unhappy. But what if people's

---

[27.]"Theory and Common Sense" (1996), 37–55, at 42. Annas agrees with this claim in *Happiness*, 428. See also Cooper, *Reason and Human Good*.

traits are neither global nor all-or-nothing, as I have been arguing? If people can be more or less virtuous (or enkratic, or akratic, or even vicious), then Irwin's thesis has to be interpreted as holding that the more virtuous are more *eudaimon* in terrible circumstances than those who are even slightly less virtuous in fortunate circumstances.

Is this true? I think not. One reason is that everyone has a breaking point, and the more virtuous person is more likely to end up in circumstances that test his virtue to the breaking point. Suppose, for example, that Admiral Stockdale ended up in a North Vietnamese prison only because he chose to do a heroic act for the sake of his men, an act that he was not obligated to do, and that saving himself instead would not have been in any way vicious. Suppose, further, that this heroic act was in character for him, not a one-time response to the exigencies of the situation. His heroism, and his consciousness of having done the best he was capable of, would have stood him in good stead in his long captivity. But for how long and under what pressures? What if had never read the *Enchiridion*, so that he could not call on it to comfort him? What if, in addition, he had never been released? Is it plausible to suppose that *nothing* his captors did could have broken him—no torture, no lies about the fate of his men, country, or family? An affirmative answer to this question bears a heavy burden of proof. The absent father in the movie, *Swing Kids*, depicts the ghastly possibilities for a heroically virtuous but unlucky person. We learn from his widow and son that his defiance of the Nazis led to his capture, torture, and eventual psychological destruction, so that, in the end, he was reduced to unquestioning obedience to their commands. His is an unusually dramatic and horrifying example of someone whose integrity and heroism leads to the loss of his very capacity for integrity and heroism, and whose loyalty to his principles and those who share his principles leads to the destruction of his agency and the betrayal of those very principles and individuals. Had he chosen a quietly noncooperative path instead of a heroically defiant one (assuming that he had this choice), he could at least have saved his moral agency.

It might be said in response that since he has lost his capacity for virtue, the claim that the more virtuous are more *eudaimon* under all circumstances no longer applies to him. It applies to him only till the last moment that he retains his agency, the last moment in which he can make a decision. But this move doesn't save the thesis that the more virtuous are always better off than the less virtuous, since the loss of this individual's very capacity for virtue is a consequence of his greater virtue in an evil world.

Can we defend the more moderate claim that the more virtuous are always more *eudaimon* than the somewhat less virtuous so long as they retain their capacity for virtue? Let us consider a less extreme real life case to test the plausibility of this claim: the fate of Soviet dissidents who ended up in the Soviet Gulag versus the fate of those who, while hating and refusing to cooperate with the Soviet regime, did not actively oppose it because they wanted to protect themselves and their families.[28] Now of course we do not know the character of any of these people in their personal or professional lives. But we can safely suppose that many of the dissidents who risked their lives and liberty to protest the inhumanity of the state had unusual courage and integrity, and that the same was true of many dissidents, especially women, who refrained from dissident activity only for the sake of taking care of their children or parents. We can also safely suppose that at least *some* of the "active" dissidents, as I'll call them, were somewhat more virtuous than at least *some* of the "passive" dissidents. But if we compare the fate of the active dissidents who were caught and physically and mentally tortured with the fate of those passive dissidents who, for all their frustration, fear, and anxiety, could live "normal" lives at home with their families, it is clear who was closer to *eudaimonia*. For some active dissidents, the torture included threats of rape, execution, or torture of their children, spouses, or parents, threats that were sometimes carried out. It stretches credulity to hold that, even so, these somewhat more virtuous dissidents were better off than the somewhat less virtuous Soviet citizens who rejected the regime but also rejected martyrdom. Indeed, if these active dissidents had regarded themselves as better off, not counting what happened to their families as a source of unhappiness, one would be right to suspect that their zeal had deprived them of some of their humanity and familial virtue.

7.5.2 A second reason for rejecting the claim that "the virtuous person is in all circumstances... [more *eudaimon*] than anyone else" is that (as the discussion just concluded illustrates), it is incompatible with the claim that external goods are necessary for *eudaimonia*. For it entails that no matter how much one loses—friends, family, bodily integrity, freedom—in short, all the external sources of *eudaimonia*—one is *eudaimon*, and more *eudaimon* than someone who has all these goods but just a little less virtue. If happiness is partly constitutive of *eudaimonia*, and external goods

---

[28] The fate of those who ended up in the gulag is described in detail by Alexander Solzhenitsyn, *The Gulag Archipelago: 1918–1956: An Experiment in Literary Investigation* (1973, 1974).

are a necessary source of happiness, it must be acknowledged that the somewhat less virtuous who are spared the tragic loss of everything and everyone they love are closer to *eudaimonia* than the more virtuous who lose everything and everyone they love.

My view is compatible with the claim that virtue is the primary element in well-being. Virtuous people are more in charge of their lives than the less virtuous, more able to enjoy things, more open to what the world has to offer, more understanding of themselves and others, and less anxious, regretful, or conflicted. In short, their greater virtue provides them with greater happiness and greater appreciation of both the possibilities open to them, and the limitations imposed by the world they inhabit. Hence the more virtuous are more *eudaimon* than the less virtuous under *the same circumstances*, and in *a wider variety of circumstances*. This claim of greater *eudaimonia* for the more virtuous is only strengthened by recognizing that even supererogatory virtue is not always exercised in situations that threaten the external sources of one's well-being.

So far I have argued that the neo-Aristotelian view that some external goods are necessary for *eudaimonia* as sources of happiness is compatible with the view that virtue is primary in *eudaimonia*, but not with the view that the more virtuous are more *eudaimon* than even the slightly less virtuous in all circumstances. In the next section I address a direct challenge to the primacy of virtue thesis by Daniel Haybron.

7.6. Should the Primacy of Virtue Thesis be Replaced by the Primacy of Happiness Thesis?

7.6.1 Haybron argues that if virtue is the primary factor in well-being, then more virtuous but less happy activities must contribute more to *eudaimonia* than less virtuous but happier ones (*Unhappiness*, 161–163). And this, he holds, is implausible. As a deep emotional state, happiness is crucial to self-fulfillment because it partially defines who we are as individuals (ibid., 178–180). Haybron uses a detailed counterexample to defend his thesis. Angela, a diplomat who has had a long and distinguished career, is getting ready to retire with her husband in Tuscany, close to where her daughter and grandchildren live. She is looking forward to "kicking back and just enjoying life" (161–162). Unfortunately, there is a political crisis overseas and she is asked to deal with it because of her wisdom and skills (162). She "could refuse the position with no regrets," but she accepts it, also without regret. The work is taxing, sometimes unpleasant, but it does leave time for family and friends and relaxation, and overall she enjoys it and succeeds admirably in averting a bloody crisis. After six years she finally retires, but a massive stroke kills her after just five pleasant years of retirement.

Haybron argues that Angela's life exhibited more virtue than it would have had she turned down the job and retired early, but that this greater virtue came at the cost of a sacrifice of a certain amount of well-being for those six years. Let us grant Haybron's claim that insofar as taking the job meant that Angela had to face and solve more difficult problems virtuously than if she had retired, her life exhibited more virtue than if she had retired. This is especially so because it is a rare politician or stateswoman who can succeed in the political arena without dirtying her hands. But is it so clear that Angela's life would have contained more well-being if she had turned down the job? The fact that she accomplished such an important goal before retiring surely afforded her a sense of fulfillment much deeper and richer than six additional years of more pleasant activities. Virtuously and successfully facing difficult challenges brings commensurate emotional rewards for the virtuous, a point that Haybron does not consider when he declares that in an early retirement she would have been "substantially happier" doing things that "bring her the greatest satisfaction." His neglect of the emotional rewards Angela must derive from her virtuous and enjoyable completion of her important work is particularly surprising in light of his own later recognition that depth and richness are important dimensions of well-being (see chapter 3). As he puts it, well-being requires authentic happiness, and the "richer, more complex" one's way of life, the greater the authenticity of one's happiness, because "such ways of living more fully express one's nature" (186).

Haybron also needs to consider—as surely Angela did in deciding to take the job—how she would have felt had she turned down the job and her less skilled replacement had failed to prevent the bloody uprising. Would she not be filled with regret? Would her pleasant retirement then seem so pleasant to her? Given who she is, it is hard to see how.

Life offers many dramatic examples of people whose lives have been enriched by virtue in difficult circumstances, especially when they have succeeded in their purpose. Perhaps the best known such example is that of Oskar Schindler. As we saw in chapter 6, Schindler was never a believing Nazi, and was always concerned about his Jewish workers' safety.[29] Over

---

[29] See Herbert Steinhouse, "The Real Oskar Schindler," *Saturday Night* (April 1994), (http://writing.upenn.edu/~afilreis/Holocaust/steinhouse.html, accessed September 2012).

time, however, his concern for his Jewish workers became his sole concern, and for three years he used his business only as a means to saving the lives of his workers and their families, exposing himself to considerable financial loss and taking great risks to his life. In the words of Paul Zweig, a reviewer of Thomas Keneally's *Schindler's List*, in the three years that Schindler spent rescuing Jews under the noses of the Nazis, he was "inhabited by a god," acting "beyond himself, living on the edge of wonder"; when the god left, he became ordinary again.[30] It is hard to deny that in those years Schindler was possessed of the passions and insights and clear purpose of the virtuous. In Becker's striking phrase, he made his life "a single spatiotemporal object" (*Stoicism*, 20). Many years later, Schindler's now ex-wife, Emilie, remarked that, since Oskar had done nothing exceptional before or after the war, he was "fortunate" that for three years he had been able to act on his real talents. It does not take what some might regard as indoctrination into *eudaimonism* to recognize that Schindler's life in those years was not just admirable, but also enviable.

Still, Haybron has a point, as we can see if we tweak his example as follows. Let us say that Angela does not enjoy her assignment overall, that although she is admirably skillful and virtuous in dealing with the situation she does not succeed in preventing the bloody uprising, and she regrets that she took the assignment instead of retiring when she meant to retire. Let us also say that had she retired, she would have exercised fewer virtues, or less admirable virtues, but would have enjoyed life more, and without regrets. This scenario is a challenge to any view that holds that she would still have had more well-being with the first choice than with the second. But this is not my view. On my view, even if Angela's virtue is greater if she carries out the diplomatic assignment well but fails miserably through no fault of her own, her well-being is greater if she opts for retirement, because it is free of the failure, frustration, and regrets that mark her years as a diplomat. But this does not suffice as a strike against the primacy of virtue thesis, because the primacy thesis does not entail that the more virtuous have more well-being than the less virtuous in every conceivable situation. Rather, what it entails is that the more virtuous have more well-being than the less virtuous in the same circumstances, and in

---

[30] Paul Zweig, "A Good Man in a Bad Time," review of Thomas Keneally, *Schindler's List*, *The New York Times*, October 24, 1982 (http://www.nytimes.com/1982/10/24/ books/a-good-man-in-a-bad-time.html, accessed September 2012). The book is a novel based on Schindler's life, but although the review is of the novel, Zweig's comment is about the real Schindler as much as about the Schindler in the novel.

more circumstances.[31] And this is explained by the fact that greater virtue makes our lives more worthwhile, as well as happier in fortunate circumstances and less unhappy in unfortunate circumstances.

My conclusion that retired Angela has more well-being than diplomat Angela in the scenario I have just sketched is reinforced if I reject what I have been granting so far: Haybron's premise that the diplomat Angela must exercise more virtue than the retired Angela.

7.6.2 Haybron's premise is intuitively powerful, but this is one of those times when analysis renders a powerful intuition less powerful. One reason for its intuitive pull is that we tend to think that "large-scale" challenges such as the one Angela the diplomat faces are always more difficult to meet successfully than the small-scale quotidian challenges of life. They are more difficult because large-scale challenges require special skills and knowledge, whereas the challenges of everyday life require only the skills we acquire as part of the normal process of growing up and becoming morally mature. But the prevalence of domestic unhappiness or at least dissatisfaction and the great number of books on how to be a good spouse, parent, or friend, and in general, how to lead a worthwhile, successful, and happy life, give the lie to this view. It is precisely the intimacy of life with friends and family that creates a challenge for living virtuously. If being virtuous when it's difficult to be virtuous makes a person's acts more admirable, then virtue in domestic life can be just as admirable as virtue in diplomatic life.

It might be thought that someone who can be virtuous in public life can also be virtuous in private life, and is therefore more virtuous than someone who is virtuous only in his private life. But the evidence suggests otherwise. Many great men, such as Mahatma Gandhi and Martin Luther King, have been unjust or unloving in one way or another in their private lives. Something similar seems to be true of intellectuals and moral reformers, such as Socrates. Perhaps the time, attention, and energy required for being morally virtuous in situations that call for heroism drains such people's resources for being virtuous in their domestic lives. Or perhaps their heroism leads them to feel justified in "letting go" when they come back home. Then there are people like Schindler, who've led humdrum lives not only domestically but also in business, but who are galvanized by danger

---

[31.] In principle, then, I can accept Haybron's verdict that Frank, a bachelor and successful artist who does the more virtuous thing by sacrificing some of his artistic ambitions and youthful pleasures in order to care for a severely autistic orphan, sacrifices some of his well-being too (*Unhappiness*, 163–164).

into reaching beyond themselves to act heroically. If Angela is one of these people, then her admirable handling of her difficult diplomatic assignment does not show that she could have handled her domestic life just as well.

Another reason that Haybron's assumption that diplomat Angela exhibits more virtue than retired Angela is intuitively plausible is that we tend to think that virtuous activities that benefit more people or prevent harm to more people are more admirable than virtuous activities that benefit or prevent harm to fewer people. However, the actual benefits of an activity are not determined solely by their virtue; many other factors are involved, including other people's virtue or lack thereof, and natural events. Moreover, a person's virtuous acts might actually produce bad consequences. For example, Angela's attempt to negotiate with the authoritarian leader of the country she is dealing with politely but honestly, rather than fawningly, might send him into an unexpected rage and lead to a break-off of talks and a bloody crackdown. Furthermore, domestic life affords as much opportunity for having a beneficial influence on others and being a moral exemplar as does public life. Thus, retired Angela who imparts important lessons in independence, honesty, fairness, and courage to her grandchildren and who is an understanding and loving friend, wife, and mother, is as much of a moral exemplar as Angela the diplomat who averts a bloody crisis through her wisdom and skills.

In short, virtue in public life is neither always more challenging, nor always more beneficial, than virtue in domestic life. Hence there is no reason to think that it is necessarily more admirable than virtue in domestic life.

I have argued that the primacy of virtue thesis is neither implausible nor incompatible with the claim that happiness, and therefore *eudaimonia*, requires an adequate supply of external goods, where "adequate supply" is relative to the individual's capacity for an enjoyable and worthwhile use of them. In the next section I will consider the theoretical and moral challenge from Stoicism. Stoic *eudaimonism* is theoretically simpler and more elegant than any Aristotelian *eudaimonism*, because it gives short shrift to the goods of fortune and our emotional investment in them, and makes virtue sufficient for *eudaimonia*. Thus it truly sees us as "masters of our fate". Hence it is easy to see why philosophers such as Lawrence Becker and Julia Annas—indeed, perhaps most of us in some moods—are drawn to Stoicism. So why not opt for the Stoic view over the Aristotelian? Because, as I argue below, this view has even graver problems. I will address Stoic *eudaimonism* in the modern guise to be found in Becker's book, where it is shorn of its implausible cosmological doctrines.

7.7. The Stoic Conception of *Eudaimonia*

7.7.1 According to Becker's "new Stoicism," the Stoic holds that:

> [T]he final end of all rational activity is virtue, not happiness; that virtue does not admit of degrees, and among people who fall short of it, none is any more virtuous than another; that sages are happy [*eudaimon*] just because they are virtuous, and can be happy [*eudaimon*] even on the rack; that they must be able to say of everything other than their virtue (friends, loves, emotions, reputation, wealth, pleasant mental states, suffering, disease, death, and so on) that it is nothing to them (*Stoicism*, 8).

The Stoic sees a virtuous life as a life according to nature, that is, a life in which we develop our agency through proper *oikeiosis* (familiarization with, appropriation of) various people and projects, so that our interests come to include virtue and other people as ends in themselves. The aim of virtuous activity is to create "a single spatiotemporal object—a life" (*Stoicism*, 20)—single, in that the dispositions, deliberations, choices, and aims all have a single purpose: "virtue, understood as the perfection of agency" (ibid., 21). The Stoic sage—the perfectly virtuous agent—makes all-things-considered practical reasoning his "most comprehensive and controlling endeavor," even if he often does it subconsciously, "or only as a retrospective corrective to intuitive or routinized behavior" (106). Virtue is necessary and sufficient for *eudaimonia*, so a virtuous life is necessarily complete and self-sufficient. The Stoics believe that what we think of as external goods, including health, friendship, pleasure, and honor, are only "*axia*," or (as some philosophers translate the term) values, not goods. Their value lies in their being necessary tools or materials for acting virtuously. Hence we should seek them for their instrumental role in our lives, not as ends in themselves; the proper attitude towards them is to see them as "preferred indifferents," and their contraries as "dispreferred indifferents." The Stoic sage makes the correct evaluations of things, so he is free of passions that embody overvaluations, such as fear or love, and has only the appropriate emotional states: *eupatheiai*, or "good feelings", such as kindness, generosity, warmth, affection; "watchfulness" (instead of fear), etc. His life is rational in that his deliberations, choices and *eupatheiai* are mutually consistent as well as in accord with nature.

The sage's controlling goal, or *telos*, is virtuous action itself, just as a surgeon's controlling goal is the best, most skillful surgery itself. Her target, or *skopos*, is the particular state of affairs she aims to bring about or preserve. But she is not invested in the target; whether she succeeds or fails to bring it about does not impact her virtue or, therefore, her *eudaimonia*. Her virtue makes her invulnerable to all external losses (except, presumably, those that destroy agency or virtue, if there are any such), and is sufficient for that sense of fulfillment and worth that is part of *eudaimonia*. There can be no conflict between prudential reasoning and moral reasoning, because the virtuous agent regards virtuous activity as necessary and sufficient for *eudaimonia*.[32]

7.7.2 Under certain descriptions, the Stoic ideal can seem compelling. The thought that we have the power to be *eudaimon* whatever our circumstances—to make of our lives a joyful, coherent, purposive, integrated object—is a thrilling one. But is it true that we have such power whatever our circumstances? And when we spell out what it takes to (attempt to) create such a life—treating external values as "indifferents" that make no difference to *eudaimonia*, becoming indifferent to the normal contours of a human life[33]—does it still provide an attractive picture of human life? Would we be decent parents to our children if we thought of them simply as "preferred indifferents"—important, but not important enough to count in our *eudaimonia*?

My view is that when we consider its implications, the Stoic ideal is neither plausible nor (partly for that reason) attractive. If life as it is lived is any evidence, the sage must acknowledge that it gains its meaning from acting to discover, create, attain, or preserve such external values as satisfying work, friendship, knowledge of important or interesting things, and so on. The Stoics themselves believe that virtuous activity is the activity of pursuing and using such values appropriately. But what could motivate us to pursue these values if we did not care about achieving them—about success? And how could we care about success if we weren't vulnerable to failure or loss? If losing something we cared about mattered not—or not enough to affect our *eudaimonia*—then failing to achieve it would matter not either. But if failing to achieve it mattered not, then neither would trying to achieve it in the first place. And if trying to achieve it

---

[32] See also Annas, "Prudence and Morality," 241–257. Annas states that reason shows the virtuous person that the interests of others are no less important than his own (ibid., 255). I assume that by this Annas means only that the virtuous person sees that the interests of others are as important *to them* as his own *to him*, and not that reason shows the virtuous person that the interests of others are no less important *to him* than his own. On the latter interpretation it would be hard to understand how *eudaimonia* can be said to be his aim, since surely *eudaimonia* requires giving a special place to his own interests in his reasoning and acting.

[33] Annas, *Happiness*, 429–431.

mattered not, why would anyone try to achieve it—in other words, why would anyone act?

The Sage could counter that the point is not to win but to play the game well. But although this is sometimes true, usually the point is to do both. If it weren't, most of human life would cease to make sense. Thus, we look for romantic love because we want to find it; if finding it mattered not, there would be no point in looking for it. We invest time and energy in the people and projects we love because they are (at least partially) irreplaceable constituents of our *eudaimonia*, and they are irreplaceable constituents of our *eudaimonia* because we love them. If losing them mattered not, and we could just transfer our virtuous loving to someone or something else, what would it mean to love them? We agonize over the choice between living with a beloved and keeping a prized job because both are crucial to our *eudaimonia;* if they weren't, we could just toss a coin to decide between them. Cancer researchers invest long years in the quest to find a cure for cancer; if success mattered not to them, they could just as well call off the search when it threatened to become frustrating and turn their attention to something else. We try to bring our children up well because what they become—creators or destroyers—matters to us deeply.

The Stoic could reasonably argue, as the Aristotelian does, that how we choose and act in these matters—honorably or dishonorably, fairly or unfairly, honestly or manipulatively, with due consideration to the other's concerns or self-centeredly—matters more to *eudaimonia*, properly understood, than success in achieving the target, because success is out of our hands. But this is not what the Stoic argues: he argues that success is of *no* importance to *eudaimonia*. Yet, if hitting the target is important enough to justify trying to become excellent (virtuous) at hitting it, how can success in hitting it become so unimportant after we have achieved excellence that we should actually regard it as irrelevant to our *eudaimonia*, and come to love only the excellence of our shots? Is there a metaphysical or moral change that justifies this change in attitude? It is not enough to say that cultivating this attitude of (preferred) indifference towards external goods makes us more secure against pain, more masters of our selves. For the same attitude also makes us less receptive to the beauty and marvels of the world, less able to delight in "the color of a bluebird," or be transported by "a phrase of music."[34] In short, the same

---

[34] In "Comments on Julia Annas' *Intelligent Virtue*" (2012), Robert Adams argues that at least some of what we are given is important to our *eudaimonia*: "If the color of a bluebird adds delight to my day, or if a phrase of music catches my soul up toward heaven, that is not just *stuff*."

attitude makes us less capable of the passionate love and excitement and delight that give depth and color to life. The Stoic must explain why protecting ourselves from pain is more important than passionately investing ourselves in this life, in the full acknowledgement that such investment brings with it the possibility of a loss that can undermine *eudaimonia*. Commonsensically, we should aim to be neither overly vulnerable nor overly detached. The Stoic needs to explain why we should reject common sense on this point.[35]

There is an even more important problem with the Stoic view that 'playing the game well' is all that matters, a problem that stems from the fact that playing well (acting virtuously), itself is defined, in part, in terms of strategies (dispositions) that are most likely to produce or constitute success, both when success is entirely external, and when it is partly internal. For example, good scientific research is defined as research that abides by the canons of rationality and the scientific method, because these have been discovered through long experience to reliably lead to the truth. If this were not the case, if respecting them was no more likely to lead to the truth than guess work or inspiration, abiding by them would not be rationally required, and sitting around playing guessing games or waiting for an epiphany might be just as rational and fruitful as following so-called scientific method. Again, good romantic relationships are defined as relationships marked by mutual love, respect, and understanding, because without these qualities romantic relationships cannot be mutually enriching. If this were not the case, if mutually enriching relationships were unequal, one-sided relationships, it would be folly to try to create I-Thou relationships, and sensible to create I-It (or I-I) ones. Or consider the virtue of generosity, the disposition to give appropriately of one's wealth or time for another's good. If giving to another tended to be harmful, there would be no such thing as appropriate giving, and generosity would not be a virtue.

In all these cases, the virtues in question are defined in terms of the values they partially constitute, preserve, or bring about. Hence it seems logically impossible to regard virtuous living as essential for *eudaimonia* while deeming these values irrelevant to *eudaimonia*; to care deeply about abiding by the canons of rationality and the scientific

---

[35] In his comments on this chapter, Becker states that "the answer is making sure that the loss and the pain are not sufficient to destroy our virtue." True enough, but this answer does not distinguish the Stoics from Aristotle. What distinguishes them is their position on what is needed for *eudaimonia*.

method but not about reaching the truth; to care deeply about mutual love, respect, and understanding, but not about mutual enrichment; to care deeply about appropriate giving for another's good, but not about whether one's giving is actually beneficial. It seems that if nothing other than virtue matters for *eudaimonia*, then virtue doesn't much matter either.

Of course, the Stoic might deny that the virtues are to be understood as dispositions that partially constitute, preserve, or bring about any values. But this denial makes a mystery of virtue—what it is, where it comes from, how it is related to excellence of practices, and why we should care about it. On Becker's own view, repeated "success at hitting" its target determines the excellence of a practice, such as what counts as good, effective medicine (133). He states that practicing safe and effective medicine as well as hitting the target (being successful) constitute the "physician's controlling goal." But when he turns to the craft of virtue, he makes acting virtuously the sole controlling goal. This creates a puzzle. How can a virtuous surgeon, a surgeon who performs surgery for the right reasons (to heal her patients) and with the right (virtuous) means—using the highest standards of skill, knowledge, and care—be indifferent to the actual outcomes of her surgeries? Doesn't her virtue lie, in part, in caring about the outcomes for her patients? The problem generalizes to other virtuous practices and projects: how can a virtuous individual have no concern about the effects of her actions on the world?

In turning all external values into so much material and tools for our virtuous activity, the Stoic view suggests that people are no more important to *eudaimonia* than things. Our children, our pet dogs, our tables and chairs: all are simply the fabric on which we embroider the *telos* of our virtuous lives. And this seems hard to see as virtuous. The Stoic ideal assumes that human beings can become pure agents, with the power to detach themselves from whatever befalls the objects of their love, so that they are no less *eudaimon* than before. It assumes that we have the power to cloak ourselves in the mantle of virtue, such that no tragedy can touch us in the core of our beings. This may well be fit for a god, but a human being is both agent and patient, both someone who acts and is acted upon. And even virtuous agency is not entirely up to us, depending as it does on our genes, our upbringing, and the society into which we are born. Neither everyday experience nor psychological research supports the view that we are capable of *eudaimonia* regardless of what tragedy befalls us; what they support, rather, is the view that if we try to detach ourselves from the objects of our love, we will end up becoming insensitive to others' suffering and repressing our own.[36]

Is there a more attractive interpretation of the Stoic doctrine? Becker suggests one in his response to Martha Nussbaum's argument that the detachment and *apatheia* recommended by Stoicism undermine our humanity, and that certain sorts of fragility or vulnerability are necessary for virtue. He protests that all that Stoics reject is the sort of fragility that might lead a flight pilot to have a meltdown in a flight emergency, or the kind that leads to "extreme depression" in manic-depressive people. He points out that there's nothing wrong with being able to "withstand anything" if there are no "offsetting effects," adding rhetorically, "Is there some good reason for wanting people to be hurtable?" (109). And in "Stoic Emotion," Becker argues that what Stoics eschew is love of people or things that compromise virtue. But if dangerous meltdowns in mid-flight, severe depressions, and virtue-compromising loves are all that the Stoic rejects in rejecting vulnerability to loss and pain, then he does not reject vulnerability per se, but only self-destructive forms of vulnerability, forms that even a non-Stoic would reject. And if the Stoic does not reject vulnerability per se, then he must acknowledge that the loss of everything and everyone we love can undermine, or even rob us of, *eudaimonia*, and therefore that virtue is not sufficient for *eudaimonia*.[37] Alternatively, he may counter that what is affected is happiness in the sense of emotional fulfillment, not *eudaimonia*, because *eudaimonia* just is a good life, and a good life just is virtuous activity. But isn't a good life that is happy a *better life* than a good life that is unhappy or even somewhere between happiness and unhappiness? Becker concedes as much when he states that without happiness, a good life is "perhaps not a blessed one."[38]

My neo-Aristotelian view is not, however, on safe ground yet. So far I have defended it against external challenges and challenges that arise from its multipart structure. Another objection arises from my claim that objective worth entails virtue.

---

[36] On this last point, see Sherman on the stoical training of soldiers in *Stoic Warriors* (2005). Russell also argues against the Stoic view that virtue is sufficient for *eudaimonia* by pointing out that virtuous activity in the particular relationships and projects that belong to us is part of the self and thus of *eudaimonia* (*Happiness*, 256–257). However, Russell does not claim that he has shown the Stoic view to be less plausible than the Aristotelian view.

[37] Becker, "Stoic Emotion" (2004), 250–276, at 272–273. Becker does not really address the issue of a loss of everything and everyone we love. He addresses only cases of partial loss in arguing that external losses don't rob the Sage of *eudaimonia*.

[38] Email correspondence, February 8, 2013.

7.8. Does Objective Worth Entail Virtue?

This objection holds that people with extraordinary intellectual, political, or artistic achievements have objectively worthy lives, even though in some cases they are sorely lacking in virtue, and may even be vicious. If these high achievers are also happy, then they meet my requirements for *eudaimonia* in spite of their injustice or cruelty. So it is not the case that *eudaimonia* entails a virtuous life or even a life according to virtue.

In Section 7.3.2, using the unscrupulous singer as an example, I argued that when someone with a great inborn talent enjoys the magnanimity of others, he does not necessarily require any other-regarding virtue to succeed, merely the absence of certain vices. I did not there tackle the question of whether such a person's life is objectively worthy. It might be thought that it is because his singing has aesthetic worth and, moreover, brings joy to millions, even if bringing joy to millions is of no interest to him.

On my view, however, although what he produces has worth, his outlook on life, his attitudes and motivations—his dispositions—lack objective worth. The only potentially creditable dispositions he has are his aesthetic appreciation of good music, and his perseverance in developing his talent. But because he is jealous and resentful of contemporary musicians, his appreciation is confined to the music of the safely dead, and his perseverance is motivated largely by his desire for applause from those he despises. Hence neither trait is very creditable after all. His musical achievement is due almost entirely to an extraordinary bounty of nature, conjoined with extraordinary help from people—in short, to extraordinary luck. In this respect, it is no different from the achievement of a very beautiful but vicious woman who becomes a top-flight model thanks to the great generosity of those who are enchanted by her beauty. It is easy to see that merely working hard to preserve her beauty and perfect her modeling for the sake of fame does not make her life objectively worthwhile, even if she brings joy to (the despised) millions. Her vices are incompatible both with happiness and with objective worth, and thus with well-being. Some other-regarding moral decency does seem necessary both for happiness and for objective worth.

Consider, now, the extraordinary achievers whose lives we do ordinarily regard as objectively worthwhile in spite of their moral mediocrity in certain respects, the lives of people like Albert Einstein and

Mohandas Gandhi. Einstein is said to have become authoritarian and contemptuous towards his first wife, Mileva, and neglectful of his children, after he fell in love with a cousin.[39] Gandhi also seems not to have been a very considerate husband or father. But this does not make any of these men unjust, *simpliciter*. Gandhi's life, as is well-known, was devoted to the cause of justice. After the outbreak of Nazism, Einstein had the courage to renounce his pacifism and call for the just defeat of Nazism. Moreover, there is no reason to think that Einstein was anything but honest and just in his intellectual life, giving credit where credit was due. Overall, these geniuses may have been no less just than the rest of us, the non-genius majority.

Even more mixed is the case of Thomas Jefferson, intellectual, politician, inventor, lawyer, farmer—and slaveholder. Unlike many others, Jefferson was aware of the injustice and cruelty of slavery, but too weak to act on his conscience. Here again, though, it is not the case that he was an unjust man, *tout court*. Rather, in fighting for liberty (except for African Americans) and the separation of church and state, he combined great injustice towards an entire race of human beings with great justice towards many others. And blame for even this great injustice must be mitigated by the times he lived in, when slavery was widely accepted as necessary, even "natural" and good for both parties. For this social sanction made it harder for someone who profited from slavery to act on his recognition of its evil.

Examples of people who combine complete or nearly complete other-regarding vice with great achievement in the intellectual or political sphere are hard, if not impossible, to come by. One reason is that most great achievements are achievements that benefit, or that by their nature (rather than accidentally) have the potential to benefit, human beings, and someone who is thoroughly unjust and maleficent towards others lacks any motivation to (intentionally) do anything that benefits them. Yet in the intellectual sphere great achievements often require this motivation, and in the political sphere they always do.[40]

[39.] See "Einstein's Wife: The Life of Mileva Maric Einstein," *PBS*, http://www.pbs.org/opb/einsteinswife/milevastory/index.htm (accessed July 2013); and "Einstein Revealed," PBS, http://www.pbs.org/wgbh/nova/physics/einstein-revealed.html, Sept. 9, 1997 (accessed July 2013). The *Encyclopaedia Brittanica*, however, suggests that he was the usual busy but not callous father: see Albert Einstein, http://www.britannica.com/EBchecked/topic/181349/Albert-Einstein (accessed July 2013).

[40.] So our contemporary palaces, pyramids, and mausoleums ("bridges to nowhere," rail systems serving practically no one, two-thousand page laws with impressive names that no legislator has read, much less understood) created to satisfy a politician's vanity and/or buy him votes don't count as worthwhile achievements.

Still, it is only "often" that great intellectual achievements require this motivation. Some achievements such as, for example, brilliant mathematical discoveries, might be motivated entirely by curiosity and a desire to solve a problem or learn the truth, rather than also by any goodwill towards others. Suppose, in addition, that a person thus motivated feels little need for friends or family. In his case, it might seem that he has little occasion for acting according to virtue, leave alone from virtue. But this is too hasty an inference, for it is highly unlikely that anyone can do worthwhile work without using the achievements of others, and thus, without incurring the obligation to acknowledge his debts to them. Furthermore, even someone who lacks close friends or family needs to interact with other people and cooperate with them, however minimally. So he both needs to, and is obligated to, act *according to* the principles of justice and honesty, even if not from the *motives* of justice or honesty, much less from the *virtues* of justice and honesty. Some other-regarding moral decency is thus essential for living a worthwhile life overall. The mathematician's chief, and perhaps only, virtues, however, are exercised in his work. His passion for solving the problem, or discovering the truth, is an intellectual and creative virtue. To succeed in his work, the mathematician also needs to be persevering and courageous in the face of difficulties. And these virtues are the source of a justified sense of worth and happiness.

No doubt he would be better off if he had other-regarding virtues, and not only the policy of acting according to the virtues. His life would be both more worthwhile and, thanks to the intellectual-emotional harmony partly constitutive of virtue, happier. Perhaps he would also be happier if he had close personal relationships. Nevertheless, two things must be kept in mind when making this judgment. One is that most individuals who have deep personal relationships and a high degree of justice and beneficence towards people in general also lack the kind of singleminded passion and creativity that brilliant mathematicians have. So they also lack a dimension of human worth and a source of happiness. The other is that the mathematician's capacity for making brilliant mathematical discoveries might, for all we know, be connected to an incapacity for close personal relationships and other-regarding virtue. The unusual mathematical (and other) capacities of high-functioning autistic people provide some evidence for this claim. So the mathematician may be no more lacking in an important human capacity than are those of us who lack his brilliant creativity. Whereas he doesn't understand people like us, most of us don't understand people like him. Whereas he lacks other-regarding virtue, most of us lack his brilliant creativity. Overall, then, his life may be just as worthwhile and happy as the life of highly just and beneficent people who lack his intellectual virtues.

7.9. Conclusion

I have defended Aristotelian and neo-Aristotelian *eudaimonism* against both external and internal challenges, and offered an interpretation of the primacy of virtue thesis that is consistent with the *eudaimonist* view that external goods are both a necessary source of happiness and, in the case of close friends and important projects, partly constitutive of *eudaimonia*. I have rejected the Stoic view that virtue is both necessary and sufficient for *eudaimonia* on the grounds that this view makes a mystery of virtue and entails an utterly implausible conception of *eudaimonia*. Finally, I have argued that someone who is highly virtuous in the intellectual sphere, but lacks understanding of other people and observes other-regarding norms without really understanding why he should observe them, can have as much well-being as those of us who lack his creativity and other intellectual virtues.

In the concluding chapter I will summarize the argument of my book, analyze some common reasons for skepticism about *eudaimonism*, and explain why they don't apply to my view.

CHAPTER 8 | Conclusion: Taking Stock

8.1 Summary of Argument

Nearly all philosophical conceptions of well-being capture some people's conception of well-being, and perhaps everyone's conception of some aspect of their well-being. In order to qualify as the highest prudential good, however, well-being must meet the formal requirements of finality, self-sufficiency, choice-worthiness, and stability. Subjectivist theories do not meet these requirements because they reject objective standards of worth. But they are not consistent on this point, as indicated by their attempts to impose conditions on well-being in order to rule out adaptive preferences (happy slaves, oppressed but satisfied housewives, and so on) and badly or barely functioning though happy lives (grass blade counters, experience machine junkies, and so on), conditions that, on analysis, turn out to be inconsistent with their own subjectivist premises.

My conception of well-being as happiness in an objectively worthwhile life satisfies the formal constraints of well-being as the HPG. Substantively, well-being conceived thus requires that we be realistic, that is, reality-oriented/autonomous, and in touch with the important facts of our own lives and human life in general. In turn, to the extent that we live realistically, we live virtuously. This makes realism both a prudential value and a moral value, bridging the alleged conceptual gap between the prudential and the moral. My conception of well-being as the HPG is also consistent with the subjectivity of well-being, because an objectively worthy life is not only a requirement of the HPG, it is a standard that the reality-oriented/autonomous person herself adopts for her well-being. If she were to discover that her fundamental values were worthless, she herself would judge her life to be a failure, devoid of the HPG.

My claim that well-being as the HPG entails a life of virtue is not, of course, true on every conception of virtue, but only on the Aristotelian conception of virtue as an emotional and intellectual disposition to think, feel, and act in certain ways. This conception of virtue seems to be made for the HPG both substantively and structurally. However, I reject the view that virtue is global, arguing instead that actual virtue is narrowly domain-specific and comes in degrees. In other words, virtue as instantiated in human beings is limited in both scope and depth. Hence so too is *eudaimonia*. I follow Aristotle in holding that the HPG requires both virtue and an "adequate supply" of external goods, such as friends, reputation, money, and health. These goods expand our lives by enabling us to exercise our various powers and capacities in virtuous and enjoyable ways and by meeting our basic human needs for love, companionship, security, and pleasure. Whereas one can be virtuous even in tragic circumstances, *eudaimonia* requires some good fortune as well. But virtue is primary because it ensures the attitudes and actions that are necessary for happiness in a worthwhile life. Moreover, if we are virtuous, we can be happy with very little, whereas if we are vicious, we can be unhappy even in abundance. Hence the more virtuous individual is more *eudaimon* than the less virtuous individual in the same circumstances and in a greater variety of circumstances. Understood thus, the view that *eudaimonia* requires both virtue and external goods, with virtue being primary, is neither unstable nor counterintuitive.

Some people are not capable of other-regarding moral virtue because their capacities for understanding other people or empathizing with them are highly limited. But if these limitations are connected to their extraordinary intellectual or other creative capacities, and they take joy in the virtuous exercise of these capacities, they can be as eudaimon as those who possess other-regarding virtue but little capacity for creative pursuits.[1]

In the next section, I ask why there is so much skepticism about the *eudaimonist* thesis and whether it can be dispelled by a better understanding of it.

8.2 Sources of Skepticism

One common source of skepticism is the belief that the *eudaimonist* thesis claims, contrary to the evidence, that the wicked *must* suffer. This, however, is a misunderstanding. What *eudaimonism* claims is that, to the

---

[1] The most famous example is, of course, Temple Grandin, *Thinking in Pictures* (1995, 2006). On the capacities of "neurodiverse" people, see Nick Dubin, "Neurodiversity: A Balanced Opinion," *Autism Asperger's Digest* (http://autismdigest.com/neurodiversity, accessed September 19, 2013).

extent that people are vicious, they cannot have well-being as the highest prudential good; it doesn't claim that they must suffer, either psychologically or materially. Whether or not the vicious suffer psychologically depends on the nature and extent of their vice. Those whose wickedness is the result or the cause of inherently unpleasant emotions, such as rage, jealousy, envy, hatred, insatiable lust, greed, malice, spite, or overweening contempt are condemned to suffer by the very nature of their vices. If their vice is thoroughgoing, they are also condemned to do without external goods that are partly constituted by virtue, such as close friendships or genuine achievements. But not all wickedness is of this type; some is due to indifference towards certain groups or individuals. Many authoritarian rulers and their functionaries, both past and present, are or have been exemplars of such wickedness. Even confronting them with the humanity of their victims does not always induce guilt, shame, or self-hatred in them for their crimes. Eichmann is only one example of such a person.[2] The cost such people incur might simply be a gaping hole in their lives: the absence of something precious they neither know nor care about.[3] For the guiltless wicked, external sanctions are the only sanctions that can inflict pain on them. Acknowledging that the idea that the wicked *must* suffer does not follow from the *eudaimonist* thesis removes one source of skepticism about this thesis.

We must accept something even harder to accept: the costs of wickedness in pain and suffering—psychic, physical, and material—might be borne entirely by their victims. This claim violates our sense of justice, our sense that, in the fitness of things, the victims, or at least the virtuous victims, ought not to suffer, and certainly not more than the wicked. But the opposite thought—that, for example, Eichmann's acts hurt him more than they did his victims—also violates our sense of justice, because it seems to belittle his victims' suffering.

The claim that virtuous victims might bear all the costs in pain and suffering, psychic, physical, and material, and the wicked none, is not one that most *eudaimonists* would accept. Socrates and Plato both declare that the just man can never be harmed in his soul (psyche) and never made unhappy, and the Stoics agree. Annas and Becker, as we have seen,

---

[2] Hannah Arendt, *Eichmann in Jerusalem: A Report on the Banality of Evil* (1963); David Cesarani, *Eichmann: His Life and Crimes* (2004).

[3] See Gregory S. Kavka, who compares the immoral man to the deaf man in "The Reconciliation Project" (1985), 297–319. Even Aristotle recognizes this possibility when he portrays the intemperate man as unconscious of his vice in *NE* III.

take the same position. Aristotle concedes that the virtuous can be made unhappy as a result of great misfortunes, but maintains that they can never be made miserable: their virtue serves to prevent the pain from going deep enough to do so, much less to destroy their virtuous agency. We know that people *can* survive grave injustice without becoming embittered or vengeful (chapter 2). But even the most virtuous are vulnerable, and it cannot be maintained a priori that no amount of cruelty or injustice can penetrate their shield of virtue and destroy their *eudaimonia*—or, for that matter, their agency (chapter 7). Denying human vulnerability can be as unjust and destructive to victims as denying human strength. More to the point, acknowledging the hard truth that the virtuous might bear all the costs in pain and suffering does not contradict the *eudaimonist* thesis. Recognizing that the *eudaimonist* thesis is compatible with the possibility that the virtuous might have to pay all the costs of others' wickedness removes a second source of skepticism about it.

A third source of skepticism stems from the unstated assumption that the virtues and vices are global, in conjunction with the common observation that apparently nasty folks often seem to be happy. For example, we see that a certain colleague is an irresponsible cad, and are shocked to discover that he is universally admired and loved by his family and friends. Confident in our assumption that a cad in the office must be a cad everywhere, we wonder if he is a con artist who has managed to fool his family and friends or if his family and friends are irresponsible cads like himself. Noting, further, that he seems to enjoy his life, we conclude that true happiness does not require virtue.

As I have argued, however, the assumption that character traits are global runs up against careful everyday observation as well as the experimental evidence from social and cognitive psychology (chapter 6). The truest, most just friend may be an unfair parent—except to one of his five children, or a harsh teacher—except when he teaches poetry. The wise statesman may be a foolish lover. The courageous, independent thinker in molecular biology may be just another cowardly conformist in his politics, joining in the year's fashionable *ressentiments* of certain groups or countries. The emotionally temperate or continent person may be gluttonous or incontinent when it comes to food—but only certain foods. In short, our virtues and (typically) vices, strengths and weaknesses are narrowly domain-specific. Hence, even though out-and-out villains cannot have well-being as the HPG, it is possible for the morally average—that is, most of us—to be unjust or cowardly or akratic in some narrow domains of our lives; just or courageous or continent in many others; and, with normal good fortune, to live fairly full, rich, worthwhile lives overall. Needless to say, we would be far more *eudaimon* without any deviation from virtue. But this, as we've seen, is psychologically impossible.

A fourth source of skepticism is the belief that the primacy of virtue thesis contradicts what is only too obvious: that sometimes an act of injustice might be necessary for preserving the chief sources of one's happiness, indeed, the very things that make one's life not only subjectively but also objectively worthwhile. However, this possibility does not contradict the primacy of virtue thesis. Suppose, for example, that, as the popular narrative goes, Paul Gauguin really was driven to paint and that he really couldn't do so without leaving his family and country. This is how he himself saw it: "My wife, my family, everyone in fact is on my back about this confounded painting of mine. But one man's faculties can't cope with two things at once, and I, for one, can do one thing only: paint. Everything else leaves me stupefied."[4] Under the circumstances, Gauguin had to choose between acting justly towards his family—and doing what he was truly good at doing and needed to do for his own fulfillment: paint. Let's assume for the sake of argument that although he recognized and regretted his injustice towards his family, suffered guilt over leaving them to be looked after by relatives, and missed his children, the fulfillment he derived from his work outweighed his sadness and guilt. Let us also assume that he treated other artists and friends justly, giving credit where credit was due, and that he faced his artistic failures with fortitude. It follows that he had a great deal of happiness in a worthwhile life. His life would have been both happier and more worthwhile and, thus, more *eudaimon*, if he could have done his work without abandoning his family. But from this it does not follow that his life would have been more *eudaimon* without this act of injustice even under the circumstances he found himself in. Abandoning his painting would have meant abandoning most of what made life worth living for him. And this too would have been a betrayal, a betrayal of himself. Had his wife demanded that he abandon his painting, the injustice would have been hers.

Sometimes, however, both acting justly and acting unjustly are incompatible with *eudaimonia*. Suppose that Gauguin's family had had no relatives to fall back on, that his wife could not support the children, and that he knew that leaving them would reduce them to penury. Then abandoning

---

[4] Quoted by Campbell Geeslin, Mary Vespa, Harriet Shapiro in their review of Yann Le Pichon, *Gauguin: Life, Art, Inspiration* (1987), *People Magazine* (http://www.people.com/people/archive/article/0,,20096555,00.html, accessed May 14, 2013).

them would have meant that Gauguin was trying to buy his happiness at his wife's and children's expense, denying them what they had a right to expect from him for the sake of his own happiness. Since he had a prior obligation to his family, abandoning them in these circumstances would have detracted from the worth of his life and thereby also undercut his happiness. At the same time, doing the just thing by them would have meant abandoning the activity that was most important for his own happiness. Although under the circumstances Gauguin would have been better off doing what rectitude required—honoring his commitments to his family— the circumstances would not have allowed him to be *eudaimon*.

A fifth source of skepticism is the belief that if virtue is the primary factor in well-being, the more virtuous person must be more *eudaimon* than the less virtuous person under all circumstances. But, as the skeptic points out, the more virtuous person is more likely to do a heroically virtuous act in risky circumstances than the less virtuous person, and hence is more likely to lose the external sources of his well-being, whereas the less virtuous person is likely to preserve them. I have already acknowledged this possibility and argued that it is perfectly compatible with the claim that virtue is the primary factor in well-being (chapters 7 and 8, Section 1). This dispels the fifth source of skepticism about *eudaimonism*.

My reply does, however, raise the question of which course of action is *rational*. On my view, either one is rational. Someone who chooses the heroically virtuous course of action stakes her all on the best that is open to her at the possible cost of her future good, whereas someone who chooses the less virtuous course of action forgoes the best for the sake of saving her future good.

In this example I have imagined a situation in which the choice is between taking or not taking a supererogatory action. But what if the choice is between an obligatory action that an individual rationally expects will lead to the destruction of her well-being, and a mildly unjust action that will preserve it without causing much harm to anyone? An example of the latter might be breaking into a house whose occupants have gone out to escape a murderer's rampage. In such a situation, there is not enough reason for the virtuous individual to choose the just act and let herself be killed or crippled—even if she knows that she will not be able to compensate the occupants for the damage. When the choice is so stark, even those who are injured by her minor wrongdoing tend to—and, I would say, morally ought to—excuse it, acknowledging that they would have done the same in her circumstances.

This example illustrates the fact that although the primacy of virtue thesis tells us that *eudaimonia* at its highest requires being a just person, it does not follow that it requires that we always *act* justly, no matter how great the cost to ourselves and how small the cost to others. Some unjust actions are rationally justifiable and morally excusable; hence a refusal to excuse them is, paradoxically, unjust.

As the example just given suggests, sometimes an individual's happiness and just behavior conflict only because of other people's unjust actions. If no one ever took advantage of anyone's weakness or ignorance. happiness would rarely conflict with just behavior, and *eudaimonia* would be much easier to achieve.

My defense of the *eudaimonist* thesis might strike some readers as too weak to be satisfying. So far as I can see, however, a stronger thesis, while perhaps theoretically more appealing, fails to apply to us, the complex and limited inhabitants of a complex and dynamic world.

BIBLIOGRAPHY

Adams, Robert. *A Theory of Virtue: Excellence in Being for the Good.* Oxford: Clarendon, 2006.

Adams, Robert. "Comments on Julia Annas' *Intelligent Virtue.*" Author Meets Critics Session on Julia Annas, *Intelligent Virtue,* American Philosophical Association, Pacific Division Meetings, Seattle, Washington, April 6, 2012.

Amenábar, Alejandro, dir. *The Sea Inside.* Los Angeles, California: Fine Line Features. 2004.

Allport, Gordon W. *Personality: A Psychological Interpretation.* New York: Holt, 1937.

Angner, Erik. "Subjective Well-Being." *The Journal of Socio-Economics* 39 (2010): 361-368.

Angner, Erik. "Subjective Well-Being: When, and Why, It Matters" (http://papers.ssrn.com/sol3/papers.cfm?abstract_id=2157140, 2012, accessed April 2013).

Annas, Julia. *The Morality of Happiness.* New York: Oxford University Press, 1993.

Annas, Julia. "Prudence and Morality in Ancient and Modern Ethics." *Ethics* 105, no. 2 (January 1995): 241–257.

Annas, Julia. "Virtue and Eudaimonism." *Social Philosophy and Policy* 15, no. 1 (1998): 37–55.

Annas, Julia. "Aristotle on Virtue and Happiness." *University of Dayton Review* 19 (1989): 7–22. Reprinted in *Aristotle's Ethics: Critical Essays,* edited by Nancy Sherman, 35–55. Lanham, MD: Rowman and Littlefield, 1999.

Annas, Julia. "The Structure of Virtue." In *Intellectual Virtue: Perspectives from Ethics and Epistemology,* edited by Michael de Paul and Linda Zagzebski, 15–33. Oxford: Clarendon, 2003.

Annas, Julia. "Virtue Ethics: What Kind of Naturalism?" In *Virtue Ethics Old and New,* edited by Stephen Gardiner, 11–29. Ithaca, NY: Cornell University Press, 2005.

Annas, Julia. *Intelligent Virtue.* New York: Oxford University Press, 2011.

Arendt, Hannah. *Eichmann in Jerusalem: A Report on the Banality of Evil.* New York: Viking, 1963.

Aristotle. *Nicomachean Ethics,* trans. Terence Irwin. 2nd ed. Indianapolis, IN: Hackett, 1999.

Aristotle. *Eudemian Ethics*, trans. J. Solomon. In *The Complete Works of Aristotle: the Revised Oxford Translation*, edited by Jonathan Barnes. Princeton, N.J.: Princeton University Press, 1984.

Arneson, Richard. "Human Flourishing versus Desire Satisfaction." *Social Philosophy and Policy* 16, no. 1 (Winter 1999): 113–142.

Arneson, Richard. "Liberal Neutrality on the Good: An Autopsy." In *Perfectionism and Neutrality*, edited by Steven Wall and George Klosko, 191–218. Lanham, N.J.: Rowman & Littlefield, 2003.

Asch, Solomon. "Opinions and Social Pressure." *Scientific American* 193, no. 5 (1955): 31–35.

Badhwar, Neera K. "Friendship, Justice, and Supererogation." *American Philosophical Quarterly* 22, no. 2 (April 1985): 123–131.

Badhwar, Neera K. "The Limited Unity of Virtue." *Nous* 30, no. 3 (1996): 306–329.

Badhwar, Neera K. "Carnal Wisdom and Sexual Virtue." In *Sex and Ethics: Essays on Sexuality, Virtue, and the Good Life*, edited by Raja Halwani, 134–146. New York: Palgrave MacMillan, 2007.

Badhwar, Neera K. "The Milgram Experiments, Learned Helplessness, and Character Traits." *Journal of Ethics* 13, no. 2–3 (2009): 257–289 (http://link.springer.com/article/10.1007%2Fs10892-009-9052-4, June 3, 2009, accessed November 5, 2013).

Badhwar, Neera K. "Reasoning about Wrong Reasons, No Reasons, and Reasons of Virtue." Forthcoming in *The Philosophy and Psychology of Character and Happiness*, edited by Nancy E. Snow and Franco Trevigno. New York: Routledge, 2014.

Bargh, John A., and T.L. Chartrand. "The Unbearable Automaticity of Being." *American Psychologist* 54, no. 7 (1999): 462–479.

Battaly, Heather: *Virtue*. Forthcoming, Polity Press, 2015.

Becker, Lawrence. *A New Stoicism*. Princeton, NJ: Princeton University Press, 1999

Becker, Lawrence. "Stoic Emotion." In *Stoicism: Traditions and Transformations*, edited by Steven K. Strange and Jack Zupko, 250–275. Cambridge: Cambridge University Press, 2004.

Belkin, Lisa. "Death on the CNN Curve." *The New York Times Magazine*, July 23, 1995 (http://byliner.com/lisa-belkin/stories/death-on-the-cnn-curve, accessed April 2013).

Benson, John. "Who is the Autonomous Man?" *Philosophy* 58, no. 223 (January 1983): 5–17.

Benson, Paul. "Free Agency and Self-Worth." *Journal of Philosophy* 91, no. 12 (1994): 650–668.

"Best of Sicily: A Guide to Sicilian Travel and All Things Sicilian" (http://www.bestofsicily.com/mafia.htm, accessed April 2013).

Bloomfield, Paul. "Justice as a Self-Regarding Moral Virtue." *Philosophy and Phenomenological Research* 82, no. 1 (January 2011): 46–64.

Brink, David O. "Mill's Deliberative Utilitarianism." *Philosophy and Public Affairs* 21, no. 1 (Winter 1992): 67–103.

Broadie, Sarah. *Ethics with Aristotle*. New York: Oxford University Press, 1993.

Burnyeat, M.F. "Aristotle on Learning To Be Good." In *Essays on Aristotle's Ethics*, edited by Amélie Oksenberg Rorty, 69–92. Berkeley: University of California Press, 1980.

Buss, Sarah. "Valuing Autonomy and Respecting Persons: Manipulation, Seduction, and the Basis of Moral Constraints." *Ethics* 115, no. 2 (January 2005): 195–235.

Cahn, Steven M. "The Happy Immoralist." *Journal of Social Philosophy* 35, no. 1 (Spring 2004): 1.

Cesarani, David. *Eichmann: His Life and Crimes*. London: William Heinemann, 2004.

Christman, John. "Autonomy and Personal History." *Canadian Journal of Philosophy*. 21, no. 1 (1991): 1–24.

Cicero. *Cicero on the Emotions, Tusculan Disputations 3 and 4*, trans. Margaret Graver. Chicago: Chicago University Press, 2002.

Cleckley, Hervey. *The Mask of Sanity*. 5th ed. St. Louis, MO: C.V. Mosby, 1976.

Colvin, C. Randall, and Jack Block, "Do Positive Illusions Foster Mental Health? An Examination of the Taylor and Brown Formulation." *Psychological Bulletin*, 116, no. 1 (July 1994): 3–20.

Colvin, C. Randall, Jack Block, and David C. Funder, "Overly Positive Self-Evaluations and Personality: Negative Implications for Mental Health." *Journal of Personality and Social Psychology* 68, no. 6 (1995): 1152–1162.

Cooper, John. *Reason and Human Good in Aristotle*. Indianapolis, IN: Hackett, 1986.

Coplan, Amy. "Feeling Without Thinking: Lessons from the Ancients on Emotion and Virtue-Acquisition." *Metaphilosophy* 41, no. 1–2 (2010): 132–151.

Cottingham, John. "Partiality and the Virtues." In *How Should One Live?*, edited by Roger Crisp, 57–76. Oxford: Clarendon, 1996.

Cox, Stephen. *Blood and Power: Organized Crime in Twentieth Century America*. New York: William Morrow, 1989.

Csikszentmihalyi, Mihaly. *Flow: The Psychology of Optimal Experience*. New York: Harper and Row, 1990.

Curzer, Howard. "How Good People Do Bad Things: Aristotle on the Misdeeds of the Virtuous." In *Oxford Studies in Ancient Philosophy*, vol. 28, edited by D. Sedley, 233–256. Oxford: Oxford University Press, 2005.

Damasio, Antonio. *Descartes' Error: Emotion, Reason and the Human Brain*. New York: Putnam, 1994.

Darwall, Stephen. *Welfare and Rational Care*. Princeton, NJ: Princeton University Press, 2004.

Davidson, Donald. "How Is Weakness of the Will Possible?" In *Essays on Actions and Events*, edited by Donald Davidson, 21–42. Oxford: Clarendon, 1980.

de Sousa, Ronald. *The Rationality of Emotion*. Cambridge: MIT Press, 1987.

Drefcinski, Shane. "Aristotle's Fallible Phronimos." *Ancient Philosophy* 16, no. 1 (1996): 139–154.

Dijksterhuis, Ap, and Loran E. Nordgren. "A Theory of Unconscious Thought." *Perspectives on Psychological Science* 1, no. 2 (2006): 95–109.

Donagan, Alan. *The Theory of Morality*. Chicago: University of Chicago Press, 1979.

Doris, John M. *Lack of Character: Personality and Moral Behavior*. Cambridge, UK: Cambridge University Press, 2002.

Dostoevsky, Fyodor. *The Brothers Karamazov*, trans. Andrew R. MacAndrew. New York: Bantam, 1970.

Driver, Julia. *Uneasy Virtue*. Cambridge: Cambridge University Press, 2001.

Dworkin, Gerald. *The Theory and Practice of Autonomy*. Cambridge, UK: Cambridge University Press, 1988.

"Einstein's Wife: The Life of Mileva Maric Einstein." *PBS* (http://www.pbs.org/opb/einsteinswife/milevastory/index.htm, 2003, website updated 2007).

"Einstein Revealed." PBS (http://www.pbs.org/wgbh/nova/physics/einstein-revealed. html, Sept. 9, 1997, accessed July 2013).

Einstein, Albert. In *The Encyclopaedia Britannica*, last updated by the editors October 17, 2013 (http://www.britannica.com/EBchecked/topic/181349/Albert-Einstein).

Elga, Adam. "On Overrating Oneself...and Knowing It." *Philosophical Studies* 123, no. 1–2 (2005): 115–124.

Eliot, George. *Middlemarch*, New Illustrated Classics. Kindle ed., 2011.

Feinberg, Joel. "Autonomy." *Harm to Self: The Moral Limits of the Criminal Law.* New York: Oxford University Press, 1986.

Feinberg, Joel. "The Idea of a Free Man." In *Rights, Justice, and the Bounds of Liberty: Essays in Social Philosophy*, edited by Joel Feinberg, 3–29. Princeton, NJ: Princeton University Press, 1980.

Feldman, Fred. *Pleasure and the Good Life: Concerning the Nature, Varieties, and Plausibility of Hedonism.* Oxford: Clarendon, 2004.

Feldman, Fred. "Replies." *Philosophical Studies* 136, no. 3 (2007): 439–450.

Fielding, Henry. *The History of Tom Jones, A Foundling* (1749) (http://www.bartleby. com/ebook/adobe/301.pdf, accessed April 2013).

Flanagan, Owen O, Jr. *Varieties of Moral Personality: Ethics and Psychological Realism.* Cambridge, MA: Harvard University Press, 1991.

Flanagan, Owen O, Jr. "Identity and Reflection." In *Self-Expressions: Mind, Morals, and the Meaning of Life*, edited by Owen O. Flanagan, Jr., 142–170. Oxford: Oxford University Press, 1996.

Flanagan, Owen O, Jr. *The Really Hard Problem: Meaning in a Material World.* Cambridge, MA: MIT Press, 2007.

Foot, Phillippa. "Virtues and Vices." In *Virtues and Vices and Other Essays In Moral Philosophy*, edited by Philippa Foot, 1–19. Berkeley: University of California, 1978.

Foot, Phillipa. *Natural Goodness.* Oxford: Clarendon, 2001.

Frankl, Viktor. *Man's Search for Meaning: An Introduction to Logotherapy.* 3rd ed. New York: Simon & Schuster, 1984.

Frankfurt, Harry. "Freedom of the Will and the Concept of a Person." *Journal of Philosophy* 68, no. 8 (January 14, 1971): 5–20.

Freiman, Christopher. "Why Be Immoral?" *Ethical Theory and Moral Practice* 13, no. 2 (2010): 191–205.

Friedman, Marilyn. *Autonomy, Gender, Politics.* New York: Oxford University Press, 2003.

Friedman, Marilyn. "On Being Bad and Living Well: Virtue and the Good Life," unpublished ms.

Gardner, Dan. *Future Babble: Why Expert Predictions Are Next To Worthless, and You Can Do Better.* New York: Dutton, 2011.

Gauthier, David. *Morals by Agreement.* Oxford: Oxford University Press, 1986.

Geeslin, Campbell, Mary Vespa, and Harriet Shapiro. Review of Yann Le Pichon, *Gauguin: Life, Art, Inspiration. People Magazine*, vol. 27, no. 25 (http://www.people. com/people/archive/article/0,,20096555,00.html, accessed May 14, 2013).

Gert, Joshua. "Color Constancy and the Color/Value Analogy." *Ethics* 121, no. 1 (2010): 58–87.

Glover, Jonathan. *Humanity: A Moral History of the Twentieth Century*. New Haven, CT: Yale University Press, 1999.

Golden, Arthur. *Memoirs of a Geisha*. New York: Vintage Contemporaries, 1997.

Goldie, Peter, ed. *The Oxford Handbook of Philosophy of Emotion*. New York: Oxford University Press, 2010.

Goleman, Daniel. *Emotional Intelligence*. New York: Bantam, 1995, 1997.

Grandin, Temple. *Thinking in Pictures and Other Reports From My Life with Autism*. Expanded ed. New York: Vintage, 2006.

Griffin, James. *Well-Being: Its Meaning, Measurement, and Moral Importance*. Oxford: Clarendon, 1986.

Griffin, James. "Replies." In *Well-Being and Morality: Essays in Honour of James Griffin*, edited by Roger Crisp and Brad Hooker, 281–314. Oxford: Clarendon, 2000.

Grim, Ryan. "Five Myths About Drugs in America." *Washington Post* (August 9, 2009) (http://www.washingtonpost.com/wp-dyn/content/article/2009/08/07/AR2009080702159.html).

Haidt, Jonathan. *The Happiness Hypothesis: Finding Modern Truth in Ancient Wisdom*. New York: Basic Books, 2006.

Haidt, Jonathan, and Fredrik Bjorklund. "Social Intuitionists Answer Six Questions About Moral Psychology." In *Moral Psychology, Vol. 2: The Cognitive Science of Morality: Intuition and Diversity*, edited by Walter Sinnott-Armstrong, 181–217. Cambridge: MIT Press, 2008.

Haidt, Jonathan, and Fredrik Bjorklund. "Social Intuitionists Reason, In Conversation." Ibid., 241–254.

Hardie, W.F.R. "The Final Good in Aristotle's Ethics." *Philosophy* 40, no. 154 (1965): 277–295; reprinted in *Aristotle: A Collection of Critical Essays*, edited by J.M.E. Moravcshik. London: Macmillan, 1968, and in Hardie, Ch. 2. *Aristotle's Ethical Theory*. Oxford: Clarendon Press, 1968.

Harlow, Harry F. "The Nature of Love" (http://psychclassics.yorku.ca/Harlow/love.htm, accessed March 4, 2013). First published in *American Psychologist* 13, no. 12 (1958): 673–685.

Hawking, Stephen. "Prof. Stephen Hawking's Disability Advice." *Annals of Neurosciences*, 16, 3 (July 2009) (http://annalsofneurosciences.org/journal/index.php/annal/article/viewArticle/48/951, accessed January 2014).

Haworth, Lawrence. *Autonomy: An Essay in Philosophical Psychology and Ethics*. New Haven, CT: Yale University Press, 1986.

Haybron, Daniel M. *The Pursuit of Unhappiness: The Elusive Psychology of Well-Being*. New York: Oxford University Press, 2008.

Hill, Thomas E., Jr. "Servility and Self-Respect." In *Autonomy and Self-Respect*, edited by Thomas E. Hill, 4–18. New York: Cambridge University Press, 1991.

Hooker, Brad. "Is Moral Virtue a Benefit to the Agent?" In *How Should One Live?*, edited by Roger Crisp, 141–155. Oxford: Clarendon, 1996.

Horgan, Terry, and Mark Timmons. "Morphological Rationalism and the Psychology of Moral Judgment." *Ethical Theory and Moral Practice* 10, no. 3 (2007): 279–295.

Hume, David. *Enquiry Concerning the Principles of Morals* (1751), edited by Eric Steinberg. Indianapolis, IN: Hackett Publishing Co., 1983.

Hursthouse, Rosalind. *On Virtue Ethics*. Oxford: Oxford University Press, 1999.

Hyman, Ray. "'Cold Reading': How to Convince Strangers that you Know all about Them." In *The Outer Edge: Classic Investigations of the Paranormal*, edited by Joe Nickell, Barry Karr, and Tom Genoni, 70–84. Amherst, NY: The Committee for the Scientific Investigation of Claims of the Paranormal, 1996.

Irwin, Terence. *Aristotle's First Principles*. Oxford: Oxford University Press, 1990.

Irwin, Terence. "Disunity in the Aristotelian Virtues." In *Oxford Studies in Ancient Philosophy*, Supplementary Volume, edited by Julia Annas, 61–78. Oxford: Clarendon, 1988.

Irwin, Terence. "The Virtues: Theory and Common Sense in Ancient Greek Philosophy." In *How Should One Live?*, edited by Roger Crisp, 37–55. Oxford: Clarendon, 1996.

Jacobson, Daniel, "Does Social Intuitionism Flatter Morality or Challenge It?" *In Moral Psychology, V. 2: The Cognitive Science of Morality: Intuition and Diversity*, edited by Walter Sinott-Armstrong, 219–232. Cambridge: MIT, 2008.

Jahoda, Marie. "The Meaning of Psychological Health." *Social Casework* 34 (1953): 349–354.

Jahoda, Marie. *Current Concepts of Positive Mental Health*. New York: Basic Books, 1958.

Jamison, Kay Redfield. *Touched with Fire: Manic-Depressive Illness and the Artistic Temperament*. New York: Free Press, 1993.

Jones, Karen. "Second-Hand Moral Knowledge." *Journal of Philosophy* 96, no. 2 (1999): 55–78.

Jopling, David A. "'Take Away the Life-Lie...': Positive Illusions and Creative Self-Deception." *Philosophical Psychology* 9, no. 4 (1996): 525–544.

Jordan, Gregory. "Into the Life of a Man Fighting for the Right to Die." *The New York Times*, December 15, 2004 (http://www.nytimes.com/2004/12/15/movies/15samp.html, accessed July 2013).

Kamtekar, Rachana. "Updating Practical Wisdom." In *Self-Knowledge and Agency*, edited by Manidipa Sen, 256–277. New Delhi, India: DK Printworld, 2012.

Kant, Immanuel. *Groundwork for the Metaphysics of Morals* (1785), trans. H.J. Paton. New York: Harper & Row, 1964. First published as *The Moral Law*, Hutchinson University Library, 1948.

Kant, Immanuel. *Critique of Practical Reason* (1788), trans. Mary J. Gregor. 2nd ed. Cambridge, UK: Cambridge University Press, 1996.

Kant, Immanuel. "The Doctrine of Virtue." In *The Metaphysics of Morals* (1797), trans. Mary J. Gregor. 2nd ed. Cambridge, UK: Cambridge University Press, 1996.

Kant, Immanuel. *Religion Within the Limits of Reason Alone* (1793), trans. Theodore M. Greene and Hoyt H. Hudson. New York: Harper and Brothers, 1934/1960.

Kashdan, Todd D., Robert Biswas-Diener, Laura A. King. "Reconsidering Happiness: The Costs of Distinguishing between Hedonics And Eudaimonia." *The Journal of Positive Psychology* 3, no. 4, (2008): 219–233.

Kavka, Gregory S. "The Reconciliation Project." In *Morality, Reason, and Truth: New Essays on the Foundation of Ethics*, edited by David Copp and David Zimmerman, 297–319. Totowa, NJ: Rowman and Allanheld, 1985.

Kidd, Sue Monk. *The Secret Life of Bees*. New York: Penguin, 2002.

Kornblith, Hilary. "What Is It Like To Be Me?" *Australasian Journal of Philosophy* 76, no. 1 (1998): 48–60.

Korsgaard, Christine. "Realism and Constructivism in Twentieth-Century Moral Philosophy." In *Special Issue: Philosophy in America at the Turn of the Century. Journal of Philosophical Research* 28, APA Centennial Issue Supplement (2003): 9–122. Republished in Korsgaard's *Constitution of Agency: Essays on Practical Reason and Moral Psychology*, 302–326. Oxford: Oxford University Press, 2008.

Kraut, Richard. "Two Conceptions of Happiness." *The Philosophical Review* 88, no. 2 (April 1979): 167–197.

Kraut, Richard. *Aristotle on the Human Good.* Princeton, NJ: Princeton University Press, 1991.

Kraut, Richard. *What Is Good and Why: The Ethics of Well-Being.* Cambridge, MA: Harvard University Press, 2007.

Kristinsson, Sigurdur. "The Limits of Neutrality: Toward a Weakly Substantive Account of Autonomy." *Canadian Journal of Philosophy* 30, no. 2 (2000): 257–286.

Kupperman, Joel J. "The Indispensability of Character." *Philosophy* 76, no. 2 (2001): 239–251.

Lear, Jonathan. *Love And Its Place in Nature: A Philosophical Interpretation of Freudian Analysis.* New York: Farrar, Straus and Giroux, 1990.

Lerner, Melvin. *The Belief in a Just World: A Fundamental Delusion.* New York: Plenum Press, 1980.

Lewis, C.S. *The Great Divorce.* New York: Macmillan, 1946.

"Libera Terra" (http://www.globalpost.com/dispatch/italy/091027/libera-terra-food, accessed January 27, 2014).

Little, Maggie. "Recent Work in Moral Realism: Non-Naturalism." *Philosophical Books* 35, no. 4 (October 1994): 225–233.

Lykken, David. *Happiness.* New York: St. Martin's, 1999.

Martin, Mike W. *Self-Deception and Morality.* Lawrence: University Press of Kansas, 1986.

Maslow, Abraham H. "Self-Actualizing People: A Study of Psychological Health." In *Personality*, Symposium 1 (1950): 11–34. Reprinted in *The World of Psychology*, edited by G.B. Levitas. Vol. 2. New York: Braziller, 1965.

Maslow, Abraham H. "A Theory of Metamotivation." *Journal of Humanistic Psychology* 7, no. 2 (1967): 93–127.

Maslow, Abraham H. *Toward a Psychology of Being.* 3rd ed. New York: John Wiley & Sons, 1999.

McCall, Nathan. *Makes Me Wanna Holler: A Young Black Man in America.* New York: Random House, 1994.

McDowell, John. "Virtue and Reason." *The Monist*, 62, no. 3 (July 1979): 331–350.

McDowell, John. "Values and Secondary Qualities." In *Morality and Objectivity*, edited by Ted Honderich, 110–129. London: Routledge and Kegan Paul, 1985.

Mele, Alfred R. *Autonomous Agents.* New York: Oxford University Press, 1995.

Merrick, Joseph. en.wikipedia.org/wiki/Joseph_Merrick, based on Ashley Montagu's *The Elephant Man: A Study in Human Dignity* (1971; 3rd ed. 2001), and other sources.

Merritt, Maria W., John Doris, and Gilbert Harman. "Character." In *The Moral Psychology Handbook*, edited by John Doris and the Moral Psychology Research Group. New York: Oxford University Press, 2010.

Milgram, Stanley. *Obedience to Authority: An Experimental View.* New York: Harper & Row, 1974.

Mill, John Stuart. *The Subjection of Women,* edited by Susan M. Okin. Indianapolis, IN: Hackett, 1988.

Milo, Ronald D. *Immorality.* Princeton, NJ: Princeton University Press, 1984.

Murphy, Jeffrie G. "The Unhappy Immoralist." *Journal of Social Philosophy* 35, no. 1 (Spring 2004): 11–13.

Nagel, Thomas. *The Possibility of Altruism.* Princeton, NJ: Princeton University Press, 1970.

Nagel, Thomas. "Moral Luck." In *Moral Luck,* edited by Daniel Statman, 57–71. Albany: State University of New York Press, 1993.

Narvaez, Darcia. "The Social Intuitionist Model: Some Counter-Intuitions." In *Moral Psychology, V. 2: The Cognitive Science of Morality: Intuition and Diversity,* edited by Walter Sinott-Armstrong, 233–240. Cambridge: MIT, 2008.

Nash, Ogden. "Kind of an Ode to Duty". In *Selected Poetry of Ogden Nash,* edited by Ogden Nash. New York: Black Dog & Leventhal, 1995.

Nietzsche, Friedrich. *Twilight of the Idols/The Anti-Christ* (1889/1895), trans. R.J. Hollingdale. New York: Penguin, 1968

Nozick, Robert. *Anarchy, State, and Utopia.* New York: Basic Books, 1974.

Nozick, Robert. *The Examined Life: Philosophical Meditations.* New York: Simon & Schuster, 1989.

Nussbaum, Martha. "Non-Relative Virtues." In *The Quality of Life,* edited by Martha Nussbaum and Amartya Sen, 242–269. New York: Oxford University Press, 1993.

Nussbaum, Martha. "Who is the Happy Warrior? Philosophy Poses Questions to Psychology." *The Journal of Legal Studies* 37, Suppl 2 (June 2008): S81–S113.

Parfit, Derek. *Reasons and Persons.* Oxford: Oxford University Press, 1984.

Peterson, Virgil W. *The Mob: 200 Years of Organized Crime in New York.* Ottawa: Green Hill Publishers, 1983.

Pistone, Joseph D. *The Way of the Wiseguy.* Philadelphia, PA: Running Press, 2004.

Price, A.W. "Emotions in Plato and Aristotle." In *The Oxford Handbook of Philosophy of Emotion,* edited by Peter Goldie. Oxford: Oxford University Press, 2010. Online at DOI: 10.1093/oxfordhb/9780199235018.003.0006, January 2010.

Prinz, Jesse. "The Normativity Challenge: Cultural Psychology Provides the Real Threat to Virtue Ethics." *The Journal of Philosophy* 13, no. 2–3 (2009): 117–144.

Prophet, Erin. *Prophet's Daughter: My Life with Elizabeth Clare Prophet Inside the Church Universal and Triumphant.* Guilford, CT: Lyons Press, 2008.

The Qu'ran, trans. M.A.S. Abdel Haleem. New York: Oxford University Press, 2008.

Railton, Peter. "Alienation, Consequentialism, and the Demands of Morality." *Philosophy and Public Affairs* 13, no. 2 (Spring 1984):134–171.

Raz, Joseph. *Ethics in the Public Domain: Essays in the Morality of Law and Politics.* Oxford: Clarendon, 1984.

Raz, Joseph. *The Morality of Freedom.* Oxford: Clarendon, 1986.

Riggs, Wayne D. "Understanding 'Virtue' and the Virtue of Understanding." In *Intellectual Virtue: Perspectives from Ethics and Epistemology,* edited by Michael DePaul and Linda Zagzebski, 203–226. Oxford: Oxford University Press, 2003.

Roberts, Robert C., and W. Jay Wood. *Intellectual Virtue: An Essay in Regulative Epistemology.* New York: Oxford University Press, 2007.

Rogers, Carl. "A Therapist's View of the Good Life: The Fully Functioning Person." In *The Carl Rogers Reader*, edited by H. Howard Kirschenbaum and V. L. Henderson, 409–429. New York: Houghton Mifflin, 1989.

Rogers, Carl. "The Person in Process." In *The Carl Rogers Reader*, edited by H. Howard Kirschenbaum and V. L. Henderson, 155–197. New York: Houghton Mifflin, 1989.

Rogers, Patrick. "Well of Darkness." May 15, 1995, People.com (http://www.people.com/people/archive/article/0,,20105787,00.html, accessed April 2013).

Royce, Josiah. *The Religious Aspect of Philosophy* (1885). Boston and New York: Houghton Mifflin, 1976.

Russell, Daniel C. *Practical Intelligence and the Virtues.* New York: Oxford University Press, 2009.

Russell, Daniel C. *Happiness for Humans.* New York: Oxford University Press, 2012.

Russell, Daniel C., and Mark Le Bar. "Well-Being and Eudaimonia: A Reply to Haybron." In *Aristotelian Ethics in Contemporary Perspective*, edited by Julia Peters, 52–69. London: Routledge, 2013.

Ryff, Carol D., and Burton H. Singer, "Know Thyself and Become Who You Are: A *Eudaimonic* Approach to Psychological Well-Being." *Journal of Happiness Studies* 9, no. 1 (2008): 13–39.

Sartre, Jean-Paul. "Self-Deception." In *Existentialism from Dostoevsky to Sartre*, edited by Walter Kaufmann, 299–328. New York: New American Library, 1975.

Sayre-McCord, Geoffrey. "The Many Moral Realisms." In *Essays on Moral Realism*, edited by Geoffrey Sayre-McCord, 1–23. Ithaca: Cornell University Press, 1988.

Schmidtz, David. *Rational Choice and Moral Agency.* Princeton NJ: Princeton University Press, 1995.

Seligman, Martin E.P. *Authentic Happiness.* New York: Free Press, 2002.

Seligman, Martin E.P. "*Eudaemonia*, The Good Life: A Talk with Martin Seligman." *Edge: The Third Culture* (2004) (http://www.edge.org/3rd_culture/seligman04/seligman_index.html, accessed October 2013).

Seligman, Martin E.P. *Flourish: A Visionary New Understanding of Happiness and Well-Being.* New York: Free Press, 2011.

Seligman, Martin E.P., and Steven F. Maier. "Failure to Escape Traumatic Shock." *Journal of Experimental Psychology* 74, no. 1 (May 1967): 1–9.

Sen, Amartya. *On Ethics and Economics.* New York: Basil Blackwell, 1987.

Sherman, Nancy. *The Fabric of Character: Aristotle's Theory of Virtue.* Oxford: Clarendon, 1989.

Sherman, Nancy. *Stoic Warriors: The Ancient Philosophy behind the Military Mind.* New York: Oxford University Press, 2005.

Skenazy, Lenore. *Free-Range Kids, How to Raise Safe, Self-Reliant Children (Without Going Nuts with Worry).* San Francisco: Jossey-Bass, 2010.

Slote, Michael. *Morality from Motives.* New York: Oxford University Press, 2001.

Smart, J.J.C. "An Outline of A System of Utilitarian Ethics." In *Utilitarianism: For and Against*, edited by J.J.C. Smart and B. Williams, Cambridge, UK: Cambridge University Press, 1973.

Smith, Dwight C., Jr. *The Mafia Mystique.* New York: Basic Books, 1975.

Smith, Jacqui and Paul B. Baltes. "Wisdom-related knowledge: Age/cohort differences in response to life-planning problems." *Developmental Psychology* 26, no. 3 (May 1990): 494–505.

Snow, Nancy E. *Virtue as Social Intelligence: An Empirically Grounded Theory.* New York: Routledge, 2009.

Solzhenitsyn, Aleksandr. *The Gulag Archipelago: 1918–1956: An Experiment in Literary Investigation*, trans. Thomas P. Whitney. New York: Harper & Row, 1973, 1974.

Sreenivasan, Gopal. "Disunity of Virtue." *Journal of Ethics* 13, no. 2–3 (2009): 195–212.

Steiner, Hillel. "The Structure of a Set of Compossible Rights." *Journal of Philosophy* 74, no. 12 (December 1977): 767–775.

Steinhouse, Herbert. "The Real Oskar Schindler" *Saturday Night* (April 1994) (http://writing.upenn.edu/~afilreis/Holocaust/steinhouse.html, accessed Sept. 2012).

Stocker, Michael. "How Emotions Reveal Value." In *How Should One Live?*, edited by Roger Crisp, 173–190. Oxford: Clarendon, 1996.

Stocker, Michael, and Elizabeth Hegeman. *Valuing Emotions*. Cambridge, UK: Cambridge University Press, 1996.

Sumner, L. W. *Welfare, Happiness, and Ethics*. Oxford: Clarendon, 1996.

Sumner, L. W. "Is Virtue Its Own Reward?" *Social Philosophy and Policy* 15, no. 1 (1998): 18–36.

Swanton, Christine. *Virtue Ethics: A Pluralistic View.* New York: Oxford University Press, 2003.

Taylor, Charles. "Responsibility for Self." In *The Identities of Persons*, edited by Amélie O. Rorty, 281–300. Berkeley: University of California Press, 1976.

Taylor, Charles. "What is Human Agency?" In *Human Agency and Language, Philosophical Papers I*, edited by Charles Taylor, 15–44. Cambridge, UK: Cambridge University Press, 1985.

Taylor, Shelley E., and Jonathon D. Brown. "Illusion and Well-Being: a Social Psychological Perspective on Mental Health." *Psychological Bulletin* 103, no.2 (1988): 193–210.

Taylor, Shelley E. *Positive Illusions: Creative Self-Deception and the Healthy Mind.* New York: Basic Books, 1991.

Taylor, Shelley E., and Jonathon D. Brown. "Positive Illusions and Well-Being Revisited: Separating Fact from Fiction." *Psychological Bulletin* 116, no. 1 (1994): 21–27.

Tiberius, Valerie. *The Reflective Life: Living Wisely With Our Limits.* New York: Oxford University Press, 2008.

Tiberius, Valerie and Alicia Hall. "Normative Theory and Psychological Research: Hedonism, Eudaimonism, and Why it Matters." *Journal of Positive Psychology* 5, no. 3 (May 2010): 212–225.

Tiberius, Valerie, and Alexandra Plakias. "Well-Being." In *The Moral Psychology Handbook*, edited by John Doris and the Moral Psychology Research Group, 403–432. New York: Oxford University Press, 2010.

Upton, Candace. "The Structure of Character." *Journal of Ethics*, 13 (2009): 101–289. Online June 3, 2009.

Upton, Candace. *Situational Traits of Character: Dispositional Foundations and Implications for Moral Psychology and Friendship.* Lanham: Rowman and Littlefield, 2009.

Walpola, Rahula. *What the Buddha Taught: Revised and Expanded.* New York: Grove Press, 1974.

Watson, Gary. "Virtues in Excess." *Philosophical Studies* 46, no. 1 (July 1984): 57–74.

Watson, Lyall. *Dark Nature: A History of Evil.* New York: HarperCollins, 1995.

Wilson, Timothy D. *Strangers to Ourselves: Discovering the Adaptive Unconscious.* Cambridge MA: Belknap Press of Harvard University Press, 2002.

Westlund, Andrea. "Selflessness and Responsibility for Self: Is Deference Compatible with Autonomy?" *The Philosophical Review* 112, no. 4 (2003): 483–523.

White, Nicholas. *A Brief History of Happiness.* Oxford: Blackwell, 2006.

Wiggins, David. "Truth, and Truth as Predicated of Moral Judgments." In *Needs, Values, Truth: Essays in the Philosophy of Value,* edited by David Wiggins, 166–184. Oxford: Blackwell, 1987.

Williams, Bernard. *Ethics and the Limits of Philosophy.* London: Fontana, 1985.

Wolf, Susan. "Happiness and Meaning: Two Aspects of the Good Life." *Social Philosophy and Policy* 14, no. 1 (Winter 1997): 207–225.

Wolf, Susan. *Meaning in Life and Why it Matters.* Princeton, NJ: Princeton University Press: 2012.

Wolfendale, Jessica. *Torture and the Military Professional.* New York: Palgrave Macmillan, 2007.

Yalanis, Christopher. "The Virtue(?) of Obedience: Some Notes for Military Professionals." *Joint Services Conference on Professional Ethics.* Springfield, VA: 2001 (http://isme. tamu.edu/JSCOPE01/Yalanis01.html, accessed Sept. 2013).

Zagzebski, Linda T. *Virtues of the Mind: An Inquiry into the Nature of Virtue and the Ethical Foundations of Knowledge.* Cambridge, UK: Cambridge University Press, 1996.

Zagzebski, Linda. "The Admirable Life and the Desirable Life." In *Values and Virtues: Aristotelianism in Contemporary Ethics,* edited by Timothy Chappell, 53–67. New York: Oxford University Press, 2006.

Zimbardo, Philip G. *The Lucifer Effect: Understanding how Good People Turn Evil.* New York: Random House, 2007.

Zimbardo, Christina Maslach, Craig Haney. "Reflections on the Stanford Prison Experiment: Genesis, Transformations, Consequences." In *Obedience to Authority: Current Perspectives on the Milgram Paradigm,* edited by Thomas Blass, 193–237. Mahwah, NJ: Lawrence Erlbaum, 2000.

Zweig, Paul. "A Good Man in a Bad Time." Review of Thomas Keneally's *Schindler's List. The New York Times,* October 24, 1982 (http://www.nytimes.com/1982/10/24/ books/a-good-man-in-a-bad-time.html, accessed Sept. 2012).

INDEX

CPSIA information can be obtained
at www.ICGtesting.com
Printed in the USA
LVOW08s2340310117
522762LV00009B/38/P